A MAP of the ENGLISH EMPIRE in NORTH AMERICA
...by Charters, and the formal Surrender of their INDIAN FRIENDS;
...the FRENCH, with the ... Forts they have unjustly erected thereon...
21

HUDSON'S

N E W B R ...

CANADA

GULF of St. LAURENCE

... LAND

BRETON I.

The several Provinces of the
English Empire in N. America
are distinguished by Red, Blue,
Green and Yellow according to
their respective Jurisdictions.
The Spanish by Brown; but
the French Colonies and Encroachments are without any
Colour.

P ...

O C E A N

T H E   W E S T E R N   O R   A T L A N T I C

A T L A N T I C K

Hatteras

The French claim all the Country within
the Hudson's Bay Company's Southern
Limits and the Brown Line.
The Purple Line represents the Western
Boundary of the hereditary & conquer'd
Country of our Indian Friends & Allies,
which has been ceded and confirmed to us
by several Treaties and Deeds of Sale.

HUDSON'S
BAY

NEW
SOUTH WALES

LABRADOR
or
NEW BRITAIN

CANADA

A T

CAROLINA

GULF of
MEXICO

O C

G 3300
1755

NEW SPAIN

PACIFICK OCEAN
OR SOUTH SEA

... And Sold by W. Herbert on London Bridge & Rob. Sayer ...

EMPIRES
COLLIDE

THE FRENCH AND INDIAN WAR 1754–63

EMPIRES COLLIDE

THE FRENCH AND INDIAN WAR 1754–63

Introduction by William M Fowler, Jr.

EDITOR RUTH SHEPPARD

First published in Great Britain in 2006 by Osprey Publishing, Midland House,
West Way, Botley, Oxford OX2 0PH, United Kingdom.
443 Park Avenue South, New York, NY 10016, USA.
E-mail: info@ospreypublishing.com

Previously published as René Chartrand, Campaign 76: *Ticonderoga 1758*; René Chartrand,
Campaign 79: *Louisbourg 1758*; Stuart Reid, Campaign 121: *Quebec 1759*; René Chartrand,
Campaign 140: *Monongahela 1754–55*; Daniel Marston, Essential Histories 6: *The Seven Years'
War*; Daniel Marston, Essential Histories 44: *The French-Indian War 1754–1760*; René Chartrand,
Fortress 27: *French Fortresses in North America 1535–1763*; Martin Windrow, Men-at-Arms 23:
Montcalm's Army; Robin May & Gerry Embleton, Men-at-Arms 48: *Wolfe's Army*; Michael G.
Johnson, Men-at-Arms 228: *American Woodland Indians*; Stuart Reid, Men-at-Arms 285:
King George's Army 1740–93 (1); Stuart Reid, Men-at-Arms 289: *King George's Army 1740–93
(2)*; Stuart Reid, Men-at-Arms 292: *King George's Army 1740–93 (3)*; René Chartrand,
Men-at-Arms 302: *Louis XV's Army (2)*; René Chartrand, Men-at-Arms 304: *Louis XV's Army
(3)*; René Chartrand, Men-at-Arms 313: *Louis XV's Army (5)*; René Chartrand, Men-at-Arms
366: *Colonial American Troops 1610–1774 (1)*; René Chartrand, Men-at-Arms 372: *Colonial
American Troops 1610–1774 (2)*; René Chartrand, Men-at-Arms 383: *Colonial American
Troops 1610–1774 (3)*; Michael Johnson, Men-at-Arms 395: *Tribes of the Iroquois Confederacy*;
Stuart Reid, Warrior 19: *British Redcoat 1740–1793*; Stuart Reid, Warrior 42: *Redcoat Officer*;
Gary Zaboly, Warrior 85: *American Colonial Rangers*; Ian M. McCulloch & Tim J. Todish,
Warrior 88: *British Light Infantryman of the Seven Years' War*.

© 2006 Osprey Publishing Ltd

A CIP catalog record for this book is available from the British Library

ISBN 1 84603 089 7

Page layout by Ken Vail Graphic Design, Cambridge, UK
Index by Alan Thatcher
Maps by The Map Studio
Originated by PPS Grasmere, Leeds, UK
Printed in China through World Print Ltd

Front cover image: *Braddock's Defeat*, Wisconsin Historical Society, WHi-1900.
Title page image: Steve Noon © Osprey Publishing Ltd
Back cover image: National Archives of Canada
Endpapers: Library of Congress

06 07 08 09 10   10 9 8 7 6 5 4 3 2 1

For a catalog of all books published by Osprey please contact:
NORTH AMERICA
Osprey Direct c/o Random House Distribution Center
400 Hahn Road, Westminster, MD 21157, USA
E-mail: info@ospreydirect.com

ALL OTHER REGIONS
Osprey Direct UK, P.O. Box 140, Wellingborough, Northants, NN8 2FA, UK
E-mail: info@ospreydirect.co.uk

www.ospreypublishing.com

CONTENTS

INTRODUCTION
by William M. Fowler, Jr.

In the early morning hours of May 28, 1754, at a place now called Jumonville Glen 45 miles east of Pittsburgh, Pennsylvania, a young Virginia militia officer led his men in an unprovoked attack against a force of French soldiers just stirring from sleep. The officer was George Washington. In that one moment Washington, according to Horace Walpole, "set the world on fire."

Walpole was right. Washington's untoward attack set in motion events that within two years swept across the globe ensnaring the world's two superpowers into a titanic struggle for imperial domination. For decades England and France had scrambled for territory in North America. Since 1689 they had fought three declared wars punctuated by incessant violent skirmishes occurring along the contested boundaries between their colonial possessions. News of the engagement at Jumonville Glen reinforced each other's fears and within a few months both powers sent naval and military forces to defend their territorial claims. Violence across the Atlantic further unsettled already fragile European alliances, and by 1756 every major European power had joined the fray. From Africa to India, in Europe and Asia and on distant seas England, France and their allies fought in what was truly the world's first world war, and although the struggle encircled the globe, North America was the most decisive theater.

To turn back the French advance in the Ohio River Valley the king dispatched a large expeditionary force to America under the command of General Edward Braddock. In addition to his own command Braddock also carried orders to organize a defense of the king's lands by seizing Fort Niagara on Lake Ontario and Crown Point on Lake Champlain. It was a debacle of the worst kind. Braddock's force ran headlong into a French and Indian force that nearly wiped them out. The expeditions against Niagara and Crown Point never even reached their objectives. The only bright spot was British success in Nova Scotia where forts Beauséjour and Gaspereau fell with little resistance, but their capture was of little strategic importance.

OPPOSITE *Wolfe wading ashore at Louisbourg, by C. W. Jeffreys. (Library and Archives Canada, C-073711)*

Buoyed by their initial victories the French pressed the attack striking south from Canada. In August 1756 the newly arrived French commander, the Marquis de Montcalm, took Oswego on Lake Ontario. The British response was feeble. The king sacked Governor William Shirley of Massachusetts who had succeeded Braddock as commander-in-chief in North America and replaced him with John Campbell, Lord Loudoun and instructed him to organize an attack against Louisbourg, the French fortress on Cape Breton Island. Although he assembled a sizable fleet and army at Halifax, after numerous delays and the arrival of French reinforcements he gave up the plan. Just as Loudoun was preparing to return to his headquarters in New York news arrived that Montcalm had captured Fort William Henry.

Bad news from America stirred political unrest in London. In the Commons William Pitt rose to assail the government's conduct of the war. His biting attacks infuriated the king. His Majesty's feelings notwithstanding, Pitt's popularity with the masses and his skillful management of the House made him the inescapable choice to lead the government.

Pitt took the reins and immediately engineered Loudoun's recall. In his place the king appointed Major General James Abercromby, the fourth commander in three years. Pitt pursued a clear strategy. Although England's forces were engaged around the world, he was determined to force the issue in North America.

In long and detailed dispatches he laid out his plan to Abercromby. The General himself would advance north towards Québec via Lake Champlain and the Richelieu River. Pitt then tasked Jeffrey Amherst to assemble a fleet and army at Halifax to take Louisbourg, and then move up the St Lawrence towards Québec to join Abercromby. Meanwhile he ordered James Forbes with a mixed force of regulars and militia to march on Fort Duquesne.

In Forbes and Amherst Pitt found able commanders. Abercromby, however, proved a poor choice. He led his army in a disastrous frontal assault against Fort Ticonderoga. In defeat and disgrace Abercromby's battered army scurried back down Lake George. Amherst and Forbes fared much better and despite the defeat at Ticonderoga, 1758 was the turning point for the British in North America. Shortly after Abercromby's repulse Colonel John Bradstreet took a force of militia and regulars west and captured Fort Frontenac. Frontenac's fall cut off the French posts toward the south including Forts Niagara and Duquesne. Thanks in part to Braddock's victory a few months after Frontenac fell Forbes captured Fort Duquesne. The most memorable victory of the year, however, was Amherst's successful siege of Louisbourg.

Pitt was pleased at the capture of Louisbourg, but he was disappointed that Amherst had not been able to carry the attack in the same season to Québec City. For 1759 the minister laid out a plan aimed at the final destruction of the French in Canada.

Pitt selected General James Wolfe to command the approach to Québec from the north via the St Lawrence. As Wolfe sailed up the St Lawrence Amherst was to close on Québec from the south via Lake Champlain. Unfortunately, Amherst moved too slowly and never got farther down the lake than Crown Point leaving Wolfe to deal with Québec alone. Wolfe, of course, went on to a brilliant victory, and his own death, on the Plains of Abraham.

Wolfe's victory did not end the war in North America. The British hold on Québec City was tenuous and in the spring 1760 the French launched a counterattack. As usual, however, British control of the sea-lanes proved decisive. France was unable to reinforce her dwindling army in North America and in May 1760 the Royal Navy arrived at Québec bringing men and supplies forcing the French to retreat to Montréal.

In an extraordinarily well-coordinated movement three British armies closed on Montréal. Amherst who had moved his command to the west, advanced down the St Lawrence; Colonel William Haviland approached via Lake Champlain, and General James Murray moved up the river from Québec. By September 7, 1760 the three armies were in place. The next day Amherst sent a message to the Marquis de Vaudreuil, governor of Canada, demanding that he surrender the city and all French forces in Canada. Vastly outnumbered and with no hope of relief Vaudreuil accepted Amherst's terms.

Vaudreuil's surrender did not end the war. It would take several weeks for orders to reach distant French posts, and in the Carolinas the Cherokees, who had been fighting against the British independently of the French, continued their struggle, but within a year they too were forced to capitulate. Meanwhile in other parts of the world the conflict continued to rage until finally on February 10, 1763 the warring parties signed the Treaty of Paris. Great Britain emerged victorious with Canada as the chief prize. This triumph helped lay the foundation for a global empire which would provide the wealth and resources to fuel the industrial revolution and transform the world.

RUPERT'S LAND

HUDSON'S BAY COMPANY

NEWFOUNDLAN

Gulf of
St Lawrence

St Lawrence

N
O
U
V
E
L
L
E

F
R
A
N
C
E

C A N A D A

ACADIA

Île
St Jean

Île Royale
Louisbourg

Québec

Beauséjour

Montréal

Halifax

NOVA
SCOTIA

Lake Superior

Michilimackinac

Lake
Huron

Lake Michigan

Frontenac

Ticonderoga

Lake Ontario

William Henry

Niagara

Albany

Boston

Detroit

Lake Erie

N
E
W

Duquesne

New York

Philadelphia

Ohio

Wabasan

Chartres

Alexandria

BRITISH
13 COLONIES

Vincennes

Williamsburg

Ohio

L
O
U
I
S
I
A
N
A

Mississippi

ATLANTIC
OCEAN

Mobile

New Orleans

FLORIDA

GULF OF MEXICO

BAHAMA
ISLANDS

Territories in North America 1753–

Britain

France

Spain

Disputed

0   250 miles

0   400 km

CUBA

HISPANIOLA

MEXICO

HAITI

PART I
WAR IN THE WILDERNESS

CHRONOLOGY

1748

October 18	The Treaty of Aix-la-Chapelle ends the War of the Austrian Succession

1753

Summer–fall	Forts Presqu'Île, Le Boeuf, and Machault built by the French in the Ohio River Valley
December 11	Washington delivers ultimatum to Commandant Le Gardeur de Saint-Pierre at Fort Le Boeuf

1754

April 16	French expel Virginians from the fort they are building at the forks of the Monongahela and Ohio rivers
May 27	Washington ambushes Jumonville's party
July 3–4	French attack Fort Necessity, and force Washington's surrender; he signs a controversial capitulation

1755

January	Vaudreuil appointed as new governor-general of New France
June	British siege and capture of Fort Beauséjour
July 9	Battle of the Monongahela River
July 13	Braddock dies near Jumonville Glen, Shirley subsequently made commander-in-chief of British forces
July 17	Remnants of the British army reach Fort Cumberland
August 8	Governor-General Vaudreuil recalls de Contrecour and passes French command in the Ohio to Dumas
August 17	British force arrives at Oswego
September 8	Battle of Lake George

RIVALRIES IN NORTH AMERICA

The French and Indian War was one of a succession of conflicts over land in North America in the 18th century between the British Thirteen Colonies (and Nova Scotia) and New France. The frontier skirmishes of 1754 prompted both France and Great Britain to secure Continental allies, and with Europe firmly divided into two camps, conflict was inevitable. By 1756, the small-scale frontier battles had developed into a fully fledged war in North America and spilled over into conflict in Europe. Initially in the French and Indian War, the French Army with its allied American Indian tribes and local colonial forces benefited from superior tactics well-suited to operating in the wilderness of North America, though throughout the war it was numerically inferior to the British forces. The British Army was also aided by colonial forces and allied Indian tribes, but in the early days suffered from inexperience and lack of tactical knowledge of fighting in the North American terrain. Deployment of French and British regular troops, and reform of the British forces, would change the later style of the war, but the early skirmishes prior to the formal declaration of war were characterized by French tactical superiority, and the importance of Indian allies.

THE COLONIES IN NORTH AMERICA IN THE EARLY 18TH CENTURY

During the 17th and early 18th centuries, the British and French colonies in North America, by the very nature of their respective development as well as the frequent wars of their mother countries, were once again moving toward a major confrontation. The British flag flew over a number of colonies stretching from Georgia to Newfoundland along the Atlantic seaboard that were, for the most part, rapidly growing and populous entities. By the middle of the 18th

century, the population of the American colonies included well over one million inhabitants of European descent. The larger colonies such as Massachusetts, Connecticut, New York, Pennsylvania, Virginia, and South Carolina had their own local legislatures, large populations, and prosperous economies thanks to the continuing development of agriculture, shipping, trade, and commerce. In spite of some efforts by the Crown to rationalize administration with royal governors, the American colonies remained very independent. They also varied considerably in character. The northern colonies, such as Massachusetts, had been settled by religious refugees who often held a religiously conservative outlook on many issues. The colonists of the middle colonies had more varied origins and New York, for instance, still had a sizable Dutch population and corresponding traditions. Pennsylvania, although a major trade center thanks to

The Thirteen Colonies

At the time of the French and Indian War there were thirteen British colonies in North America, ranging along the Atlantic coast: Massachusetts, New Hampshire, Connecticut, Rhode Island, New York, New Jersey, Pennsylvania, Maryland, Delaware, Virginia, North Carolina, South Carolina, and Georgia. The settlers of the colonies were in no way a homogenous group. Ranging from the Quakers in Pennsylvania who had come to America to practice their own religion, through the factory workers of Maryland, to the plantation owners of Virginia and Georgia, they all had different reasons for leaving Europe, and wanted different things from the New World.

King George II of Great Britain relied on the advice of his ministers, such as William Pitt, and his reign was a landmark in the development of constitutional monarchy. The king's support of his minister's policies eventually saw outstanding victories across the globe and established Britain as a major world power. Painting by Robert Edge Pine. (Topfoto)

the city of Philadelphia, was still politically dominated by the pacifist sect known as the Quakers. Of the southern colonies, Virginia was the most important and it depended largely on the expanding plantations that gave its society a more distinctive class structure with the large estates and more genteel way of life of its social elite. The government of the British colonies in North America was very decentralized, with each colony having its own legislative assembly and policies. For all these reasons, in time of war it was difficult to mobilize the colonies into a concerted effort.

New France, by contrast, penetrated deeply into the hinterland of North America thanks to outstanding explorers such as Samuel de Champlain who went to the Great Lakes in the early 17th century; Robert Cavalier La Salle who reached the Gulf of Mexico during 1682 by navigating the Mississippi River; and a captain of colonial troops, de la Veréndrye, and his sons who built trading forts in the Canadian prairies and penetrated as far as the Rocky Mountains in present-day Wyoming in the 1730s and 1740s. Except for Cape Breton Island and its fortress and naval base of Louisbourg, built from 1720, France had few

15

coastal settlements until one reached Mobile and New Orleans on the Gulf of Mexico. New France had developed in the interior of the vast North American continent, happy to leave the British colonists to the eastern seaboard and a few posts on Hudson's Bay, and the Spanish to Florida and northern New Spain.

The Ohio River Valley

The Ohio River Valley, formed by the Ohio and its tributaries, encompasses about 200,000 square miles and covers major portions of the modern states of Indiana, Ohio, Kentucky, and West Virginia, as well as smaller portions of several other states. The Ohio begins in Pittsburgh, where the Allegheny and Monongahela rivers flow together, and ends at Cairo, Illinois, where it flows into the Mississippi. The valley is rich in natural resources, and valuable for hunting and agriculture, which has led to centuries of conflict over its control.

In the 18th century communication between Canada and Louisiana was usually along a route west to lakes Erie and Michigan and down the Mississippi via smaller rivers. This route was guarded by a string of forts along the shores of the lakes and rivers. The route along the Allegheny and Ohio rivers was known but seldom used other than by occasional roaming traders. During the 1730s and 1740s, as the importance of communications between Canada and Upper Louisiana (or Illinois) increased, the vital geostrategic position of the Ohio Valley became apparent to the French. At this time thought to be of negligible economic or political significance and rather wild, with a collection of American Indian nations, the Iroquois, reputedly hostile to strangers, the route was not yet considered worth protecting with forts. However, in the mid-1740s, increasingly frequent reports of British traders roaming into the Ohio Valley reached the governor-general of New France in Québec. Governor-General de la Galissonière was alarmed by the news. He realized that gradual British penetration into the Ohio River Valley might persuade the tribes of the area to switch their trade and diplomatic allegiance to the British. For France, the consequences of this were dramatic – loss of trade and influence, and increasing British activity along the shores of the western Great Lakes, which would eventually drive a wedge into the great arc of French possessions in North America. Dispatches from Québec to New Versailles spoke of disaster looming over New France. However, with the War of Austrian Succession raging in Europe, the problem of the Ohio Valley could not be dealt with by simply building a string of forts. New France's limited resources were at the time focused on expeditions on the frontiers of New York, Massachusetts, and New Hampshire. The French had so far built only one post near the Ohio, Fort Vincennes, and even this was much further west. Physical occupation of the territory would be the deciding factor, however, and as soon as the war ended in 1748 attention turned to the Ohio. To buy time and make it known to interlopers that the territory was French, an expedition of 30 soldiers and 180 militiamen with a few Indians, led by Captain Céléron de Blainville, left Montréal for the Ohio in June 1749. For the next few months Céléron's party roamed the Allegheny and Ohio valleys burying lead plates along the shores of the rivers, effectively claiming the territory for France.

The British were also acting to exploit the Ohio Valley. In 1747, the Ohio Company was founded to extend settlements of Virginia westwards. The members, mainly Virginia planters interested in land speculation and fur trading, were not at all impressed by the French attempts to prove their occupation of the valley. In 1749, King George II granted the company a royal charter of 200,000 acres of land around the forks of the Ohio, and the frontier trader Christopher Gist began explorations of the area in earnest, much to the chagrin of the French. Soon, settlers, and the young surveyor George Washington, would arrive in the area.

In 1752, a new governor-general of New France, the Baron de Longueuil, arrived in Canada with strict instructions to secure the Ohio Valley. It was clear that a fort-building program was the only way to achieve this efficiently, and in the spring of 1753 a large force of 300 soldiers, 1,200 militiamen, and 200 Indians left Montréal for the Ohio. Forts Presqu'Île, Le Boeuf, and Machault were built during the summer and fall.

This detail of a 1777 map shows a discussion between fur traders and American Indians. The fur trade was at the root of the rivalry which led Britain and France to war. In the middle of the 18th century, the French largely controlled the interior of North America and its fur trade, but mounting pressures caused by increasing numbers of British traders using the Ohio River Valley led to confrontation. (National Archives of Canada, C-7300)

There was no gold or silver found in New France and its economic mainstay was the fur trade. To facilitate this trade and maintain its territorial claims, a far-reaching network of forts was built at strategic sites along the shores of the hinterland's rivers and lakes. This network formed a great arc running from the Gulf of the St Lawrence River through the Great Lakes to the Gulf of Mexico. The European population of New France was miniscule and concentrated at the ends of this arc: Canada in the north with approximately 60,000 inhabitants concentrated along the shores of the St Lawrence River; Louisiana with only 5,000 or 6,000 settlers on the Gulf coast and another 2,000 or so established in the "Illinois Country," also called Upper Louisiana, in the area where the Missouri and Ohio rivers flowed into the Mississippi. Several thousand African slaves had also been transported into Louisiana. As for as the indigenous American Indian population, it is practically impossible to calculate an accurate figure; many eastern nations had been decimated by epidemics of diseases from Europe in the 17th century, but sizable populations remained, while many western nations were all but unknown to the Europeans.

The government of New France and its components were autocratic. The governor-general in Québec had overall authority and was commander-in-chief. He was assisted by the intendant in financial and civic matters, and the bishop in religious issues, with powers devolved to local governors, commissaries, and senior priests. The great hereditary seigneurs held huge land-grants from the crown, worked by the peasantry. In spite of a seemingly rigid autocratic structure, it was necessary to exercise power wisely, as all actions had to be approved by senior officials in France who had channels of information and news over and above official reports. One of the benefits of the centralized system of governance in New France was that it was comparatively efficient at mobilizing the colonies' relatively meager resources for military purposes.

THE FIRST SPARKS

Since the conclusion of the War of Austrian Succession (also known as King George's War) in 1748, French and British colonists, motivated by a desire to expand their domains into the rich Ohio River Valley, had edged closer to armed conflict. The area along the river was considered uncharted, and so formally unclaimed by either side. The British contended that the area should be open to both sides for trade, and thus established the Ohio Company in 1747. The French saw this as a British attempt to claim the entire area and so they had responded by sending militia and troops into the area to build forts and eject British settlers or traders found there (for more details see page 16).

Tensions had also been rising in Acadian Nova Scotia, particularly along the Bay of Fundy. The French had established several new forts in locations which the British colonial government felt violated the 1748 Treaty of Aix-la-Chapelle. Both sides claimed large areas of present day New Brunswick, and considered the other the transgressor. The insult of these encroachments was compounded by the French government's relations with the Acadians, a French-speaking population who, as a result of treaty agreements, had become subjects of the British Crown. The French authorities deliberately stirred the Acadians' aspirations to independence, incensing the British governors. The establishment of Fort Beauséjour in the disputed area was the last straw, as this made it apparent to the British colonists that the French had them surrounded.

The Right Honorable William Pitt, first Earl of Chatham (1708–78), entered Parliament in 1735. He made a name for himself while paymaster-general 1746–55. However, his criticism of the Duke of Newcastle and his government's war policy led to his dismissal. After Newcastle's resignation in 1756, Pitt formed a government with George Grenville and the Duke of Devonshire. Disagreements again led to his dismissal; however, several months later he was recalled to form a coalition government with Newcastle. He was very effective as a wartime prime minister, and his policies led to victory over the French in India, North America, and on the seas. He resigned in 1761 following opposition to his plans to further the war. He spent the next five years criticizing the government, denouncing British policy towards the American colonies. In 1766, Pitt was recalled to form and lead another coalition government, but his second term as prime minister was not successful. His most loyal ministers resigning around him, a depressed Pitt resigned in 1768. After this, he remained in the political arena, speaking out against British policy in the colonies, and fighting for parliamentary reform. He collapsed while speaking in the Lords, and died one month later in 1778. (Topfoto/The British Library/HIP)

The British were not simply being paranoid – it seems the French did intend to construct a series of forts from Louisbourg to New Orleans, effectively enclosing the British colonies. The two countries were now very close to the outbreak of hostilities.

Governor Robert Dinwiddie of Virginia was not prepared to let the French derail the British claim to the Ohio Valley. The area was of great interest to Virginians, especially with the continuing activities of the Ohio Company in the area. The valley was also considered to be an area subordinate to the Iroquois Six Nations, allies of the British, and there were some Iroquois there under Chief Tanaghrisson, better known as the "Half King." Therefore it was clear to the governor that the British claim was justified, and the French were seizing British territory. If nothing was done, the French forts would, by actual occupation, legitimize their claims, and the area would be lost to Britain, and particularly to Virginia.

Propaganda through cartography. This 1755 map, sold in London, is entitled "A new and accurate map of the English empire in North America: Representing their rightful claim as confirm'd by charters, and the formal surrender of their Indian friends; likewise the encroachments of the French, with the several forts they have unjustly erected therein. By a Society of Anti-Gallicans." (Library of Congress)

19

The first step was to make it clear to the French that they were intruders. This task Dinwiddie allocated to the young Major George Washington, who though inexperienced was eager to deliver the ultimatum. Accompanied by Christopher Gist and a few men including his translator Jacob Van Braam, and the Half King, Washington made the long journey into the wilderness to Fort Le Boeuf. On December 11, 1753, Washington delivered Governor Dinwiddie's letter to Commandant Le Gardeur de Saint-Pierre, whom Washington described as an "elderly Gentleman, and has much the Air of a Soldier." Washington started back with Gist for Williamsburg to report to Dinwiddie, while de Saint-Pierre had the translated ultimatum sent to Québec. The ultimatum signaled to both sides that they should occupy the area as fast as possible. In the spring of the following year, Washington, now a lieutenant-colonel, led 132 Virginian provincial soldiers toward the fork of the Allegheny, Monongahela, and Ohio rivers. A detachment of the Virginians reached the spot which would later become the city of Pittsburgh and started building a fort. A few days later, on April 16, a large force of French and Canadians, under the command of Claude Pécaudy de Contrecoeur arrived and ordered the Virginians to withdraw immediately. Heavily outnumbered, the Virginians had no choice but to obey. De Contrecoeur's men then continued construction of the fort, which they named Fort Duquesne. It was seen, by Dinwiddie and others, as tantamount to an act of war on the part of the French. It was now only a matter of time until the first major confrontation.

REDCOATS AND COLONIALS
THE BRITISH FORCES IN 1755

A t the time of the French advance to secure the Ohio Valley, there were very few British regular troops in the old Thirteen Colonies. To defend Lake Champlain, Lake Ontario, and New York City there were just four independent companies in the colony of New York, with three more in South Carolina to guard against potential Spanish and Indian forays. The "Fourteenth Colony" Nova Scotia, and Newfoundland had three regular regiments with artillery and ranger companies as they had as their neighbor the powerful French naval base and fortress of Louisbourg on Cape Breton Island. In addition there were the French forts Beauséjour and Gaspereau on their western borders and most of the local population were neutral Acadians, the descendants of the settlers of French Acadia before it was ceded to Britain in 1713. In all, the British colonies had about 2,500 British regular troops of variable quality in 1754. Therefore many of the first soldiers to fight for the British in the French and Indian War were colonial troops raised in America, both militiamen and provincial troops, and the colony of Virginia took the lead in opposing the French in the Ohio Valley.

ROYAL TROOPS IN NORTH AMERICA

The Independent Companies and Royal Regiments

In 1754 there were no British line regiments stationed in the Thirteen Colonies. The settlement patterns and politics of the American colonies did not favor much involvement from the royal government in Britain; puritans and others who had come to America to leave behind the religious intolerance in England were not eager to see royal soldiers in their new home. There were more royal troops in garrison following the 1713 Treaty of Utrecht, but these

American-raised Regular Units

The private on the left is from Shirley's 50th or Pepperell's 51st Regiments of Foot in 1755; the sergeant in the center is from Pepperell's regiment. The men of these regiments had identical, plain clothing for reasons of economy. It was red faced with red, with white metal buttons and lace. Much of the arms and equipment issued to the regiments turned out to be defective, including the muskets and cartridge boxes, causing regular complaints. In contrast, the clothing seems to have been of decent quality. On the right is a private from one of the New York independent companies, wearing the green jacket, leather buckskin breeches and green "Indian stockings" first adopted as a duty uniform in 1756 by Captain Cruikshank's company. The outfit was very popular with that company, and spread to the other companies by 1760. The regular uniform of the independent companies continued to be red coats with green lapels and cuffs, red waistcoat and breeches, white metal buttons, and tricorn hat laced with white. Officers had silver buttons and lace. (David Rickman © Osprey Publishing Ltd)

troops were largely posted on the northern and southern frontiers to watch the French and the Spanish.

During 1740–41 a new element appeared: thousands of American colonists were recruited locally to form Gooch's 61st Regiment, a large unit on the British regular establishment which was sent to serve against the Spanish in the West Indies. The campaigns were disastrous, and only one man in ten returned, and this had a negative impact on the future enlistment of Americans in the British Army. In 1745, following the capture of Louisbourg, the government in London commissioned two American heroes of the hour, William Shirley and William Pepperell, each to raise a regiment of 1,000 men in America for the British regular establishment, to be numbered 65th and 66th in precedence. Neither regiment reached its authorized establishment, however, and they were sent to garrison the newly won fortress. There were disputes over the men's treatment and the low number of commissions granted to Americans, and the regiments were disbanded in 1749. The colonists felt they were badly treated and led, and thus preferred to serve in their own provincial colonial units, which assumed a more permanent character from the late 1740s.

Nevertheless, the British authorities tried to attract recruits once again during the French and Indian War, with mixed results. In the fall of 1754, Shirley and Pepperell were again appointed by the Crown to each raise an infantry regiment on the regular British establishment. There was once more some discontent over the low number of officers' commissions granted to Americans, as well as various financial difficulties. Both regiments did muster enough recruits to be formed by early summer 1755, though neither had more than half of its establishment strength. The 60th (Royal Americans) Regiment of Foot had even more severe problems recruiting. Originally planned as a four-battalion regiment raised in North America, eventually only one quarter of the regiment were Americans, the remainder filled with British and European recruits. Despite these early issues, the battalions of the 60th participated with distinction throughout the war.

In 1754, the Thirteen Colonies had seven regular units named Independent Companies, posted along areas of the South Carolina and New York frontiers. Detachments from the three South Carolina independent companies formed into the temporary Independent Company led by Captain McKay were the first to join the war. They joined Washington's Virginians at Fort Necessity in June 1754. Used to garrison duty, these troops were quite unsuited to the frontier, and, in any event, were too few to face the French regulars. These troops were also present at Monongahela, and in November its remaining men were drafted into Shirley's 50th while the officers and NCOs went back to South Carolina to recruit anew. The companies raised garrisoned forts, and fought the Cherokees, until disbandment in 1764.

Clarke's and Rutherford's companies were sent to Virginia and joined Braddock's army in 1755. The battle of Monongahela was the first action seen by these New York independent companies, and they were badly mauled. Further detachments from the New York independent companies served through the war, and following service in the West Indies, when strength fell from nearly 300 to 101 men fit for duty and recruitment was impossible, they were disbanded in 1763.

In 1755, Philip's 40th Regiment of Foot formed part of the expedition which captured Fort Beauséjour on June 25. In 1757 the main body of it was at Halifax, and the 40th took part in the siege of Louisbourg in 1758. Left there in garrison, its grenadier company was part of Wolfe's "Louisbourg Grenadiers," a three-company temporary unit which served with distinction in the 1759 Québec campaign. The regiment was sent to Canada in 1760, and was present at the capitulation of Montréal.

Shirley's and Pepperell's regiments of foot, both well under strength, were ordered to garrison the forts at Oswego on Lake Ontario, and both regiments remained there until August 1756 when, after a short but brave resistance, they surrendered to the Marquis de Montcalm. Almost all of both regiments were taken as prisoners to Canada, and eventually to France for exchange. Only two companies of the 51st escaped the disaster. Both units had practically ceased to exist, and were formally disbanded on March 7, 1757.

Regiments of the Line in 1754

When news of the first clashes reached Britain, attempts were being made to improve the armed services, which were in a pitiful condition. The navy had 200 over-extended ships and the army was down to less than 20,000 men. A large number of battalions had been disbanded in 1748 after the end of the War of Austrian Succession. The disbanded regiments were mainly the least senior, but the Duke of Cumberland had managed to retain some because they were good regiments, including the 54th to 59th Foot, which subsequently became the 42nd to 48th Foot.

The Duke of Argyll had remarked in 1740 that the soldiers of the British Army were for the most part "too stupid or too infamous to learn or carry on a Trade." But recorded behavior rarely bears out the expressed contention that the army was the refuge of the desperate and criminal classes; instead there are many recorded instances of courage of the 18th-century British soldier. Most recruits were young, and frequently unmarried at the time of enlistment. The most basic motivation for enlistment was probably economic – the army would at least promise a relatively secure source of food, shelter, and clothing. The majority of recruits were probably youths picked up at country fairs or after the harvest. There is no real reason to doubt that many volunteers for the British Army in the 18th century were drawn by the promise of an easy life and military glory, a more attractive vision than laboring dawn till dusk for the rest of their lives in the parish where they had been born. There were also those men who did not choose to join: in time of crisis Parliament often passed Temporary Acts allowing local authorities to conscript a broad range of men. Known as "vestry men," they could include every petty criminal for miles around. These men were very much a mixed blessing and hardly served to raise the status of soldiers.

The British Army of the early to mid-18th century was an advocate of the linear style of warfare (see page 37), and consequently British infantry soldiers were required to be rigorously trained in weapons, fighting tactics, and discipline. Such training was carried out centered around the manual exercise and platoon firing much more than on the Continent, mainly because there were few training facilities for complete battalions and larger formations. An important factor in the British Army's success with linear warfare in Europe was the superior Land Pattern flintlock and its derivatives, commonly known as the "Brown Bess." Contemporary French firearms are generally held up as being of a superior quality, but testimony from British officers is unanimous in stressing the real edge which they reckoned to have from the heavier weight of ball.

Infantry regiments at this time usually only mustered a single battalion, though several were authorized to raise a second during the early years of the French and Indian War. In peacetime infantry battalions could sometimes muster as few as eight companies, but on active service usually mustered ten. In wartime some regiments had "Additional Companies" which functioned as recruit depots.

In July 1754, before the news of Fort Necessity had reached Europe, money and arms were sent across the Atlantic, and in late September, when the worst was known, Colonel Sir Peter Halket's 44th and Colonel Thomas Dunbar's 48th Infantry Regiments were ordered to sail from Cork to North America. Each battalion was about 350 strong with additional drafts of variable quality added to them, bringing them up to 700 each, and it was hoped that Americans would later be recruited. Recruiting in America proved most disappointing and Dunbar's 48th was even below its initial establishment when it marched west in June 1755. It was accompanied by a company of the Royal Artillery under Captain Ord to serve the field guns of the expedition. In preparation for the expedition, Major-General Braddock ordered that soldiers leave behind their hangers (short swords), belts, and heavy equipment, and bring only a spare shirt, a pair of spare stockings, a pair of spare shoes, and wear their brown marching gaiters. Thin pads of leather were placed in hats between lining and crown as protection against the hot sun and they were issued new clothing more suitable for the climate, including linen waistcoats and breeches rather than those made of warm red wool, but no bush-warfare training was provided.

Sir William Shirley (1693–1771) was born in England and emigrated in 1731 to Massachusetts, where he was very successful in business and politics, becoming its governor in 1741–45 and 1753–57. Shirley was one of the most influential leaders advocating the conquest of New France. He was commander-in-chief in 1755–56 following Edward Braddock's death, until Lord Loudoun's arrival in North America. Colonel of British royal regiments in 1746 and 1754, lieutenant-general and knighted in 1759, governor of the Bahamas 1761–69, Shirley retired to his beloved Massachusetts in 1770. (Library of Congress)

Although the British regulars were good soldiers, they were totally unprepared and untrained for the kind of fighting they would face in the wilderness. North America came as a shock to most British veterans, accustomed as they were to the open countryside of Europe, with level roads and small settlements interspersed along the way to provide billets. Although some British soldiers and officers were used to irregular warfare from experiences in Scotland or on the battlefields of Europe, most were daunted by the conditions in North America. One veteran on Braddock's expedition was dismayed by the "Trees, Swamps and Thickets…the very Face of the Country is enough to strike a Damp in the most resolute Mind." He concluded "I can not conceive how War can be made in such a country."

Braddock's defeat and death made it obvious to the Duke of Cumberland, the Captain-General of the British Army, that the North American theater demanded a special type of soldier. In Europe, the tasks of scouting, screening, and skirmishing for an army on campaign were usually assigned to the cavalry. However, the wilderness was totally unsuitable for cavalry, and the British heavy

infantry would need to adapt to survive and defeat an opponent already skilled at forest fighting. British success would hinge on a transformation of the tactics of the British forces, but this would not begin until the tenure of John Campbell, Earl of Loudoun as commander-in-chief in 1756.

COLONIAL TROOPS

Militias

In nearly all the American colonies, males between the ages of 16 and 60, whether freemen or servants, were compelled to be listed into their local militia company and attend the company musters and regimental training days. Such occasions in colonial America during the 17th and much of the 18th centuries were considered serious events, and generally bore little resemblance to the carnival-like atmosphere which characterizes many descriptions of 19th-century militia musters. In early colonial times the survival of a community and the lives of its members could well depend upon the proficiency of the militia. The frequency of training varied. In the early 17th century it could be as often as once a week in Massachusetts and Virginia, but this schedule decreased as time went on, to a few days throughout the year. The regimental muster of a unit took place at least once a year and was usually well attended.

Colonel James Kennedy's 43rd Foot served in North America from 1758 to 1765. Facings were white, and the white lace had two white stripes with a row of black stars between. The cap had white scroll-work relieved in black, a dark blue cipher, and a blue and white tuft. Sir Peter Halket's (later James Abercromby's) 44th Foot was one of the regiments involved in the battle at Monongahela, but served on in America until 1765. They wore yellow-ochre facings and white lace, with a blue and black zigzag divided by a yellow stripe. The grenadier-corporal has white scrolls and a black cipher on his cap front. The strip of lace on his right shoulder holds the knot of his rank, hanging down the back. Hugh Warburton's 45th Foot served in America from 1758 to 1765. Its facings were a dark bluish green, its lace white with green stripes and stars. The mitre cap has white scrolls and cipher on its green front, and a green and white tuft. (The Royal Collection ©2006 H.M. Queen Elizabeth II)

Officers had various military and administrative obligations besides bearing arms, and senior officers – generally the community's wealthiest men – were usually obligated by law to furnish drums and colors. No one was paid, but the prestige then associated with being a militia officer was substantial and such service was considered an honor. The appointments of senior officers were made by the legislature while captains and subalterns were chosen locally, often by election. The men who became officers were called by their military rank for the rest of their lives as a mark of respect.

There were some exemptions from enlistment in the militia, for magistrates, public notaries, deputies to a legislature, ministers of the church, schoolmasters, students, physicians, masters of ships, fishermen, herdsmen, and invalids. There were few Jewish families in the early colonies and prejudice against non-Christians was such that they were not welcome in the militias.

The enlistment of African Americans, be they slaves or free, was generally forbidden by law. Since the great majority of African Americans were slaves, it was considered that their duty to their master superseded any obligation to the colony and that, in any event, their owners would have to be compensated for a loss of property rights. It was also widely believed that arming and giving military training to African Americans was inviting future difficulties. Thus, legislation in nearly every colony forbade the arming of African Americans. In

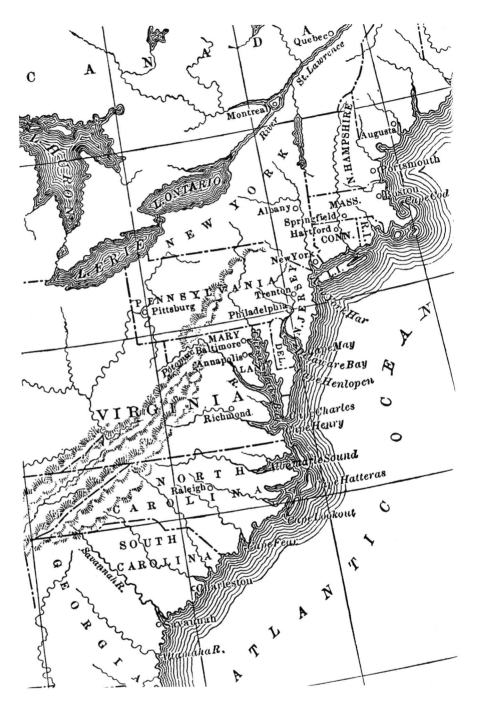

Virginia they were nevertheless allowed to be enlisted as drummers or trumpeters from 1723. They might be drafted as pioneers. From 1707 it was specified that African Americans in Massachusetts would "do service equivalent to trainings" by providing "so many days' work yearly" for community labor. Rhode Island had initially allowed free African Americans in the militia in 1667, but they were limited to being unarmed musicians or laborers from 1708. Such limitations were general because of the fear of slave uprisings in the south and just "trouble" in the north. There was a notable exception in South Carolina between 1715 and 1740, when African Americans were allowed in the militia. Naturally in actual practice, a few African Americans might nevertheless be found in some units.

The early colonial militia units were organized in imitation of the English "Trained Bands," with proportions of musketeers and pikemen. Indeed, they were commonly called "Trainbands" right up to the early 18th century, particularly in New England. A Trainband would usually be a company-sized unit of about 50 men drawn from a village or a town ward, which would form part of a county regiment. Early artillery gunners were individual specialists but might be grouped, the first such unit being raised in Boston in 1638. Troops of mounted militiamen appeared in the 1640s.

All militiamen were obliged by law to possess arms. Many obligations were specified in the colonial militia laws and the men would be fined if they did not meet the requirements, the money usually being used to purchase the unit's drums and colors. Early Trainbands in New England included pikemen, but very few remained by the middle of the 17th century. The armament of early musketeers generally consisted of heavy matchlock muskets with rests, but the light flintlock "snaphance" muskets became plentiful from the 1630s and predominant by the next decade. The snaphance muskets referred to by the early American colonists were in fact conventional flintlocks, as there were actually few true snaphance arms in the settlements (the distinction lay in the design of the lock).

Swords and edged weapons were varied as they were largely owned by individuals, but cutlasses – relatively short, heavy, broad-bladed weapons – were especially popular. By the end of the 17th century many militiamen had given up carrying the cumbersome swords, and militia laws eventually omitted them from the list of required arms. Bayonets appear to have been scarce unless furnished with government muskets. Halberds were common for sergeants, but half-pikes for officers much scarcer, especially in rural communities. Armor and protective clothing was favored by the early settlers, but went out of use by foot troops from the 1640s. However, cavalrymen in Massachusetts wore buff coats, helmets, and breast- and back-plates to the end of the 17th century. Officers' gorgets were rarely seen. Uniforms for militias were rare until the eve of the French and Indian War.

Provincial troops

From the late 17th century, the North American colonies raised a variety of troops to serve for limited periods of time against the Indians and later against the French. The legislature of the province would vote laws enabling these units to be raised, usually consisting of infantry regiments, together with a few companies of rangers (see page 119). They were recruited from volunteers lured by bounties and wages. The length of service was usually reckoned to be for the time required by the expedition.

The coming of age of American provincial units as quasi-regular troops came during the French and Indian War. They were usually authorized in May of each year and were kept in pay for service until November, when the men would be discharged. In some colonies a few companies were maintained during the winter to guard the frontiers. The great majority of these units had uniforms. Some wore red but, perhaps to differentiate themselves from the British regulars, they were generally dressed in blue or green. Officers were appointed by the provincial governor and thus received "provincial" commissions. Many officers would be the same individual from one year to the next. Thus by 1759–60, units had a good proportion of officers and soldiers who were veterans of several campaigns. Recruiting was, however, consistently below the establishments authorized by the colonial legislatures. In 1759 provincial legislators voted for 20,680 men but 16,835 were actually enlisted. In 1760, 21,180 were voted for, but only 15,942 enlisted. Nevertheless, these were substantial numbers of troops which added considerable weight to the British war effort.

In terms of tactics, the militias and provincials mostly served as support to the British regulars; their rangers and light troops could to an extent check the marauding frontier raids of the French and Indians, but could not make forays deep into the wilderness. American provincial infantry regiments were generally not as disciplined, nor as well-drilled or as steady in action, as British regular troops. Provincial officers lacked military education and experience in the field. All this surprised no one as these were temporary units best suited for support or garrison duty. On the other hand, Alexander Hamilton noted that the "courage of our Americans demonstrates that they would make excellent soldiers." Some would gain considerable experience and distinction during the French and Indian War, but in 1754–55 American provincials and militias were very new to the art of war as waged in North America. This was because the vast majority of Americans at that time resided safely in the extensively settled farming areas, fishing villages, and towns found all along the Atlantic seaboard and most did not venture into the continent's primeval forest wilderness; that was the domain of their "French and Indian" opponents.

Virginia

The structure and organization of the colonial and militia forces varied between the colonies. Prominent in the defense of the colonies during the French and Indian War was the colony of Virginia which responded to the call for men throughout the conflict.

The Virginia Regiment

These three men represent the uniform of the Virginia Regiment during the French and Indian War. The man on the left is a private from 1754. Initially the men of the regiment were expected to wear civilian clothing, but in early March 1754 George Washington found many recruits to be "quite destitute" and reported that they were willing to be clothed at their own expense by deductions from pay. Governor Dinwiddie agreed, and approved a "coat and breeches of red cloth" for the men. Officers too procured some regimentals. By the end of 1754 the color of the uniform had changed from red to blue. In February 1755, Dinwiddie felt that "blue turned up with red" made very proper uniforms for his troops. The private on the right wears this uniform, which the Virginia Regiment maintained until 1762 when it was disbanded. Generally the regiment was one of the better-equipped provincial units in the American colonies. In the center is an officer of the regiment dressed in accordance with the uniform order of September 17, 1755. (David Rickman © Osprey Publishing Ltd)

The first permanent English settlement in the present USA was begun at Jamestown, Virginia, in May 1607. The first structure finished was a triangular fort, within which the houses of the settlers were built. From the very beginning the colony had to fight for survival. Virginia had to organize and maintain troops and weapons for its protection, and the early years were characterized by raids and countless skirmishes against the American Indians who wished to drive the colonists out.

At the outbreak of the French and Indian War, the Virginia militia was divided into four districts. Each district had adjutants to train both officers and men. The militia was estimated at 36,000 men able to bear arms, who were according to Governor Dinwiddie, in "want of a martial spirit," being a "lazy, indolent set of people." What is more, a period report noted that "not above half that number are armed, and the arms of those who have any are of different bores." The province's arms store had no small arms left in it, but did contain 28 halberds, 12 drums, and some powder and shot. The governor was proved somewhat pessimistic, as arms were eventually found, and the militia on the frontier did mobilize and gave good service. However, more than this was needed, and in January 1754 the Virginia legislature authorized funds to raise two companies of 100 men each to form the Virginia provincial regiment. The men were to be drawn from volunteers, one company from Augusta County under Lieutenant-Colonel Washington, and the other, mainly traders and woodsmen, under Captain William Trent. This establishment quickly grew to six companies by March, organized as a regiment under Colonel Joshua Fry. Captain Trent's men were tasked with building a fort at the forks of the Monongahela and Ohio rivers, but were repulsed on April 16. It was Virginian provincials under Washington who ambushed the Jumonville party, and who suffered badly at Fort Necessity in July. The Virginia Regiment was finally broken up in the fall of 1754.

In 1755, Major-General Edward Braddock raised men in Virginia, forming them into six companies of rangers, two companies of carpenters, and Stewart's Company of Light Horse. The emphasis was now on the royal troops, which the few provincial companies accompanied toward Fort Duquesne. The battle of Monongahela left the companies badly mauled. Dinwiddie ordered out the militia, but finding them panicked, quickly raised three companies of rangers. Fort Cumberland was immediately garrisoned with another 50 men from Virginia.

Following the battle of Monongahela (see page 63), men in frontier communities grouped themselves into "associations" to form volunteer companies. In August, a troop of light horse led by Captain Nathaniel Terry already patrolled the area about Lunenberg; another 50 men under Captain Samuel Overton was to "range" at Hanover. In the fall some 200 militiamen in several companies were reported on guard in Hampshire County, keeping the frontier lands safe "from the Incursions of the Indian enemy." Units were not only raised on the frontier, a cavalry association of about 200 gentlemen — apparently lawyers — was formed by Colonel Peyton Randolph, the attorney-general of Virginia, from May 7, 1756. They gathered at Fredericksburg on May 20 for service, and marched toward Winchester, but, the alarm on the frontier having subsided, they were retained for further service.

On August 14, 1755, Washington was commissioned colonel of a new Virginia Regiment with 1,000 men, and was appointed commander-in-chief of all Virginia forces. Unlike most provincials, the Regiment was kept on service during the winter of 1755–56. The following March, authorization was passed for 1,500 men in provincial service, including 1,000 for the Virginia Regiment. Over the next two years the regiment was augmented, and on March 30, 1758, the colony increased its forces to 2,000 men in two regiments. The 1st Virginia Regiment continued under Washington's command; the 2nd Virginia Regiment was under Colonel William Byrd. Both served with the army of General Forbes which marched on Fort Duquesne, destroying it in November. The elimination of this major threat to Virginia led to the disbanding of the 2nd Regiment in December. The 1st remained on guard along the frontier, with part of it serving in Pittsburgh during 1759. The regiment underwent various other changes until 1762 when the Virginia Regiment was disbanded.

TENSIONS

Commissioned officers in the provincial forces, even as high as the rank of general, were degraded to the level of senior captain when serving alongside regular forces in the field. This was a major source of resentment for the provincial forces in the early years of the war. Loudoun was uninterested in resolving this issue with colonial governments, and the Pitt-Newcastle ministry did not make concessions to the colonial governments on disputes over command and payment until 1758 with the appointment of Major-General James Abercromby as commander-in-chief. In an effort to resolve past issues of reinforcements and supplies and make the way smoother for Abercromby, Britain agreed to pay for a portion of the raising, clothing, and arming of provincial units recruited for future campaigns, and to discontinue the custom of de-ranking provincial officers. Now the provincial officers retained their rank, but were junior to regular officers of equivalent and higher rank. Pitt considered this necessary to appease the colonial governments and persuade them to recruit more men for the campaigns. Even though the British government ultimately funded colonial units, they had to rely on the colonial governments' efforts to fill the ranks. In the end, Pitt's tactic was successful, with the colonial governments providing more soldiers than before in 1758 and 1759. The constant need for soldiers and supplies from the colonies was a continual source of friction between British military officials and colonial assemblymen. Both sides accused the other of not carrying its share of the load or of being autocratic. The debate became so acrimonious that even the end of the war didn't resolve it and the argument continued through the financial crises of the postwar period.

COLONIALS AND MILITIA OF NEW FRANCE

THE FRENCH FORCES IN 1755

The only uniformed French presence in North America until the arrival of Jean-Armand Dieskau's regulars in 1755 were the independent companies of the *Compagnies Franches de la Marine*. The Canadian militia also played an important role in the war. The French regular troops, the *troupes de terre*, were not sent to New France until later in the war.

Battalion color, Île Royale Compagnies Franches de la Marine, *1740s and 1750s. In 1758 the colors had to be surrendered to the British, who took them, with other colors, to St Paul's, where their silk had totally disintegrated by 1840. Meanwhile the Île Royale* Compagnies Franches *were repatriated to France and granted new colors in 1759. Following their disbandment in December 1760, the new colors were stored for a few years until sent to the garrison infantry of French Guyana. Reconstruction by Michel Pétard. (Department of National Defence, reproduced with the permission of the Minister of Public Works and Government Services Canada)*

COMPAGNIES FRANCHES DE LA MARINE

The *Compagnies Franches de la Marine* were so-called because they were independent companies, and because the colonies were under the administration of the Ministry of the Navy. This meant the troops in the various colonies were raised, paid, clothed, and regulated by that ministry. The service had been created out of an earlier organization in the 1690s. For most of the first half of the 18th century there were only about 800 men – some 28 companies of 30 or so men led by three officers. By 1750 the strength had risen to 30 companies of 50 men; in 1756 it went up to 30 of 65, and in 1757 it would rise again to 40 companies of 65. Officers and men were recruited in France, and encouraged to settle in the colony on completion of eight years' service. As the war dragged on and manpower became more of a problem, local men were accepted into the *Compagnies Franches*. A proportion of the officers had, in practice, been drawn from the local *noblesse* for many years, Canadian-born descendants of regular officers who had settled in Canada during the 17th century. The sons of officers often served as cadets with the troops until they could secure a commission. Thus a powerful network of military families dominated Canadian society. Most of the Canadian officers were familiar with

Compagnies Franches de la Marine

The regulation gray-white and blue uniforms worn by the *Compagnies Franches de la Marine* in the French colonies in America were very similar whether in New France, the West Indies, or Guyana. The officer on the left is dressed for a full dress parade, carrying a spontoon and sword, and wearing a gorget, and the coveted Cross of St Louis on a scarlet ribbon on his breast. Created in 1693 by Louis XIV, the Royal and Military Order of St Louis knighted officers who had long and distinguished service careers. Hundred of colonial officers earned the cross, especially in Canada. Center front is a sergeant. NCOs were armed with halberds for formal occasions. In the 1750s, their rank was shown by edging lace at the cuffs and pocket flaps. On the right is a *cadet à l'aiguillette*. Cadets only existed in Canada, Île de Royale, and Louisiana. They were distinguished by a blue and white aiguillette, but otherwise were dressed, armed, and equipped as private soldiers. The drummer at back left is dressed in the king's livery, as the *Compagnies Franches* were royal troops. Back right is a private; corporals and fusiliers were armed with muskets, bayonets and swords, and were equipped with the *gargoussier* belly box and powder horn with its own narrow sling well into the 1750s. (Eugène Lelièpvre © Osprey Publishing Ltd)

frontier warfare and had often spent years serving in outposts in the wilderness. Many had learned American Indian languages from the time they were cadets detached to live and serve with allied Indian nations. In theory, the rank system of the officers went no higher than captain. In fact the governor-general, who exercised overall control, appointed the senior captains as commandants of an area or a fort. He would also appoint commandants to lead allied Indians, this role being reserved for officers with great experience and diplomacy in relations with the Indian nations, like Ensign Joseph Coulon de Villiers, Sieur de Jumonville, 36 years old and an experienced officer.

From their observation of Indian warfare and their way of life, Canadian officers devised an unwritten tactical doctrine that combined the best elements of European organization and discipline with the American Indians' extraordinary ability to travel great distances largely undetected and mount very fierce attacks. From the last decades of the 17th century, mixed parties of Canadian militiamen and allied Indians put these tactics to the test. They were led by a cadre of selected regular officers, almost always Canadians, assisted by officer cadets and those regular soldiers experienced in the ways of the wilderness. The doctrine was an outstanding success; not only did it keep the colonists of the British colonies away but, just as important, it gave the French military superiority over hostile Indian nations. First the Iroquois confederation, and especially its Mohawk nation, was humbled, and later the Fox nation was almost annihilated in the southern Great Lakes region. This ensured that from their string of forts on the shores of the Great Lakes and the upper Mississippi valley, the French enjoyed substantial control over a vast area of North America's wilderness.

In peacetime some units looked more like settlers than soldiers, even before discharge. The companies were scattered as garrisons and escorts all over the frontiers of the settled areas, often far out in the wilds. There was little to do of a military nature, and before Governor-General Duquesne tightened discipline it appears that many of the officers were mostly concerned with fur-trading. Some of the officers and men of the more isolated commands "went native," and adopted certain aspects of American Indian customs which did not endear them to the regular troops, who considered them, at best, provincial.

As well as the issue uniform (see page 35) officers and men in Canada and upper Louisiana had other dress for expeditions. Officers had discovered that Canadian militiamen were ideally dressed for expeditions which took them hundreds of kilometers deep into the wilderness in canoes and on foot. The officers and men adopted the same dress, which consisted of a cap and a *capot* (a naval hooded cloth coat fastened by a sash at the waist); the garments below the waist were Indian, a breech clout, *mitasses* (long leggings of cloth or soft leather), and moccasins. It seems that the uniform waistcoats were sometimes used in summer instead of the *capot*.

Soldiers in distant outposts would keep their European-style uniform for more formal occasions and wear *capots* for ordinary duties.

Although there was a total of some 1,850 men on the establishment, they were answerable primarily to the governor, and were not always placed at Montcalm's disposal, although some companies took part in virtually every one of the frontier battles. In 1757 the number of companies serving in Canada, as distinct from Louisiana and the maritime colonies of New France, was set at 40. For the most part they were scattered in far-flung garrisons, but eight of the companies were formed into a provisional marching battalion that year to serve alongside Montcalm's *troupes de terre*. In 1758 there were 24 companies on detached service in Louisbourg, reducing the Canadian force to about 1,000 men.

The companies took part in just about every battle from the end of the 17th century until the surrender of Montréal in 1760. The remnants were sent to France and incorporated into the eight army battalions that had served in Canada on December 25, 1760.

Linear vs. irregular warfare

Warfare in the mid- to late-18th century was characterized by two different fighting styles: linear and irregular warfare. The linear or Continental style was designed to maximize the effectiveness of the flintlock. Troops deployed in a line and delivered a synchronized volley of fire; the aim being to offset the musket's inaccuracy with sheer volume of coordinated fire. Once the battalions had deployed, the forward line would fire, then move back to reload. They would be replaced by the second line, which would repeat the process and so on. The French Army deployed its battalions into four lines, with a frontage of 162 men. The British Army deployed its battalions into three lines, with a frontage of 260 men; some experts argue that this gave the British an advantage by providing a bigger volley, while others claim that the French system was more compact and more maneuverable, and thus superior. In 1758, the British expanded their frontage even further by deploying their battalions in only two lines.

The ability to deliver coordinated heavy volleys on the main body of the enemy line was paramount to an army's successful performance. The main intention of this tactic was to create havoc and disorder within the enemy's ranks. It was common for a soldier to require 18 months of training to perform the various drills required and troop discipline was critical.

The French and Indian War was instrumental in the further development of irregular or frontier-style warfare. This approach was characterized by the use of lightly armed troops who could march easily in heavily wooded terrain and fight in small, flexible units. The system was not an entirely North American phenomenon; however, as the majority of the fighting in North America took place in woodlands, the terrain necessitated the development and deployment of light troops and other specialists in much greater numbers than had ever been used before. The theater also demanded that successful armies be proficient in road-building, fort-building, and moving and supplying troops through difficult terrain, and armies had to adapt to this.

While both France and England had a core of woodland expertise among their fighting men, each side perceived that the war was not going to be won solely on familiarity with the ways of the woods and the American Indians. Strategy for both sides involved deploying large numbers of regular troops from Europe who would be able to wage a traditional linear-style battle when terrain permitted. The senior commanders of both armies recognized, to varying degrees, the usefulness of the irregular troops, but preferred linear-style engagements to provide a decisive conclusion to the conflict.

The various companies of the Canonniers-Bombardiers *all had an identical uniform of blue faced with red during the French and Indian War. Officers (left) had uniforms of finer quality cloth, and wore gilt gorgets when on duty. When serving guns, gun crews would leave their coats and equipment aside for ease of movement. (Eugène Lelièpvre © Osprey Publishing Ltd)*

Colonial Artillery corps

From the mid-17th century, individual master gunners, also called *Commissaires de l'artillerie* were posted in the colonies with a few assistants to oversee artillery matters and provide training. Gunnery schools were eventually established to provide trained artillerymen. The first was organized in 1697 at Québec City where a soldier from each of the colony's 28 companies was detached to be trained as the master gunner in what soon became known as an unofficial artillery company. Similar schools were organized at Louisbourg in 1735, Mobile in Louisiana in 1744, Martinique in 1746, and Haiti had several from 1755.

On June 20, 1743, the king signed an ordinance creating a company of *Canonniers-Bombardiers* to serve at Louisbourg. Other companies were soon raised elsewhere: Haiti on December 19, 1745, Martinique and the Leewards on April 30, 1747, and Canada on April 10, 1750. On March 15, 1757, a second company was ordered raised in Canada, another at Martinique on November 20, 1757, and a second company for Louisbourg on February 1, 1758. On November 1, 1759, a company was ordered raised in Louisiana. In general, a company would have about 50 men, many of whom would be detached elsewhere. For instance, gunners from Martinique were detached to Guadeloupe, Grenada, St Lucia, and Marie-Galante.

All companies generally had the same conditions, pay, uniforms, equipment and weapons. Those in Canada, Louisbourg, Martinique, and the Leewards fought with distinction against much stronger British forces. The companies in Louisbourg ceased to exist following the fall of the fortress in 1758, those in Canada in 1760, and the company in Louisiana was disbanded in 1763.

NEW FRANCE MILITIAS

From the late 1660s in Canada, every man able to bear arms from the age of 16 to 60 was enrolled in a company of militia. Each parish had at least one company, usually numbering about 50 men, and each led by a captain, plus lieutenants and sergeants. The parish companies belonged to one of the three districts of Québec, Trois-Rivières, and Montréal. Each district had an administrative staff consisting of a colonel, assisted by majors; in wartime, regular colonial officers had overall command. In 1750 the militia amounted to some 13,000 men, including 724 officers divided into 165 companies, and to over 15,200 ten years later.

A Canadian militia company assembled once a month for muster, and often for some target shooting instead of drill. Besides military matters, the company was

An early 20th-century watercolor depicting a French Canadian militiaman of the late 1750s, dressed against the cold. (Mary E. Bonham, National Archives of Canada, C-006217)

concerned with many local government duties such as the pursuit of criminals and road construction. Generally, only a small proportion of men, usually volunteers, would be detached to serve in military expeditions. Many Canadians were employed in the fur trade as *voyageurs* or as small traders, either part-time or full-time, and thus made ideal candidates for wilderness expeditions when called up for militia duty. They were fierce and outstanding bush fighters and raiders who could move very fast in the wilderness during any season with almost incredible endurance. As they handled guns from childhood, many were outstanding marksmen with their favorite weapon, the lightweight and dependable smoothbore hunting and trade musket made in Tulle, France. A key difference between the Canadian militia and the militias of the American colonies was that the former operated under a highly effective central command system: whatever the governor-general decided was the order of the day.

Canadian militiamen had no official military uniform. Although they received no pay, clothing and equipment was supplied to the militiamen going on campaign. This generally consisted of a cloth cap, a *capot*, breeches or breechclouts, *mitasses*, deerskin mitts, and moccasins. As well as a gun, the armament also consisted of a powder horn, a bullet and ammunition pouch, a tomahawk, and often up to three knives: one at the knee garter, one tucked into the sash, and another hanging from the neck. Officers were similarly dressed and equipped, but distinguished by a gilt gorget and, when not on campaign in the wilderness, a sword and, frequently in cities, a spontoon.

During the French and Indian War, increasingly large numbers were embodied as the British armies approached from all sides. In 1759, nearly all able-bodied men were called out, and some 600 were incorporated into the eight metropolitan battalions. In 1760, some 2,264 Canadian militiamen were incorporated into the eight metropolitan and two marine battalions, so that 38 percent of the "French" regulars were actually Canadians. They all fought with distinction in countless engagements and skirmishes until the surrender of Canada.

There were a few specialist units. From 1723, about 20 militiamen in Québec City were trained as gunners, and this unit had grown to a company by 1750. Another militia artillery company had been raised at Montréal by that date. In 1752, Governor-General Duquesne ordered two uniformed bourgeois *Compagnies de Réserve* raised, one in Québec and one in Montréal. A company of militia *Ouvriers* was raised in 1759 to serve as firemen in Québec.

The militia was far less important in Île Royale. Only in 1740 were two companies organized at Louisbourg, four more, and perhaps as many as seven, being organized during the 1745 siege. Port Toulouse also had a company. There is little evidence of a sustained organization between 1749 and 1758, although numerous townsmen assisted the regulars in the 1758 siege of Louisbourg.

A CHARMING FIELD FOR AN ENCOUNTER
FORT NECESSITY, 1754

Following the building of the French Fort Duquesne, Washington and Dinwiddie made alternative plans to conquer the Ohio Valley. The Virginia troops were to assemble at Redstone Creek, around 70 miles from Fort Duquesne and construct a road suitable for wagons and guns toward the fort, to enable a force to advance and dislodge the French. At first, however, there were no supply wagons or horses, no additional troops, and no American Indian allies. Moving west from Will's Creek (Fort Cumberland), Major Washington's talents as a surveyor proved useful for planning the road. His plan required a road about 100 miles long through some very difficult and mountainous terrain, but he and his officers were determined to open the route to the Monongahela as it was the only practicable way to transport the artillery necessary to overcome Fort Duquesne. Despite the strong French presence, the Virginians considered it vital that they maintain a presence on the frontier to sustain their claims in the Ohio and encourage their Indian allies.

The actual building of the road turned out to be a difficult and backbreaking labor for the Virginians. There was no easy, obvious route. The Virginians finally found an opening through the mountains called Great Meadows and established a temporary camp there. They could not have known the fame that future events would bring to this spot, although Washington prophetically described Great Meadows as "a charming field for an encounter."

In May 1754, the building of Fort Duquesne was nearly finished and Commandant de Contrecoeur sent out some French and Indian scouts toward the east. He knew the Virginians had to be somewhere out there and after a few days the scouts came back with worrisome news. According to them, the Virginians were building supply depots (this would have been the camp at Great Meadows) and the scouts felt it could only be in preparation for mounting an

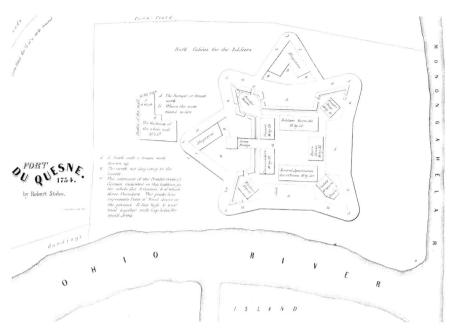

Plan of Fort Duquesne in 1754 by Robert Stobo. The remarkable detailed plan shows the fort's ramparts still under construction on the banks of the Ohio and Monongahela rivers. Robert Stobo was one of the two hostages left with the French to ensure British compliance with the capitulation signed by Washington. Stobo spent his time at Fort Duquesne drawing sketches of the fort, and writing plans for its destruction. He managed to get these papers to the British, but they were discovered by the French following Monongahela. Stobo was subsequently sent to Québec, where he was sentenced to death for spying, but he managed to escape, and rejoin the British army before Louisbourg where the knowledge acquired during his imprisonment proved very useful. (Print after Robert Stobo, photo René Chartrand)

attack on Fort Duquesne. If this was true, de Contrecoeur faced something of a dilemma, as France and Great Britain were not at war. The best course of action seemed to be to send an officer with an ultimatum to be delivered to the first British officer he encountered. This ultimatum would request that the intruders "leave in peace" and advise that there would be no more warnings. Should any hostile act occur, the British would have to bear the responsibility as de Contrecoeur fully intended to "maintain the existing union between two princes that are friends," referring to the kings of France and England. Whatever the particular plans of the English officer, de Contrecoeur was confident that his envoy would enjoy every consideration and be sent back with an answer. Ensign Joseph Coulon de Villiers, Sieur de Jumonville was selected for the task.

Jumonville left Fort Duquesne on May 23, with an escort of 32 men including an interpreter, heading east toward Great Meadows bearing the ultimatum. A drummer named La Batterie was also part of the detachment. This appears to confirm that Jumonville was not leading a war party. A drummer was considered necessary to deliver an ultimatum according to the protocol in force amongst European armies at the time. As the party marched through the forest, the weather was rainy and unpleasant. It rained on May 26 and, seeking some cover from the elements, Jumonville's party settled down in a low spot below a rocky ridge deep in the forest, about 5 miles (8km) from Great Meadows and remained there the next day as the weather conditions were not much better.

Major Washington had been warned by the Half King on May 24 that a French party was approaching. The following day he sent some scouts on

Jumonville Glen, where the ensign and his party were camped when they were ambushed on May 27, 1754. It is clear how Washington and his men could have crept close enough to spy on the French party from above. (René Chartrand)

horseback to patrol the area, but they came back having seen no one. On May 27, Christopher Gist arrived reporting that a party of some 50 French had sacked his settlement. Then, at about eight in the evening, a messenger from the Half King came to report that the French party was seemingly encamped in a nearby gully. In case it was a French trap, Major Washington had the ammunition in the camp at Great Meadows hidden and left a party to guard it. Then Washington and the Half King along with 40 Virginians and 20–30 American Indians quietly moved to attack. It was a difficult trek in the darkness, but they reached the rocky ridge overlooking the French encampment without being detected. Precisely what happened next has never really been clearly established. The evidence is both scarce and contradictory. George Washington's version, as outlined in his *Remarks*, mentioned that "the French sent a detachment to reconnoiter our Camp and obtain intelligence of our strength & position; notice of which being given by the Scouts, G W [George Washington] marched at the head of the party, attacked, killed 9 or 10, & captured 20 odd." His report of May 29 to Virginia's Governor Dinwiddie was written in a similar vein, overall a rather sketchy account of the incident which sparked a war on three continents.

There are other accounts from witnesses, but all are second- or third-hand. The one man in the French party who escaped was a Canadian militiaman named Monceau. He delivered the first news of Jumonville's death, and it was his version of events which Commandant de Contrecoeur sent to Governor-General Duquesne. It stated that:

[in] the morning, at seven o'clock, they [the French] found they were surrounded by English on one side and Indians on the other. They received two volleys from the English, and none from the Indians. Through an interpreter M. de Jumonville told them to stop, as he had to speak to them. They [the English] stopped. M. de Jumonville had read to them my summons to retire... While it was being read, the said Monceau saw all our Frenchmen coming up behind M. de Jumonville, so that they formed a group in the midst of the English and Indians. Meanwhile, Monceau slipped to one side, and went off through the woods.

A gunner, "J.C.B.," who was at Fort Duquesne at the time, also obtained his version from Monceau who had "heard musket shots, and a few moments later, a second volley with cries of the dying." He concluded his party had been ambushed and defeated and decided to run back to Fort Duquesne to bring news of the battle. By making detours in the forest to evade the British-allied American Indians, he reached the fort six days later.

A more direct witness of the event was Ensign Pierre-Jacques Drouillon, an officer of the *troupes de terre* captured by Washington's men. His version was given in English through a translated letter to Governor Dinwiddie in which he stated that Washington should have taken notice, when he attacked, at "about 7 or 8 o'Clock in the morning," that the French detachment did not take "to our arms: he [Washington] might have heard our Interpreter [call out] ... instead of taking that opportunity to fire upon us." Although Drouillon was part of the French detachment, and his recollection is thus essentially first-hand, he was not with the interpreter and as such his account must involve some supposition.

Tanaghrisson, the Half King

Tanaghrisson was taken captive when only a child by the French and their American Indian allies, and was later adopted into the Seneca nation. He was called the "Half King" by the British because he was a sub-chief or representative of the Iroquois leaders in the Ohio Valley. Although the Iroquois leaders wanted the Half King to be neutral in this task, he sided with the British, advising in 1752 that the Virginia colony should build a fort at the forks of the Ohio. In 1753 he and three others accompanied George Washington when he went to Fort Le Boeuf to deliver the ultimatum to the French.

In May 1754, he aided Washington again, informing him of the presence of French soldiers near his camp, and taking part in the attack on Jumonville's party. At the end of the skirmish, the Half King saw that Jumonville was wounded, and killed him with his tomahawk. It was both a horrifying and symbolic act. To the Half King and his people, Jumonville represented the French in the Ohio River Valley. Killing him showed that they wanted the French to leave.

Washington asked the Half King and another leader, Queen Alliquippa, if their warriors would fight the French with him, but they decided not to fight with Washington. The Half King and his people moved to central Pennsylvania, but the Half King did not live to see much of the French and Indian War, dying in October 1754.

Upon hearing of the incident, de Contrecoeur made a rough note on his copy of the summons that Jumonville had been killed by the English while reading it. Amongst those killed by the Virginians was the drummer, which adds credence to the assertion that Jumonville tried to read the summons. De Contrecoeur received another message, this time from la Chauvignerie who commanded an outpost at Chiningue, that allied Indians had reported the killing of Jumonville and many of his men while the summons was being read. The American Indians also said that they saved the other French from being killed by intervening to stop the shooting. However, this must have been hearsay because no French-allied Indians are known to have been with Jumonville's party. The Indians were not above inventing some facts to gain favor. Other versions of the encounter include the de Villiers family story wherein Jumonville was hoisting a flag of truce when attacked.

Although the exact events will never be fully known, the immense consequences of the incident are impossible to dispute. Perhaps Governor Dinwiddie foresaw the explosive impact the incident would have when the news reached Versailles and London as in his dispatch relating the event, he tried to downplay events calling it "a little skirmish [that] was really the work of the Half-King and ... [his] Indians. We were but auxiliaries to them..."

Following the successful ambush, Washington and his men returned to nearby Great Meadows. While pleased by his success, Washington felt that a "fort of necessity" should be built at Great Meadows as a more secure base and for protection against the probable French retaliation. Situated near modern-day Farmington, Pennsylvania, Fort Necessity, as it came to be called, was a small circular log palisade with trenches covering some two thirds of its exterior.

As soon as Commandant de Contrecoeur learned of the ambush from Monceau, he at once wrote of the event to Governor-General Duquesne at Québec and, with the resources available to him at Fort Duquesne, immediately set about organizing a strong force to go after the Virginians who had killed Jumonville and his men. Within a few days, de Contrecoeur had collected a force of some 500 French soldiers and Canadian militiamen, along with a few American Indians, who were prepared to move east. The command of the party was given to artillery captain le Mercier. However, on the morning of June 26, a convoy of canoes and boats arrived at Fort Duquesne. It was Captain Louis Coulon de Villiers, an experienced frontier officer who also held the title of Commandant of the Indians in the area, with some 300 Indians accompanying about 50 French soldiers and Canadian militiamen bringing supplies for Fort Duquesne. Captain de Villiers was deeply shocked and angered to hear of de Jumonville's death as de Jumonville was his younger brother. As he was senior to Captain le Mercier, de Villiers asked Commandant de Contrecoeur to allow him to command the expedition preparing to march against the Virginians. This was certainly within de Villiers' prerogatives as a senior officer. Commandant de Contrecoeur agreed, presumably hoping that de Villiers would persuade the American Indians to join him.

De Contrecoeur's and de Villiers' first action was indeed to summon a war council with the Indian chiefs on June 27. De Contrecoeur had the respect and confidence of many chiefs; as they knew he spoke for "Onontio" – the governor-general of New France. He explained the recent events, and that the expedition was being led by de Villiers, not only much respected by the chiefs, but the brother of the slain officer, wishing for revenge. After some deliberation, aided no doubt by a couple of French casks of wine, the chiefs decided to take up the war tomahawk.

The very next morning de Villiers left Fort Duquesne at the head of his force. To his 500 French and Canadians were now added at least 300 American Indians. De Villiers proceeded swiftly yet cautiously, leaving his dugout canoes and moving by land from July 1. His main force was preceded by numerous small parties of scouts. The next day, some of Villiers' scouts spotted a few Virginians on patrol and captured a Virginian soldier. From this man, who claimed he was a deserter, de Villiers learned that Washington's men could hold out in a small fort they had built at Great Meadows. Later that day, de Villiers arrived at Gist's abandoned settlement. The trails were now getting very difficult to travel on and they were further hindered by the rainy weather.

On July 3, de Villiers marched on; his scouts captured three more Americans and learned that the fort was not very far. The rain continued. The French and Indians came up to Jumonville Glen, the site of the incident, and found four scalped decaying bodies that were given a decent burial. From there, a cautious de Villiers ordered a screen of scouts. As they got nearer to Fort Necessity, some scouts reported to de Villiers that they had been spotted by British scouts. He immediately ordered his troops to assume the formation "most convenient to fighting in the woods" and continued to advance. The French and Indian force was now in the hills overlooking Fort Necessity, whose swivel guns opened fire, while a body of about 50 British was sighted to the south in battle formation. If it was an attempt to lure de Villiers into an engagement in the open field near the fort, it had no effect on this experienced wilderness commander. Instead, the French and Indians made their terrifying war cries as they advanced under cover; enough to drive the British soldiers back into the entrenchment around the fort.

The French troops and their allies surrounded Fort Necessity and approached as near as possible without exposing themselves to enemy fire. Although the fort was well situated in the meadow, the woods and nearby heights were within musket range.

Inside Fort Necessity was George Washington's force of some 400 men. Initially flushed with optimism following their victory over Jumonville's party, the Virginians had been much encouraged by the arrival in June of Captain James McKay leading an independent company of about 100 soldiers from South Carolina. These were regular British colonial troops and there were soon strains between young Washington, the upstart militia officer with his band of provincials, and McKay with his soldiers. Captain MacKay, as a regular, outranked Colonel Washington, a mere volunteer, a regular occurrence during the early period of the war, and one which naturally upset commissioned officers of the provincial forces. The regulars would not participate in building Washington's road to the Monongahela without extra pay, something that the

George Washington (1732–99)

Born in Westmoreland County, Virginia, on February 22, 1732, George Washington, "the Father of his country," was the eldest son of planter Augustine Washington and his second wife, Mary Ball Washington, who were prosperous Virginia gentry of English descent. Despite little schooling, the young Washington's talent for mathematics led him to become a surveyor of new territories in Western Virginia when only 15 years old. He inherited Mount Vernon plantation in 1752 when his older brother died. His military career started in the Virginia militia, and by 1753, when tasked by Governor Dinwiddie with delivering a summons to the French, he was already a major.

Following his service during the French and Indian War, he resigned his commission in 1758 and went back to his plantation. Over the next decade he, like many other Americans, became increasingly unhappy about the British government's attitude toward the Old Thirteen Colonies. When the dispute developed into conflict on June 15, 1775, his reputation led to his being elected commander-in-chief by the American Congress. He took command of his ill-trained troops at Cambridge in Massachusetts on July 3, and led them in a grueling war for six long years. He developed a strategy of harassment of the British, falling back and then striking unexpectedly.

Finally, in 1781, he forced the surrender of the British at Yorktown, after which the fighting in North America stopped almost entirely. Washington was not a great tactician, though he could hold his own with contemporaries; his strength lay in his strategic vision, and ability to identify and use talent in others, while securing their total loyalty by exceptional and inspired leadership.

After the war, he retired to a quiet life on his plantation. However, his service to his country was not yet complete, and in 1783 his expression of his ideas on how the United States should be led and governed led eventually to his inauguration as the first President of the United States in 1789. To his disappointment, two parties were developing by the end of his first term. Wearied of politics, he retired at the end of his second term in 1797. In his Farewell Address, he urged his countrymen to forswear excessive party spirit and geographical distinctions. He enjoyed just a few years of retirement, passing away on December 14, 1799, at his beloved Mount Vernon.

At the time of his death, Washington was lauded as one of the world's great statesmen, and he was greatly mourned, both in America, and internationally. General Henry Lee said of Washington in the funeral oration he made, "First in war, first in peace, and first in the hearts of his countrymen." (Topfoto/ARPL/HIP)

provincials did as part of their duty. However, Washington was encouraged to receive six swivel guns, which were installed at Fort Necessity.

A more significant worry for both Washington and McKay was the reluctance of the local American Indians to join them against the French. By mid-June, the Half King had gone and few others apart from some Senecas, most of them being women and children, were eager to join the British troops at Fort Necessity. The news of the Virginians' ambush of Jumonville must have had a sobering effect among the American Indians; they knew that Onontio, although far away, would have his men strike back. The wiser course was not to get involved and, as days went by, rumor of a strong French force caused even the few Indians left at Fort Necessity to vanish.

The truth of the rumor was confirmed to soldiers working on road construction some 13 miles (21km) from Fort Necessity. French and Indian scouts appeared in the area and a few men disappeared. Obviously, the place was no longer safe and the soldiers returned to Fort Necessity. When they arrived at the fort on July 1, conditions were far from ideal in the garrison, with as many as 100 men too sick to continue work to improve its defenses. Within two days, de Villiers' French and American Indians had them surrounded.

De Villiers had no artillery to bombard the fort so he had his men pour musket fire into the British position. Well covered by the trees, the soldiers opened up such a heavy musketry on the fort and its entrenchments that de Villiers worried that they would soon run out of ammunition. The returning fire from the fort's swivel guns and muskets was largely ineffective. The shooting went on until eight in the evening.

Meanwhile, de Villiers took advice from Captain le Mercier to start building fascines to completely seal off Fort Necessity. His force was also very tired, having marched and fought under constant rain. At this time, de Villiers wrote, "the Indians said they would leave us the next morning, and that there was the report that drums and the firing of cannon had been heard in the distance." Faced with the sudden withdrawal of his sometime allies and the possibility of a British relief force on the way, the time seemed ripe to open negotiations. Hoping that the British were in disarray within their fort, de Villiers then decided to call on them to surrender. Some French shouted to the fort's garrison that if they wanted to parlay, they would cease fire. The offer was accepted and a British officer came out; Captain le Mercier went out to meet him and offered to grant the honors of war should the garrison surrender, adding that it would otherwise be difficult to control their Indian allies.

Washington and McKay knew they were doomed. Their fort was being targeted from all sides and there was no hope of escape; well-aimed shots had already left 31 killed and some 70 wounded. Clearly, Fort Necessity and its surrounding trenches did not provide enough cover and more men would be mowed down. The torrential rain was turning the interior of the fort into a morass, filling the trenches with water, and wetting the ammunition. Some of the men, discouraged and afraid, had turned to their bottles of spirits and were said to be drunk.

Despite all this, Washington declined the first French invitation to talk. When it was renewed, he agreed. However, there was a problem of communication. Nobody on the French side knew English, Washington's French was not up to the task and only Ensign Peyroney and Captain Jacob van Braam knew it relatively well. Washington was not satisfied with the verbal terms and sent Captain van Braam as his interpreter to the French commander to draft a suitable document. van Braam came back to Washington bearing the surrender documents written in French. In spite of considerable misgivings, Washington and McKay had little choice if they wanted to get out alive and save their men. Some of the clauses were altered and, possibly at van Braam's insistence, the capitulation was finally signed at about midnight. By then, shooting had stopped for some hours.

As the capitulation agreement granted the honors of war, the garrison evacuated, with drums beating, to Virginia carrying its weapons (including a cannon) with colors and personal baggage; hostages were left for the safe return of the men of Jumonville's party who had been taken prisoner. The agreement also stipulated that this area was the domain of the king of France, that the garrison of Fort Necessity was not to bear arms for a year, and that every effort would be made to contain the American Indians. The French version of the document contained the word "assassinat" which van Braam translated as the "death" of Jumonville. It is unknown whether Washington realized that in signing the document he was admitting to the assassination of Jumonville.

Captains Robert Stobo and van Braam were left with de Villiers as hostages until they could be exchanged. The garrison left Fort Necessity early on the morning of July 4, even before the French arrived to take possession of it. According to J.C.B., they found the place quite messy with remains of demolished rum and salted meat barrels, 25 wounded or sick men left behind, and the unburied bodies of 12 men killed. The American Indians had agreed to the capitulation, but wanted booty that now escaped them. When they learned that Washington's men had departed, some warriors went after the column of retreating soldiers and captured ten stragglers, whom they brought back to de Villiers. The French commander chastised the Indians as this was contrary to the capitulation agreement and asked them to return these men. The Indians were upset and killed and scalped three but let the rest go back.

Meanwhile, the French soldiers and Canadian militiamen razed Fort Necessity to the ground and broke the swivel guns left behind. The French victory had demonstrated their tactical superiority in the wilderness, and ensured continued allegiance from the American Indian nations in the area. De

Washington and his men built Fort Necessity in June 1754 as the strong force led by Captain de Villiers approached. It was a very simple, small, round stockade fort with trenches outside. This reconstruction was built by the US National Parks Service. (René Chartrand)

Villiers returned to Fort Duquesne having seen to it, as Francis Parkman put it, that "not an English flag now waved beyond the Alleghenies."

Washington and his troops eventually reached Will's Creek. The proud young lieutenant-colonel must have feared for his career after presiding over a decisive defeat. Yet within a few months Washington's name, if scorned in Versailles, would become internationally famous and he would be hailed as a hero in London.

Governor Dinwiddie reacted to the news of the capitulation with praise for the bravery of Washington and his men who had no chance of success against "900 French & Indians." He squarely laid blame on the considerable delay of the two New York independent companies to reach the area; had these additional 160 regulars been there, things might have been different. At first, Dinwiddie felt compelled to respect the terms of the capitulation in order to recover the hostages safely, but as time passed, this attitude changed. Once back to the safety of Fort Cumberland and then Virginia, Washington, McKay, and other officers openly proclaimed that they had no intention of respecting the terms of the capitulation they had signed. They interpreted the terms to apply only to the sick men and baggage that had been left behind and had given "no parole for themselves" and stood ready "to proceed with other Forces" against the French. This was without a doubt a highly spurious interpretation of the document they had signed and extremely weak justification for annulling the terms of the capitulation.

By late August, Dinwiddie had the necessary justification to break the terms and accuse the French of cruelty and duplicity. He had now received information that the French and allied Indians had "acted contrary to the Law of Nat[ion]s

in taking our People Prisoners after the Capitulat[io]n agreed upon, offering [th]em to Sale, and at last missing of the Sale, sending them Prisoners to Canada, an unprecedented, unjust and barbarous Usage; they pretended they were Prison[e]rs to the Ind[ian]s; the same reason subsists in regard to our Prisoners, the Half King insisting on their being his." In short, while the French prisoners were safely kept in Virginia, the French had abandoned some of the British to the Indians. Thus, the unwarranted capture of a few departing British soldiers by French-allied Indians provided the pretext to render the terms of the capitulation null and void.

A month earlier, Governor-General Duquesne, no doubt sensing the opportunity given to the British to break the terms, had instructed Commandant de Contrecoeur to inform the Indians that it was his personal order to release the prisoners they had brought to Fort Duquesne. By early September, Duquesne's mood had changed for the Baron de Longueuil, acting as chief of staff, had brought him a translation of Washington's journal that had been seized by de Villiers' men at Fort Necessity. Duquesne found it a "priceless document" revealing the putridity "of the English" and of the Iroquois Indians. The governor-general concluded that there could be "nothing more undignified and low and even darker than the feelings and the way of thinking of this Washington."

The royal courts and ministers of both France and England were outraged; there had been other incidents, notably in India, but this was much more serious. The French were convinced Jumonville had been assassinated, while the British would have none of it. Both sides were mobilizing troops and, in the spring of 1755, battalions were embarking for North America.

WAR PATHS AND TOMAHAWKS
THE AMERICAN INDIANS

The so-called "Woodland" cultural area, a quite arbitrary distinction useful only in the widest sense, has at various times been assigned to all the tribes living east of the Mississippi river between the Gulf of Mexico and James Bay. Historically the area is the most important in the development of the early United States, and the tribes in this region played the most important role of all the native Americans in shaping the New World's history.

The Atlantic coastal tribes suffered the first European invasion and lost the greater part of their population from diseases and war resulting from contact with whites. The Iroquois league, on the other hand, living some hundreds of miles inland, were able to successfully come to terms with the white man, given

Many of the early encounters between the American Indians and European explorers were brutal. This is a depiction of Samuel de Champlain's 1609 battle against the Mohawks at Ticonderoga. The battle heralded many decades of warfare between the Iroquois and the French. (National Archives of Canada, C-5750)

a few generations more to work out political and military adjustments to the new arrivals. The legendary purpose behind the Iroquois confederacy is phrased as a desire to unite warring brother nations. The story tells that five tribes conferred under the "Tree of the Great Peace," a conference declined by their neighbors who consequently became potential enemies. The formation of the league is thought to have occurred just prior to the arrival of the white man in the New World. The Iroquois confederacy, comprising the Mohawk, Onondaga, Oneida, Cayujga, and Seneca tribes, destroyed and controlled many other tribes, establishing itself as the most important native confederacy on the continent, and the nucleus of Woodland culture. Between 1713 and 1722, wars with British colonists forced the Tuscarora tribe of North Carolina north to join the confederacy, and the confederacy was then the Six Nations.

The Iroquois who were won over to French interests in the 17th century formed a league with the Algonkians, Abenakis, and Hurons of Lorette as an adjunct to the Six Nations Confederacy, and were at times in a state of war with their relatives. They were known as the Seven Nations of Canada, or French Indians.

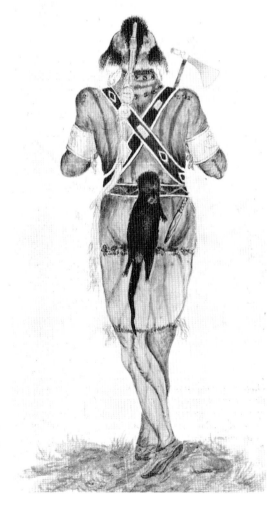

Back view of a "Canadian Indian," covered in tattoos and warpaint. He wears ornate belts and silver arm bracelets and holds a pipe tomahawk. This watercolor study probably dates from the second half of the 18th century. (National Archives of Canada, C-108983)

AMERICAN INDIAN WARFARE

Woodland American Indian men seem to have revered war above all else and, despite the great message of peace enshrined in the Iroquois league's constitution, a conflict between the old men and the young over war policy was endemic. The councils could only adopt a policy of peace or neutrality; they could not force young men to observe it. War had been a major cause of the decline of the native population during the 17th century, for which the Iroquois compensated by the adoption of captives; in fact, war parties were often organized for this purpose. So despite the ideal that men were brothers and that killing should stop, the Iroquois were the major native disruptive military force in the northeast.

A warrior who wished to lead a war party would send a messenger with tobacco to ask others to join his expedition. The messenger would explain the purpose of the expedition followed by a ceremonial smoking of the pipe with those who enlisted. Later the warriors arrived near the camp of the leaders, who prepared a feast asking for a final pledge of support. The leader usually appointed lieutenants to act as his aides during the proposed raids. War dances and

British-allied American Indians of the 18th century. On the left is an Iroquois warrior from about 1759. He is tattooed, and is armed with a painted trade musket. The Mohawk in the center is from the early 18th century, and is carrying a Hudson Valley fowling piece. He has complex tattoos on his face and body, and wears ear ornaments of swan down. He has a European blanket and shirt. On the right is a Mohawk warrior from about 1764. He carries a bow and arrows, and a trade tomahawk. He wears feather and quillwork head ornaments, wampum ear ornaments, and a "gorget." In the foreground are ball-headed clubs, and a red-painted scalp with decorative stretcher rim. (Richard Hook © Osprey Publishing Ltd)

striking-the-warpost ceremonies were held before the war party left the camp together with the collection of "medicine," and materials for making and repairing moccasins. Amongst many of the eastern tribes parched corn was the standard provision of the warrior when on the trail; when mixed with maple-sugar it provided quick sustenance. The final event before the departure of the war party was often the dog feast, which was considered as a final pledge to meet the full fortunes of war. Dog war feasts were not acts of piety. They were organized by the warrior or clan societies in order to receive blessings from spirits. The dogs would be killed, singed, then boiled, and prepared in the same way as deer. The meat symbolized the flesh of captives that they might later eat, these enemies being

Algonkian wampum belt, of the 18th century, possibly from New Brunswick. The belt is woven of cylindrical beads; the two colors act as mnemonic devices commemorating agreements and events important in politics, history, and religion. The design of three rectangles suggests an alliance of three groups in war, indicated by the use of purple which comes from the edge of the quahog clam. The white comes from the columns of univalve whelks. Wampum beads were made by Algonkian-speaking peoples and by the Iroquois, and later by white manufacturers. In ancient times a treaty was not considered binding without the presentation of wampum belts, which were also frequently used as a standard of exchange by American Indians and European settlers. (Topfoto / The British Museum / HIP)

compared to dogs. The attendant ceremonies, involving the ritual use of tobacco, evoked help from the night spirits, and also the bear and buffalo spirits.

On the warriors' journey to the enemy village many songs and dances were held at the nightly camps, the warriors frequently singing of their former victories. The pipe bearer, a noted warrior, often led the war party with the leader walking last. A Chippewa war party could travel 25 miles a day. As the warriors neared the enemy they began preparations for actual warfare: singing medicine songs, making litters for the wounded, and designating individuals to carry extra supplies of medicine, corn, and water. An eagle-feather banner was often carried by one of the bravest warriors during the fight; another beat a drum to inspire his comrades.

The warriors would array themselves in the most colorful body-painting, trappings, feathers, and charms for the attack, which was often made at daybreak after taking ambush positions near the enemy village. The attackers usually rushed the enemy while they were sleeping. Occasionally one warrior might inspire the others by making himself a target, throwing away his weapons and clothing, and charging the enemy.

Returning victorious war parties sent runners in advance to carry the news of the warriors' approach to their home village. The women would meet the warriors and carry the scalps, painted red, fastened inside hoops on the end of poles; frequently scalps were given to the women. The women led the procession, waving the scalps and singing, into the village. After the return preparations were made to hold a victory dance, and a feast of dried meat, wild rice, and maple sugar followed. The victory or scalp dance seems to have been common to almost every tribe in eastern North America. Wives and

American Indian tactics

Though apparently crudely armed by European standards, American Indians had an undeniable advantage in North American warfare. Their knowledge of the forests and wilderness of their homeland was built up over centuries, and they could use the topography against any enemy. Having hunted since childhood, Indian warriors were well used to traveling vast distances at speed, dealing with fatigue and hazard, and being aware of every detail of their surroundings. They were lightly armed, highly mobile fighters, able to disappear into the environment at will, and supply themselves from their surroundings while on campaign for extended periods. Complete command of stealth tactics made Indians invaluable as scouts, and gatherers of intelligence. Colonial military leaders learned that spying on, and defeating, Indian warriors in battle was only possible with the expertise and knowledge of other Indians. Eventually, native scouts and tactical knowledge became legendary, and success in the Revolutionary War was partly attributed to the use of American Indian tactics and stealth.

sweethearts of warriors usually carried the poles with the attached scalps at celebrations in neighboring villages. Unsuccessful war parties were generally ignored by villagers.

Amongst the Iroquoian tribes the taking of prisoners was an important part of warfare. They were often adopted into families who had lost warriors in battle, thus helping to maintain population strength. Ceremonial torture of prisoners and the eating of vital organs were also reported by early observers of the Iroquois.

The war dance was usually performed on special occasions such as council meetings to recall past deeds. In the dance itself attitudes of battle, watching, listening, acts of striking the foe, and throwing the tomahawk added to the war songs, rapid drumming, recitals, and speeches, giving the effect of passion, excitement, and violence. Most deeds of valor were recorded by symbols worn in public, usually eagle feathers worn upright, crosswise, hanging down, or colored red. Other warrior insignia were armbands, ankle and knee bands of skunk or otter skin, painted legs, painted hand designs on body or face, and raven's skin around the neck. Sometimes the skulls of slain enemies were used as lodge weights, and their flayed skins were used as mats and doorflaps.

The Woodland American Indians fought bravely to defend their lands from neighboring tribes and whites. Their methods of warfare were culturally determined, and any atrocities committed were equally matched by their foes. The torture and burning of captives were often abandoned at the instigation of their own chiefs. Scalping was a New World custom, although it was later much encouraged by the payment of bounties by the English and French. However, killing and scalping were sometimes secondary objectives to prisoner-taking by

Iroquois war parties. Scalping for bounty became a feature of white frontier life, as did the severing of heads. King Philip's head was carried to Plymouth at the close of the 1675–76 war, where it was placed on a pole and remained exposed for a generation as a reminder to Indians and whites of the brutality of colonial warfare.

The disruptive use of gifts by both the French and the British during the 18th century did much to undermine the stability of the frontier and the dependability of American Indian auxiliaries. Braddock's Indian scouts reconnoitering Fort Duquesne reported few men at the fort; following the death of the leader's son by friendly fire only constant presents bribed the scouts to continue their duties, and they did so with little enthusiasm. A better understanding and treatment of the Indian allies by the British could probably have avoided the ambush of the column at Monongahela altogether.

Before the trade tomahawk and gun came into popular use by the eastern Indians, their principal weapons were the bow, the stone tomahawk, and the war club. The war club was a heavy weapon, usually made of ironwood or maple, with a large ball or knot at the end. Some antique clubs in museums have a

American Indian warriors were adept at traveling and fighting on snowshoes and were expert marksmen. This warrior is dressed in French woolen tucque, a capot and moccasins. His mittens lie on the ground as he reloads. (National Archives of Canada, C-122387)

warrior's face carved on the ball, sometimes with inlaid wampum (beads cut from the shell of the clam or conch), a long-tailed carved serpent on the top of the ball adjoining the shaft, and a cross motif. The shafts were also occasionally carved with war records and decorated. It appears to have been a devastating weapon at close quarters.

In the Great Lakes region the so-called "gun stock club" was popular, often having a sharp-pointed horn or steel trade spike at the shoulder. These were largely replaced with the trade tomahawk of English, French, or later American manufacture in iron or steel. Originally of a hatchet form, these later incorporated a pipe bowl, thus symbolizing a dual role in peace and war: to smoke – to parley; to bury it – peace; to raise it – deadly war.

Poisoned blow-gun arrows were used by the Cherokee and Iroquois but not to any extent in the major conflicts, and perhaps for hunting only. Bows were usually of one piece, made from ash, hickory, or oak. Arrows had delicately chipped triangular chert heads, and were usually kept in sheaths or quivers of cornhusk or skins. Early reports suggest that a type of wooden slatted armor made of tied rods was used by the Huron and Iroquois.

The gun replaced the bow throughout most of the eastern regions between about 1640 and the late 17th century, and partly rendered obsolete the bow and arrow and rod armor. However, as late as 1842 (due to lack of ammunition) an eyewitness reported that a battle between Chippewa and Sioux was waged with club and scalping knife.

Between the 17th century and early 19th centuries the practice of American Indian warfare changed little. A warrior's equipment in later years included a blanket, extra moccasins, a tumpline used as a prisoner tie, a rifle, powder horn, bullet bag, and his own medicine. Delaware and Shawnee scouts in the US Army out west are said to have administered warrior medicine to white soldiers. The calumet ceremony was often performed for war and peace. It appears to have been of Mississippian origin and spread east to the Ottawa via most central tribes, together with the ritual use of tobacco and steatite and catlinite pipe bowls. Calumets were highly decorated wands of feathers, painted tubes with animal parts (including the heads and necks of birds) with or without the pipe. The use of the calumet and pipe for ritual smoking at treaty councils led to the term "peace pipe."

Although the horse was adopted by the eastern tribes as a beast of burden, there seems to be little reference to its use in warfare except in the later 18th and early 19th centuries and particularly by the western tribes Sauk, Fox, Winnebago, etc. However, the Iroquois and Cherokee had large numbers of horses from the mid-18th century on.

The Iroquois conquered or exterminated all the tribes upon their immediate borders and by 1680 had turned their arms against more distant tribes, the Illinois, Catawba, and Cherokee. According to Iroquois tradition the Cherokee

were the original aggressors, having attacked and plundered a Seneca Iroquois hunting party, while in another story they are represented as having violated a peace treaty by the murder of Iroquois delegates. The Iroquois war party usually took 20 days at least to reach the edge of Cherokee territory. Such a war party was small in number, as the distance was too great for a large expedition. The Cherokee often retaliated by individual exploits, a single warrior going hundreds of miles to strike a blow which was sure to be promptly answered by a war party from the north. A formal and final peace treaty between the two tribes was arranged through the efforts of Sir William Johnson in 1768.

About the year 1700 the Iroquois reached the apogee of their empire. From the start their relationship with the French was difficult, and from 1640 to 1700 a constant warfare was maintained, broken by periods of negotiated peace, the exchange of prisoners, and periods of missionary influence, which drew a portion of the Mohawks from their homelands to Canada. Their friendship with the English remained largely unbroken during the 17th century, but during the 18th century frontier politics were such that the league weakened and individual tribes no longer acted in one accord with league policy.

The Jesuits had established missions in eastern Canada by 1639, and by 1700 they were as far west as the Mississippi river. Thus France had a secure route to its southern territories, and secured French dominance of the Great Lakes fur trade until 1761. New France now encircled the Thirteen Colonies through the western wilderness. However, it was not always a friendly relationship between the French and the various American Indian tribes and several wars resulted with the Mesquakie (Fox), Sauk, Dakota (Sioux), Huron, and Chickasaw. While inter-tribal warfare seems always to have been the norm, the arrival of the Europeans added to inter-tribal rivalry within the fur trade. Indeed, the Iroquois' conquests seem to have been largely to establish their superiority in such commerce. At times Indians took their furs to the British posts of the Hudson's Bay Company in the far north, or even to Albany. By the 1730s the focal point of Indian and frontier colonial warfare was the Ohio River Valley, now populated along its tributaries by tribes forced across the Appalachian mountains by white population pressure. These were principally the Delaware and Shawnee, with portions of many tribes forming a multi-tribal population, including fragments of all six Iroquois tribes, Mahican, New England groups, Abenaki, and Chippewa (Mississauga).

ALLEGIANCES DURING THE FRENCH AND INDIAN WAR

The commercial trade between the Ohio American Indians and French or British agents and traders during the 18th century was of a different nature to previous trading. It degenerated into competition for Indian alliances by means of gifts. War gifts of cutlasses, scalping knives, hatchets, guns, powder, and bullet molds were added to vermilion paint, flints, cottons, blankets, scissors, needles, thread, cloth, watchcoats, and stockings. Once the Indians had become accustomed to the white man's goods, they could not live without them. Unscrupulous traders plied Indians with rum, which often resulted in intoxication, brawls, and death. The French gradually regained the upper hand in the Indian trade during the first half of the 18th century, and they were in control of the Ohio area in 1754.

A commission given by the French governor of Louisiana, Louis de Kerlérec, to Cherokee chief Okana-Stoté. It is dated February 27, 1761. The ornate documents were meant to impress and rally the leaders of allied American Indian nations. This one includes the full coat of arms of France above those of Louisiana, and those of the governor, who is pictured speaking to the chief. (United States National Archives)

The eastern Woodland Indians, especially the Canadian Iroquois and Abenakis, were among the most steadfast allies of the French in Canada. Their villages were often close to the French settlements and they served with the Canadian militia. Most of the western Woodland tribes – Ottawa, Ojibwa, Potawatomi, and Shawnee – were also allies of the French. The Hurons who had finally settled in the Ohio Valley following the dispersal of their confederacy by the Iroquois in the mid-17th century were known as the Wyandot. Allied with the Ottawa, they were the "eldest children" of Onontio, the governor-general of New France, and the cornerstone of the French alliance with the Great Lakes Algonkians. Although their relations with the French were tempestuous for many years, when war broke out in the Ohio Valley, the Wyandot sided with the French, and with the other French allies went east to fight in the French campaigns in northern New York.

The Iroquois for the most part fought on the side of the English, in part due to the influence of the British Superintendent of Indian Affairs, Sir William Johnson. The Irish trader George Croghan, in the British service of Sir William Johnson, won over the friendship of the western Indians at a great council in Pittsburgh in 1758.

Following the battle of Lake George, Sir William exerted himself to keep the Iroquois friendly to Britain's cause, or at least neutral, despite a series of disheartening military failures. The Iroquois fulfilled a campaign of diplomatic pressure by bringing the Delawares and Shawnees to heel at the treaty of Easton in October 1758, and they played a major part in the final British victory. However, following the end of the war, the actions of Amherst destroyed the relations with the western nations and led to Pontiac's War.

William Johnson and the Mohawks

William Johnson, a young Anglo-Irishman, came to the Mohawk Valley in 1738. He built a huge commercial empire from the fur trade and land deals. Within three years he had built a fortress-like home, Mount Johnson, and had begun a long association with the Mohawks. His second wife, Caroline, was the niece of old "King Hendrick." After her death he married as his third wife Molly Brant whose younger brother, Joseph Brant, was destined to become a captain in the British Army during the American Revolution. In 1745 Johnson was appointed British Commissioner of Indian Affairs, and in 1755, Superintendent of Indian Affairs. His victory at Lake George, supported by hundreds of Mohawks and Oneidas, was heartening to the British colonists, although King Hendrick was one of those killed in the fighting. Through this victory Johnson united the Iroquois behind him, and was rewarded by the Crown with a baronetcy and cash grant. Johnson spent the rest of the war trying to keep the Iroquois friendly to Britain's cause. He took Fort

Niagara in 1759 with a force augmented by over 900 Iroquois warriors. Johnson's home was palisaded in 1755 and became known as Fort Johnson, but with the return of peace he built a stately home called Johnson Hall at Johnstown, NY, where he sheltered Indians and entertained other distinguished guests. This illustration shows various distinguished Indian visitors to Johnson Hall, from left, an Ottawa chief, a Wyandot chief, a clan matron, Joseph Brant, a Fox chief, and a Huron chief. As many as 60 to 80 Indians often camped in the grounds. His actions helped to bring about the end of Pontiac's War in 1766, and in 1768 he made a formal treaty with all the Indians which set out the boundaries between the American colonies and Indian country. Johnson was adopted as a war chief of the Canajoharie Mohawks; his nickname was Orihwane, "Big Business." He had a unique influence with the Mohawks, and through his many children he has descendants among them today. (Jonathan Smith © Osprey Publishing Ltd)

BRADDOCK'S DEFEAT
MONONGAHELA, 1755

Early 1755 saw a flurry of ships crossing the Atlantic, as both France and Britain sent reinforcements to North America. The British planned to capture forts Duquesne, Saint-Frédéric, Beauséjour, and Gaspereau. The French, meanwhile, were reinforcing new France with six battalions. The Royal Navy attempted to intercept the French convoy, but, except for two ships, the French continued their voyage safely. Edward Braddock, commander-in-chief of all British troops in America, arrived in Virginia in March, and started preparations for the expedition to take Fort Duquesne.

PREPARATIONS

The general and the staff officers of an army setting out to capture Fort Duquesne faced many difficulties, and of a type not usually encountered by an army campaigning in Europe. Perhaps the first and possibly the most significant problem was the lack of any reliable detailed maps of the wilderness of mountains and forests it was necessary to traverse. There might be trails of a sort, but there was no road worthy of the name; yet Braddock's army would have a considerable number of wagons, as they would have to transport all their food with them. Even water might present a problem; ideally, in North America, the army would move by river, with ample water available for drinking, cooking, and washing. A river could also be used for transporting the army and its supplies. Although the British army would initially move along the Potomac River as far as Will's Creek, the Potomac then turned southwest. The army had to march on northwest to reach Fort Duquesne and there was no practicable waterway between the Potomac and the Monongahela almost as far as its junction with the Allegheny.

The difficulties, however, were not insurmountable. Although General Braddock and his staff officers could not rely on maps, scouts could be depended upon to provide reliable information, as would Lieutenant-Colonel Washington, who had certainly become familiar with the area in the previous couple of years. It was obvious to all that crossing the wilderness by land was the best course. As for a road, the existing trails going west would simply have to be improved to allow passage of the army with its artillery and supply wagons. Braddock met the logistical challenge by enlisting American provincial companies as carpenters more than as front-line fighting troops. More American companies would be enlisted as rangers and light horse to provide advance warning in the forest. A detachment of sailors was brought along to deal with the navigation of the Allegheny, Monongahela, and Ohio rivers once Fort Duquesne was invested. Taking a sizable army across a substantial wilderness to reach its objective was undoubtedly no ordinary challenge, but the British planning was equal to the task and they had every reason to be confident as they assembled at Fort Cumberland at the end of May 1755.

The French geostrategic situation on the Ohio was very different from that of the British. New France's basic strategy rested on control of the main rivers for transport and communications. Although a long way from their main base at Montréal, the French and Canadians could carry impressive quantities of supplies, arms, and men far into the wilderness with relative ease. Great canoe brigades assembled at La Chine west of Montréal and traveled along the rivers and lakes, punctuated by occasional portages, to their destination: a fort in the middle of the wilderness. From that wilderness base, they would venture in smaller parties along smaller waterways and eventually leave their canoes and continue on foot, as they had done to invest Washington and his force at Fort Necessity.

Captain de Beaujeu was a French officer of legendary fame in New France, renowned for the brilliant part he had played in the triumphant raid on Grand Pré (Nova Scotia) eight years earlier and greatly respected by the American Indians as a result of his postings on the frontier. De Beaujeu had left Montréal on April 20 to relieve Captain de Contrecoeur as commandant of the Ohio at Fort Duquesne. Arriving at Fort Presqu'Île in early June, he received a dispatch from Commandant de Contrecoeur written on May 18 stating that a large British army had arrived in Virginia and was about to invade the Ohio Valley. Instantly perceiving the urgency of the threat, de Beaujeu stayed some days at Presqu'Île and Le Boeuf, obtaining all the supplies and manpower available to strengthen the fort. He also received more dispatches from de Contrecoeur providing news of the British army. On June 8, de Contrecoeur wrote to de Beaujeu that a British deserter had brought the news that the British troops were on the march. Following this intelligence, de Contrecoeur sent out a party of some 60 Indians with 11 cadets of the *Compagnies Franches de la Marine* to harass the British column. De Beaujeu finally reached Fort Duquesne in late June.

Although the officers and men at Fort Duquesne knew that France was reinforcing both regular and colonial forces in New France, this was of little

Major-General Edward Braddock (1695–1755)

Born in 1695, Braddock followed his father into the army, and at the age of 15 joined the Coldstream Guards, and served in Flanders at Flushing, but took no part in the fighting itself. After 43 years, he left the Guards in 1753 to become the Colonel of the 14th Foot at Gibraltar. He was acting governor of Gibraltar, and in April 1754 was promoted to major-general. Appointed commander of the expedition to occupy the Ohio Valley in September, he was back in England in November, and sailed for North America in January 1755. On arrival, the commander-in-chief of British forces in America was anxious to get the expedition underway, and brushed aside most local suggestions, both on strategies to defeat the enemy, and warnings about French and American Indian tactics. He knew nothing of American conditions but realized that he would have to cut his way "through unknown woods." His response to the Indian threat was: "these savages may, indeed, be a formidable enemy to your raw American militia, but upon the King's regular and disciplined troops ... it is impossible that they should make such an impression."

He was 60 years old when he led the army toward Fort Duquesne. Fatally wounded during the battle of Monongahela, he died on July 13. Washington saw to it that he "was interred with the honors of war." The spot where he was buried was then hidden, with wagons passing over it "to hide every trace by which the entombment could be discovered" lest it should be found and desecrated by the French and American Indians. A monument now marks the spot where what are believed to be his remains were found, near Fort Necessity and Jumonville Glen. Washington said of Braddock's character that he "was brave even to a fault and in regular service would have done honor to his profession. His attachments were warm, his enmities were strong, and having no disguise about him, both appeared in full force. He was generous and disinterested, but plain and blunt in his manner even to rudeness."

comfort to them, as none of these troops would reach them in time to confront the British forces marching toward the forks of the Ohio River. Nevertheless the French could call on other warriors. The call had gone out to all *Compagnies Franches de la Marine* officers in wilderness outposts and forts of the Great Lakes to rally all the friendly American Indians they could and send them to Fort Duquesne. They informed the Indians that the English and the scorned American long knives were marching to vanquish the French, and if they won the British would chase the Indians away from their hunting grounds forever. As June wore on, more and more canoes filled with warriors arrived at Fort Duquesne, where Commandant de Contrecoeur met and reassured the different Indian groups. His words were no doubt well received. Some of the most influential chiefs were gathering at Fort Duquesne: Pucksinwah, Athanese, White Eyes, and Pontiac. And from Michilimackinac, the young man who was both an Indian chief and a French officer: Ensign Charles-Michel de Langlade who, in spite of his youth, could influence the Indians to act in unison thanks

The Braddock Expedition, 1755. In the foreground is a private of the 44th Regiment of Foot, just behind him is a private of the 48th Regiment of Foot. Both privates wear their uniform adapted as prescribed by Braddock for the expedition. Officers would have worn boots, sashes, and gorgets. On the right is an officer on Braddock's staff. He wears a plain red frock over a gold-laced waistcoat. Many officers wore fairly plain gold-laced red or blue coats on campaign. The officer here wears old riding breeches and boots, but unfortunately his horse has been shot from under him. Center back is a petty officer from HMS Norwich. The seamen of the Royal Navy did not have a formal uniform at this time, but bulk purchases of clothing led to a certain uniformity, and this man's clothing is typical. In the background is a private of the Virginia Regiment wearing civilian clothing. (Gerry Embleton © Osprey Publishing Ltd)

to his unique background and exceptional talent. Captain de Beaujeu was to lead this mixed force. Desperate as the situation may have seemed to the French and Indians, and heavy as the odds stacked against them undoubtedly were, capitulating was never considered for a moment. On the contrary, the French and Indians were determined to give the enemy a fight he would remember.

BRADDOCK MOVES WEST

On May 30, the assembled British army at Fort Cumberland was ready to move west into the wilderness. The army was divided into two brigades under Colonel Sir Peter Halket, and Colonel Thomas Dunbar. There were about 200 wagons, and the train of artillery with Braddock's army consisted of six brass 6-pdr cannons, four brass 12-pdr cannons, four 8in. brass howitzers, and 15 4⅖in. brass Coehorn mortars, and the hundreds of horses needed to transport them, as well as 500 packhorses. As well as the 1,600 or so British and American officers and men, there were hundreds of wagoners and camp followers. So, as it started from Fort Cumberland into the wilderness, Braddock's army would have included at least 2,000 people and over 900 horses.

On May 29, a strong vanguard of 600 men under Major Russell Chapman with 50 wagons loaded with supplies left Fort Cumberland heading west to try and find a way through the mountains and clear a road 12ft wide to Little Meadows some 20 miles away. The construction of the road was a formidable enough task for the soldiers of the army, but getting over Will's Mountain just west of Fort Cumberland proved to be even more challenging. Luckily a pass was found that went through a valley around the mountain, the road through the pass was built in less than three days, and the army pressed on. For the next ten days, animals and men toiled constantly, moving the heaviest pieces of artillery and somehow coping with the 16 heavy army wagons that had come over from England with the British troops. The American draught horses were lighter than the heavy English horses the wagons were designed for, and they simply could not pull these wagons over such a road without constant help from the men themselves. The rough wilderness road itself was unable to take the immense weight of the artillery for long, nor could it support the army's heavy wagons. As a result, the army's progress seemed painfully slow to General Braddock and his officers, as little as two miles a day with little prospect of improvement.

On June 11, the army had progressed only as far as Spendelow Camp, about 25 miles, and thus was still in Maryland. General Braddock determined to lighten the army by asking officers to return unnecessary baggage to Fort Cumberland, and contribute any private horse they could spare to the army's transport. This had an excellent effect on the officers and most of them complied. It was also decided to send back to Fort Cumberland two of the 6-pdr cannons, four Coehorn mortars and some of the ordnance stores with an escort of 50 men. Other dispensable troops and dependents were sent to Philadelphia. The 16 very heavy army wagons were also ordered to return; their content was unloaded into ordinary farm wagons.

Braddock's march to Fort Duquesne.
(Ann Ronan Picture Library)

SKIRMISHES IN THE FOREST

Thus "lightened" the march continued, with the often twisting narrow trail being transformed into a narrow road over the coming days. The terrain was rugged, and on each side of the road a silent and seemingly impenetrable forest of tall pines and dark foliage bore down on the column of troops. There should have been scouts on either flank but, more often than not, the woods proved almost impossible to traverse and the flank guards feared becoming isolated so that almost everyone was on the road. The formation of Braddock's army was thus reduced to a winding narrow column of mixed wagons, horses, teamsters, and soldiers that might stretch some four miles. This certainly left it exposed to possible raids and hit-and-run attacks, but the British troops felt they were too far away from Fort Duquesne to be at serious risk. Yet the army was being constantly watched: the French officers at Fort Duquesne were frequently receiving information from allied Indians as to the progress of the army. They also knew from many previous scouting forays that the terrain was difficult for such a force to cross. Their scouts simply observed the column from a safe distance and were rarely if ever seen. Although no blood was yet shed, the British were growing apprehensive. Captain Chomley's servant wrote as early as June 13 that "We Expect the French Indians to attack us Every day."

A wood engraving of the battle of Monongahela. (Library of Congress)

The British army was nevertheless slowly marching west. The road remained very difficult and even the lighter wagons were proving unsuitable. On June 16, the 1st Brigade reached Little Meadows where the army would regroup at the stockaded camp erected there. A new development that passed largely unnoted was a brief skirmish with lurking "French" Indians noted by Chomley's servant. The army's progress was still too slow for General Braddock. He shed more dependents, and had officers' baggage reduced yet further; Washington's baggage was down to a single portmanteau. Sir John St Clair had also received information from an Indian, who claimed to have left Fort Duquesne on July 8, that its garrison was no more than 100 French and 70 Indians. Such a low figure was hardly believable but was encouraging; General Braddock also received information that the garrison of Fort Duquesne was certainly much weaker than his army, which increased his determination to get to the fort faster, before French reinforcements could arrive.

The only way to increase the speed of the march was to split up the army, a calculated risk. It was decided to leave some of the artillery, troops, the supply wagons, and wagoners, and other non-combatants at Little Meadows under the command of Colonel Dunbar who was to regroup the supply train. Braddock would lead a faster-moving detachment of about 1,200 men, including the 44th and 48th regiments, the New York Independent Company, three companies of

Virginia rangers, a company of Virginia artificers/carpenters, Stewart's Virginia light horse, the detachment of seamen and some gunners. Colonel Dunbar and the remainder of the army would follow later. This way, General Braddock reasoned, he could rapidly cut off Fort Duquesne before it was reinforced and Colonel Dunbar would join him with additional artillery, the remaining troops, and all the necessary supplies during its siege.

On June 18 the 400-man vanguard left to scout a route. The following day, General Braddock went on with Sir Peter Halket (acting as brigadier) and about 800 men including the two grenadier companies of the 44th and 48th, 500 soldiers, gunners, the detachment of seamen, 18 of Stewart's Light Horse, and the artillery train. Packhorses carried provisions for 35 days. The march started rather inauspiciously. The British-allied Indians under Chief Monocatuca were ordered to act as scouts for the advance party, but Monocatuca was soon ambushed and captured by some French and American Indian warriors. He was left tied to a tree and soon released as troops came up, but the incident confirmed the enemy to be lurking, well hidden, and possibly more numerous and more adept at forest warfare than the few American Indians allied to the British. It might have just been an unlucky brush, however, and in any event was certainly no reason to halt. On the column went, along the rough and hilly road; block and tackle was sometimes needed to help the artillery and wagons up and down slopes, and when not dealing with rocks and hills the men sometimes found themselves knee deep in a sticky mud. Nevertheless, the army pressed on, slowly getting closer to its target. On the 21st, it crossed the modern-day border from Maryland into Pennsylvania. By June 24/25, it was turning north past Great Meadows and the site of Fort Necessity, approaching Gist's abandoned settlement. There were now almost daily incidents with lurking French and American Indians. De Contrecoeur's men were looking out for anyone who might wander just a little too far from their comrades, and they regularly wounded or killed members of the column. British efforts to attack Indians seen in the woods were generally unsuccessful. On July 2 the army stopped for the night at Jacob's Cabin. Next day, a council of war was held to decide whether to wait for Dunbar or carry on. Considering their provisions, and the importance of reaching Duquesne before the French reinforcements, it was decided to press on.

Incidence of French and Indian harassment had been fewer for the last few days. General Braddock was anxious to have his allied American Indians "go toward the fort for intelligence," especially as they had declined to scout for the last eight or nine days. He tried again with promises and presents, but to no avail; they would not go out. Thus, the British army was practically blind. The next day, Gist did go out with a couple of Indians; they returned on July 6 with "a French officer's scalp" and word that they had seen "very few men" at the fort, had seen no one between the column and Fort Duquesne, and believed very few French and Indian raiders and scouts were out. The officer's scalp story is dubious as the French did not report losing any officer, while Gist had narrowly escaped when set upon by two French Indians. As for the absence of lurking enemies, it was an illusion; they showed up raiding the baggage later that very morning causing quite an alarm, with nervous soldiers firing at anything that moved; unfortunately, their "friendly fire" killed the son of Chief Monocatuca, a devastating blow to relations with the allied Indians even if he was given a military funeral with a guard of honor firing over his grave.

The important thing was to press on now that the objective was near. On July 7, the army reached Turtle Creek. Braddock opted to cross to the west bank of the Monongahela, turn north and then, as the river bent westward, cross it again to the north bank as he neared Fort Duquesne. Once on the north bank, the British army would be only about 8 miles (12.9km) from its objective. There was no time to lose and the army set out at once since General Braddock hoped to invest Fort Duquesne by July 10. Sir Peter Halket worried that the army was advancing almost blind. Sending in scouts before approaching the fort would be wiser, but time was of the essence. Lieutenant-Colonel Thomas Gage was sent forward with a group of chosen men to secure the crossings and ground

A painting by J. B. Stearns of George Washington at the battle of Monongahela. (Library of Congress)

71

ahead. By early on July 9, the ground had been secured and St Clair's workmen began constructing the road. At 6.00am, the army crossed the first ford and at 11.00am the second ford. It re-formed its column and continued its march into the forest. Fort Duquesne was now tantalizingly close.

Meanwhile, in the fort itself, de Contrecoeur, de Beaujeu and the other officers were pondering the daily reports of the progress of the British army. It was obvious that, despite the natural obstacles and Indian resistance, the enemy was determined to reach and capture the fort. On July 7, a war council of officers was called to consider what to do. There were really only two options for the French: blow up the fort and retreat, or put up a fight. The officers quickly dismissed the idea of destroying the fort and leaving; there was only one honorable option and that was to confront their enemies. A general engagement might have been brought on earlier but its outcome would have been risky and these experienced frontier officers had dismissed this option. Apart from the logistical problems over a longer distance, their more numerous enemies might have detected a large party. A failure would, furthermore, have discouraged many allied American Indians, and they were crucial to French success.

The situation now was different. As General Braddock's army was closing in, all available men were being mustered and, even more important, the Indians were expected to join in. The French officers knew that Fort Duquesne was indefensible against an army with artillery; the only option was to ambush and attack it while on the march. The French plan was simple: Commandant de Contrecoeur would remain at the fort with a small garrison while Commandant de Beaujeu led a mixed attack force. A force of regulars and militiamen was put together: a total of 254 French regulars and Canadian militiamen. With them were about 650 American Indians with their chiefs. De Beaujeu had initially wanted to attack Braddock's army at the second ford of the Monongahela, but it appears the Indians were somewhat reluctant to do this. It would seem that they preferred, possibly at Ensign de Langlade's suggestion, to ambush the British column from both sides once contact had been made. Finally, on July 9, de Beaujeu, with some 900 French and Indians, left Fort Duquesne at 8.00am and headed east into the forest.

THE BATTLE

The British army had crossed the second ford of the Monongahela River "Colours flying, Drums beating and Fifes playing" and marched inland to an abandoned trader's house. Washington remembered it well as he had rested there on his way back from Fort Le Boeuf a year and a half earlier. From there the army marched west.

At the forefront were some scouts and six troopers of Stewart's light horse, then the vanguard of the advanced party, the advanced party under Lieutenant-

Colonel Gage, a working party under Sir John St Clair, followed by gunners and the rearguard of the advance party. Next came Stewart's light horse, sailors, artificers, and more gunners, General Braddock with his ADCs and staff with a guard, the main body of troops on each flank of the convoy of packhorses and cattle, a few gunners with a 12-pdr at the rear of the convoy, and the rearguard. The long and narrow column also had small parties of troops detached as "Flank Guards" off to each side. They followed the trail moving west and entered a heavily wooded area.

It seems that de Beaujeu thought that Braddock's army might have been further away than it actually was. Like Braddock, he does not appear to have had scouts far ahead of his force probably hoping the many Indians with him would have scouts out already. Thus it was that neither force had precise knowledge of the exact whereabouts of the other. Commandant de Beaujeu's fast-moving force rapidly covered the seven miles, while the British army was moving much more slowly from the ford. At about 2.00pm, Gage's vanguard had just crossed a wide valley when its lead scouts and Virginia light horsemen, who were about 200 yards ahead, suddenly stopped, came back and reported a considerable number of enemy troops, mainly Indian.

The opening clash

The two companies of British grenadiers accompanied by another 150 soldiers came up; Gage ordered them to fix bayonets and to form in order of battle. The front rank kneeled, and they opened fire into the woods in front of them. The volley's initial effect startled two cadets with the Canadian militiamen who started to panic; half of the militia, about 100 men, broke and ran yelling, and French return fire was sporadic. The British brought up the two 6-pdrs, which also opened fire while the troops continued to fire volleys for a few minutes. On the third volley, Commandant de Beaujeu was killed. Seeing some of the Canadians and Indians flee, the British let out some cheers.

At about 300 yards behind the vanguard was the main body under General Braddock. They could hear some shooting and the cheering of the soldiers up front. The troops in the main body made ready for action. They expected, however, that the regulars in the vanguard would naturally soon prevail and scatter the small number of "savages" ahead.

But all this confidence was about to vanish. With de Beaujeu killed, command of the French and American Indians devolved to Captain Dumas. The situation looked desperate, but Dumas bravely called on the French soldiers, Canadians, and Indians who had not panicked to stand and fight with him. He then went forward with the courage "given by despair." His men were inspired by his example; many followed him and they soon came within close range of the column of redcoats. Finding good cover in the woods as they approached either

THE BATTLE OF MONONGAHELA, 1755

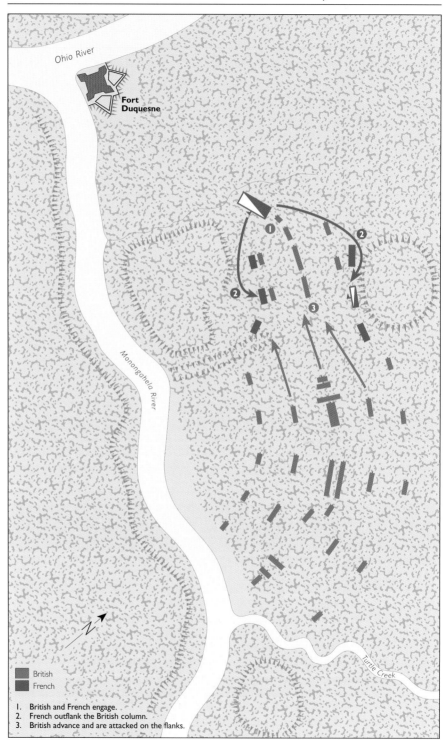

1. British and French engage.
2. French outflank the British column.
3. British advance and are attacked on the flanks.

side of the column, they opened a very heavy fire into the British ranks. The startled British soldiers stopped cheering as their invisible enemies had redoubled their shooting from both sides while shouting Indian war whoops.

The hundred or so Canadians and American Indians who had started to flee, hearing the shooting and war cries, recovered their nerve. They ran back to help their comrades and join in the action. The detached flank guards were quickly cut off from the main column. In spite of the heavy odds against the French and Indians, the tactics of the "Canadian style of warfare" were starting to reap results. At this point, Captain Dumas sensed things were starting to turn in his favor. He was with the French troops and Indians shooting at the front of the British vanguard. He now saw an opportunity to surround and engage the enemy at close range from cover and he seized it. By now, the Indians and Canadians with their regular officers and cadets were deployed in the woods on either side of the British army. He sent orders to the officers leading Indians, such as de Langlade, to attack both sides of the British column.

General Braddock had meanwhile sent an aide-de-camp, probably Captain Morris, to find out how things were going with the vanguard engaged in front. He expected they would have rapidly cleared the band of French and American Indians they had run into; instead, shooting continued, and, indeed, grew more intense while Indian war whoops seemed to echo everywhere in the dark forest all around. Quite suddenly things were not going according to plan. Hearing the "excessive quick and heavy firing in the front," General Braddock ordered more troops to join the vanguard, and halted the march of the rest of the column. Leaving Sir Peter Halket in command of the remaining 400 troops to safeguard the artillery and baggage in the rear, General Braddock then spurred his horse toward the action followed by his ADCs Lieutenant Orme and Colonel Washington, and the rest of his staff.

A desperate fight

Up front, the vanguard's line of grenadiers with the two 6-pdr cannons were firing into the woods in front of them, but to little effect as most of Captain Dumas' men were now pouring their fire into the redcoats from both flanks. As grenadier after grenadier was hit and fell, the others wavered and then their line broke. Lieutenant-Colonel Gage saw he was outflanked and ordered a withdrawal so as to re-form about 30 yards behind. In doing so, Gage's men ran into the front of Lieutenant-Colonel Burton's command as they came up. Burton's men too were being fired upon and, as Orme related, he was forming his men "to face a rising ground to the right" from which "Indians" were firing down on his men. Burton's men were trying to form themselves into a firing line, according to Gordon, "in the greatest Confusion," and the arrival of Gage's men, some of them near panic, caused even more disarray. The confused forces were huddled together, forming superb targets for their foes who, safely under cover, took full advantage of this. The British force now rapidly degenerated into "Confusion and Panic."

The officers tried to restore order, separating the 44th and 48th regiments by rallying the men to their colors, but officers were falling even faster than the men and the rally to the colors failed. General Braddock ordered the officers to form the men into small divisions and advance, but to no avail. The French and American Indians were practically invisible, and now that a fog of musket smoke hung over the scene, even the flash and smoke from a hidden foe's musket had become indiscernible. The irregular tactics meant that the British soldiers were running back and forth trying to cover all angles, while the provincial troops further added to the disarray. The 900-man French force was now deployed along the full length of the British column on both sides. The terrain, heavily wooded with numerous large trees, suited their tactics perfectly. They moved around, confusing the enemy as to their location and numbers. Consisting largely of Canadian militiamen and Indians, most of the force was armed with light-caliber Tulle hunting and trade muskets rather than the heavy-caliber military muskets. They were handling very familiar weapons and were proficient at aimed fire, which explains the vast numbers of British casualties and also the high proportion of officer casualties, who were naturally prime targets. Their one potential weakness was the lack of bayonets, a disadvantage in hand-to-hand combat with regular troops. The Canadians could withdraw very quickly, however, and were about to demonstrate that expert handling of the tomahawk more than compensated for the lack of a bayonet at close quarters.

Death and defeat

While General Braddock was trying to rally his men, the French and Indians at the rear moved closer to the baggage and ammunition train, which they attacked. Many horses were hit as well as some of the wagoners – the rest of the horses panicked and ran off. Sir Peter Halket tried to form a defense with the men he had and ordered the three 12-pdr cannon with the baggage train to open a rapid fire into the woods. Their ammunition was quickly being expended but the 12-pdrs had little or no effect on the scattered French and Indians in the woods. Colonel Halket was hit and fell mortally wounded.

Under fire from all sides, General Braddock was himself a prime target for the Canadians and American Indians and four or five horses were successively shot from under him. Several more shots went through his clothes but he remained as yet unscathed. The panic and confusion around him was supreme, with the crazed soldiers crowded against each other loading and firing into the air as quickly as possible. He ordered a party to advance toward the left to support the gunners and men with the two 12-pdrs, who were in danger of being overwhelmed. He also now knew that the two 6-pdrs with the vanguard had been left in the field and captured by the French, who could turn them on their former owners. Each gun had by then fired between 20 and 30 rounds, despite the gunners being prime targets for the Canadians and Indians. General Braddock ordered that the hill to the right be captured, hoping to execute some sort of pincer attack. By now two of General Braddock's three aides-de-camp, Morris and Orme, were wounded, with only Washington left unscathed. Braddock tried in vain to rally what men he could to clear the hill. Lieutenant-Colonel Burton at last managed to get together about 100 men of the 48th Foot and, Orme says, "prevailed upon them, by the General's order, to follow him toward the rising ground on the right, but he being disabled by his wounds, they faced about to the right, and returned." It was while Braddock was attempting to rally his troops that he was finally struck and fell with a mortal wound to the shoulder and the chest according to Washington, through his lungs according to Orme. It was around 4.00 or 4.30pm.

The troops escorting the wagons in Braddock's column were fired upon and were soon in disarray. (Photo René Chartrand)

As the French and American Indians fanned out around Braddock's column, the British became confused and dismayed as this unseen enemy began to tear holes in the exposed ranks of the regulars. (Stephen Walsh © Osprey Publishing Ltd)

By now, all the senior officers had been hit: Gage, Burton, and St Clair were wounded, and now Braddock had suffered a grievous wound. Scores of regimental officers lay dead or wounded along with hundreds of soldiers. The enemy's shooting was clearly quite accurate and the British soldiers' instinct to close ranks simply offered excellent targets even through the thick musket smoke. Many British soldiers were now seized by panic at the slaughter around them and ran, making their way as best as they could toward the Monongahela River.

The French soldiers, Canadian militiamen, and Indian warriors were shooting as fast as they could, some starting to run low on ammunition. They were in excellent cover and all but invisible in the forest, concealed not only by the foliage but by the smoke. Thus, they had seen hardly any of their number fall while they could see British redcoats falling in droves. Captains Dumas, de Ligneris, and other officers now had an increasing command and control problem with the American Indians, and probably with many Canadian militiamen as well. They were eager to rush in to finish the job with tomahawk and scalping knife and get some booty. It was the only "pay" Canadian militiamen could expect, and, for the Indians it was important to get some prisoners to sell to French officers or to keep for their own purposes, ranging from adoption to a ghastly fate at the torture post. For Captain Dumas, the issue was obvious and he knew he had to let them charge in; the question was whether there might be a trap or reinforcements that might yet turn the tide. He and his officers had no way of knowing that all the British commanders had been hit and that panic had set in among the British troops, but they did not expect a relief force to be nearby.

Colonel Washington faced a hopeless situation. He was seemingly the only officer of rank who had not been killed or wounded. Four bullets had pierced his coat and two horses had been shot under him, but he had escaped any injury. Nobody knew the true extent of the army's disorder or who was now the commanding officer. The British force was now in chaos and the battle was lost. The cannon fell silent, and the whole body gave way and crossed the river. The few American Indians with the army were determined, but the rest of the army would not stand.

RETREAT

The issue was now to try to organize some sort of orderly retreat to save as many wounded as possible and prevent a total disaster. General Braddock was still alive, though very weak, and ordered Washington to retreat to Dunbar's camp. Colonel Washington managed to rally some officers and men as a rearguard, and retreated in some order to the ford of the Monongahela leaving the dead and wounded, all the artillery, and baggage on the battlefield. Near the ford, Washington's improvised rearguard formed up, and allowed many of the survivors to cross the river. Lieutenant-Colonel Burton, although wounded, tried to rally the soldiers and "made a speech to the men to beg them to get into some order," but they were overwhelmed with panic. In the end, everyone hurried off from the Monongahela River as fast as possible.

At the site of the action, the shooting subsided while the American Indian war whoops had redoubled. Seeing what was left of the enemy column on the run and hundreds of bodies strewn around, the excited Indians, Canadian militiamen, and French soldiers had left their covered positions and descended in a rush, yelling Indian cries, and scalped and finished off all they could. The "pillage was horrible," reported Captain Dumas who now had lost all control of his force. The majority were warriors of allied Indian nations, for whom this was their reward and glory. However, a good many Canadian militiamen were equally fierce warriors, and a number had adopted Indian customs through contact over the years. Even some French regulars, long stationed by choice in such forts as Michilimackinac, had adopted wilderness ways.

OPPOSITE *The grenadiers are shaken by heavy fire at the battle of Monongahela. Print by Howard Pyle illustrating George Waashington's account of the battle published in* Scribner's Magazine *in May 1893. (Photograph René Chartrand)*

Meanwhile, the wounded French officers were left without assistance in the nearby woods when all had descended on the field. Captain Dumas ordered officers to the field to call on some soldiers busy looting to help their wounded officers. Eventually, the wounded were carried to Fort Duquesne. Having now too few soldiers left to carry the body of Commandant de Beaujeu, he was lain hidden in a small ravine for the time being. Meanwhile, on a field given over to indiscriminate looting to the sound of war whoops, the sergeants of the *Compagnies Franches de la Marine* kept their cool, seized and destroyed the British powder kegs, and dismantled the British guns.

Flushed with such an extraordinary victory, Captain Dumas was also dismayed at the sudden disintegration of his own force. He only had a handful of regular officers and men left. The Canadian militiamen were out of control for the moment, and the Indians had done their part and most were already on the way back to Fort Duquesne with their prizes and prisoners. Some unfortunate prisoners were also brought into the Indian camp near the fort and tortured and put to death. The rest of the Indians had found liquor in the abandoned baggage, probably the issue army rum, and stayed on the battlefield to get utterly drunk. Amidst all this carnage, Captain Dumas was concerned about a British counterattack. Following confusing reports, and a council with his officers, Captain Dumas ordered a withdrawal to about a mile from the action so as to regroup and be ready should the British advance again the next day.

On July 10, Captain Dumas greeted "the Indians who had spent the night drinking on the battlefield" who were coming back "with a few officers who had stayed with them." These would have been officers operating with the American Indians such as Ensign de Langlade. They reported that the British were marching toward them and that they had heard drums beating. Captain Dumas did not give much credence to such reports by hungover men smelling of rum, and returned to the battlefield with a hundred soldiers and Canadian militiamen to recover the British artillery. These were transported to the fort by canoe. While on the battlefield, Captain Dumas received more reports from the Indians that the enemy was returning, but Dumas was relying on the reports of his two scouting parties, who had reported that the British were nowhere nearby.

For Captain Dumas, a pursuit was impossible. Besides his officers, he had almost no soldiers left with him. Although later criticized for not pursuing, Captain Dumas was undoubtedly right when he told his critics that the force left to him could not have prevailed; even if he had wanted to "push his luck," he did not have the means to do it. Thus, after being assured that the British were soundly beaten and would not be back, Captain Dumas and his men returned to Fort Duquesne. The Ohio Valley remained within the realm of King Louis XV of France and as far as ever from British control.

The French and allied American Indians fire into Braddock's column at the battle of Monongahela. (State Historical Society of Wisconsin)

Far from plotting a counterattack, the British were in a complete rout. Attempts by some officers to rally the men had no success at all, and fearing further desertion by the troops, the officers were obliged to go along with their hurrying men. The survivors of Braddock's army were in such fear of American Indian pursuers that they marched all night. George Washington recalled this night march as horrific with "the dying, the groans, lamentations, and crys along the road of the wounded for help... The gloom and horror of which was not a little increased by the impervious darkness occasioned by the close shade of thick woods." The survivors marched throughout the next day until about 10.00pm when they came to Gist's abandoned settlement. There they decided to stop, no doubt totally exhausted after marching for about 30 hours without a break and covering an incredible 60 miles (97km) from the field of battle. The men slept there, no doubt posting guards, as they remained nervous of lurking French and Indians.

Colonel Dunbar became aware of the disaster when terrified wagoners galloped into his camp early in the morning on July 10. Later that day, a wounded Sir John St Clair rode in giving a more complete account. There seemed little point in mustering a force to advance, but rather to prepare for the hundreds of survivors who started to reach Dunbar's camp on July 11. It was now obvious that the remnants of the army, including Dunbar's force, would have to return to Fort Cumberland. As the senior surviving and unwounded officer, Dunbar was now in command of the army. On July 12, therefore, he ordered provisions and ammunition destroyed and the next day the army abandoned Dunbar's camp and marched toward Fort Cumberland. At last, on July 17, the army reached the fort. The campaign to capture Fort Duquesne and secure the Ohio Valley had ended in a resounding defeat.

The count of dead and wounded on the British side was horrendous. Participants usually estimated about 1,000 casualties out of some 1,200 or 1,300 souls in the column, including at least 450 killed. Lieutenant-Colonel Washington commented that "our poor Virginians behaved like men and died like soldiers." The leading officers had been killed or wounded, including the commanding general. All the artillery and baggage had been lost. It ranked as one of the worst disasters in the annals of the British Army. The French casualties were trifling by comparison, although they included the death of Captain de Beaujeu. The total killed came to 23 killed including the 15 Indians, and 20 wounded including 12 Indians. French and American Indian casualties thus came to 43 including 27 Indians.

The two sides drew different lessons from the battles of Fort Necessity and Monongahela. The French saw little to improve upon in terms of woodland warfare tactics and Indian diplomacy. Despite this triumph, metropolitan tacticians in France continued to ignore tactical doctrine championed by the Canadian officers.

By contrast, the sheer scale of the disaster forced the British to reassess the way they had undertaken the Duquesne campaign. Washington said of his men: "our poor Virginians behaved like men and died like soldiers," and before his death, Braddock praised the conduct of the Virginians, then whispered that he could not bear the sight of a redcoat. Indeed though the panic of the regulars was understandable, their reputation, and that of British soldiers in general, had taken a terrible beating. Obviously change was overdue for the British forces. Their victory over an army of redcoats also reinforced American Indian confidence in their irregular tactics. However, the next time they faced a regular army, in 1763, the American Indians fought alone against the British, who had long since become adept at light infantry tactics, and Chief Pontiac's Indians were defeated at Bushy Run, not far from the battle site of Monongahela.

THE BRITISH CATASTROPHE

Elsewhere in North America, the French were not as fortunate as in the Ohio Valley, and by the end of the year, the British had seen some success from their bold plans. Overall, however, the year was catastrophic for the British forces.

Amongst the items found by the French on the Monongahela battlefield were General Braddock's papers, including his instructions from King George II and those from the commander-in-chief, the Duke of Cumberland, as well as copies of letters from the duke to several ministers. These were real prizes and were sent to Québec. There, Governor-General Vaudreuil saw their political importance and had copies sent to the Count Maurepas, the Minister of the Navy at Versailles. Once translated, the papers were useful to French diplomats determined to prove the British guilty of aggressive usurpation and oppression of the rights of France. The French government published them in 1756. More immediately, the papers provided details of the main British aims for the campaign season, and allowed them to preempt the British forces at Niagara and Fort Saint-Frédéric, known to the British as Crown Point.

OSWEGO

Following General Braddock's death, Governor (Major-General) Shirley became commander-in-chief of the British forces in North America. Shirley was designated to lead the expedition against Fort Niagara, primarily using two newly raised regular regiments filled with raw recruits and various provincial units. He assembled his force in late July. The plan called for the column to travel overland and by river to Oswego, a British-Indian trading center situated on Lake Ontario. Oswego was the British foothold on Lake Ontario, situated between the French forts of Frontenac on the north shore, and Niagara on the south. It was more than 200 miles from Albany to Oswego, and a further 150 miles to Fort Niagara via Lake Ontario.

Shirley and the major part of his expedition arrived at Oswego on August 17, 1755. They encountered no opposition, either en route or when they arrived. The difficult passage to Oswego, followed by numerous delays in the arrival of supplies and troops once there, prevented Shirley moving on toward Fort Niagara as quickly as planned. The last troops arrived in Oswego on September 2, but supply problems continued and desertions had begun. In the interim, the French, taking advantage of the delay, had moved troops to Fort Frontenac, on the north side of Lake Ontario, and to other posts to protect Niagara. Shirley, aware of the growing threat from the north and the decreasing time left to lay siege to the fort, decided to call off the attack until the next campaign season and build up defenses in the Oswego area in preparation for taking Frontenac as a necessary prelude to Niagara.

LAKE GEORGE

In late July 1755, the spirited but inexperienced Lieutenant-Colonel William Johnson headed from Albany toward Lac du St Sacrement, which he renamed Lake George. With him were 2,000 provincial soldiers, and hundreds of Mohawk and Oneida Indians in support. He had orders to construct a fort on the Hudson River, south of Lake George. Upon completion of this task, he was to proceed to Lake George, sail north, and attack the French positions on the north side of the lake. From there, he was supposed to continue to Fort Saint-Frédéric at the southern end of Lake Champlain, just north of Lake George. Having established and manned Fort Edward, named for one of the king's grandsons, Johnson and the majority of his men reached the southern end of Lake George in late August where he received reports from Indian scouts that the French were in position at Ticonderoga, but they had not yet constructed fortifications. Baron Dieskau had been warned by the papers found on the Monongahela battlefield that Johnson was planning to attack Crown Point, and reports had then informed him that Johnson was stationed at Fort Edward. He led 3,500 French regulars, militia, and American Indians to Ticonderoga, and leaving the majority of these troops there to construct Fort Carillon, took 1,000 regulars, militia, and Indians to attack the British at Fort Edward. As the French forces moved down the lake in bateaux, they realized that Johnson was in fact encamped at the southern end of Lake George, several miles north of where they expected to find him. They then reached the road between Fort Edward and Lake George. In the meantime, Johnson learned of Dieskau's presence, and on September 8 he sent about 1,000 men to attack the French force, despite a warning from the Mohawk

A paramount influence over the Mohawk nation, Sir William Johnson led them into battle on the side of the British in many of the battles of the French and Indian War and worked hard to keep them on the side of the British, or at least neutral. (National Archives of Canada, C-005197)

war chief Hendrick. The troops were led by Colonel Ephraim Williams, and accompanied by Indians led by Hendrick. The British force set off down the road toward Fort Edward, but Dieskau was warned, and set an ambush with his Indian and militia troops. They surprised the head of the column, which crumpled. The regulars behind managed to regain order, and fell back to the British camp. About 200 were killed, including Williams and Hendrick. This encounter became known as "The Bloody Morning Scout."

The British camp was quickly fortified with available logs, boats, and carts against possible attack by the French army, and the two armies met there later that day. The French regulars marched in open order toward the camp, but their fire only pounded the felled trees surrounding the British position. The provincials retaliated with musket and artillery fire. The French attempted to shift their fire, but despite their efforts were unable to inflict heavy casualties upon the British. During the fighting several hundred Canadians and American Indians were fiercely attacked by the British, and their bodies thrown into a small lake which is still known as "Bloody Pond." After a few hours the Canadian and Indian troops melted away, but, as Johnson noted, the French regulars "kept their ground and order for some time with great resolution and good conduct." Eventually, however, the French began to lose ground, and the provincials seized the advantage, launched a counterattack, and captured the wounded Dieskau. The battle ended when a relieving force arrived from Fort Edward, forcing a conclusive French withdrawal.

Johnson did not pursue the fleeing French, which has been held against him by critics. The British and French had each lost more than 200 men in the battle at Lake George. The Mohawks had suffered heavy losses in the campaign, but found Johnson a brave and reliable new leader, who united the Iroquois behind him, which Johnson would use to British advantage in the years ahead. The British campaign toward Fort Saint-Frédéric came to a halt when news was received that the French had begun to fortify Ticonderoga and renamed it Fort Carillon. The British were content with their victory, and fortified the southern end of Lake George with the construction of Fort William Henry. The true significance of the battle of Lake George lay in the fact that mere provincials had decisively defeated French regulars. Dieskau said of them: "In the morning they fought like good boys, about noon like men, and in the afternoon like devils."

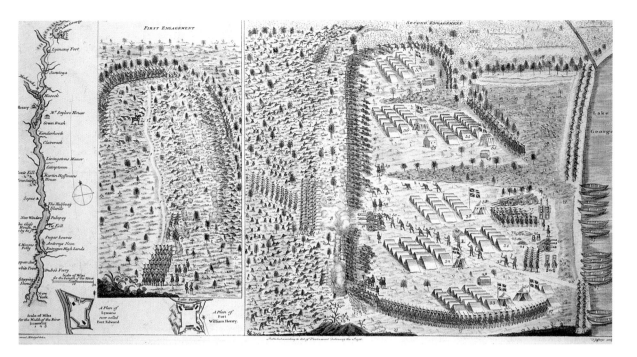

FORT BEAUSÉJOUR AND THE ACADIANS

Ironically, the smallest British expedition was also the most successful of the 1755 campaign season. Lieutenant-Colonel Robert Monckton led 2,000 provincials and 280 regulars against the French Fort Beauséjour in Nova Scotia. The invasion force sailed from Boston on May 26 for (Fort) Annapolis Royal in Nova Scotia. Artillery and supplies were sent in from Halifax to Fort Lawrence, on the route to the expedition's final destination, in time for the arrival of the Boston contingent on June 2. The troops stopped just long enough to re-supply, marching out on June 4 toward the fort.

British troops spent the next week clearing the areas surrounding Fort Beauséjour of Acadians who were providing support to the French cause. The displaced Acadians flooded toward the fort for protection. Beauséjour was manned by a few companies of regulars, plus nearly 1,000 Acadian militia. By June 14, most of the area around the fort had been cleared and the British artillery was in position to begin the bombardment of the fort. A French observer described in the *Journals of Beauséjour*, "on the morning of the 16 [June] an enemy bomb exploded on one of the casements to the left of the entrance … [I]t was enough to bring about the surrender of the fort because fire combined with inexperience made everyone in that place give up."

The nearby French Fort Gaspereau also capitulated, creating a significant breach in the French strategy of a continuous line of forts from Louisbourg to

The first and second engagements of the battle of Lake George in 1755. The British fortified camp is illustrated in the second engagement, with the lake to its rear, and the French attacking from the left. (Anne S. K. Brown Military Collection, Brown University Library)

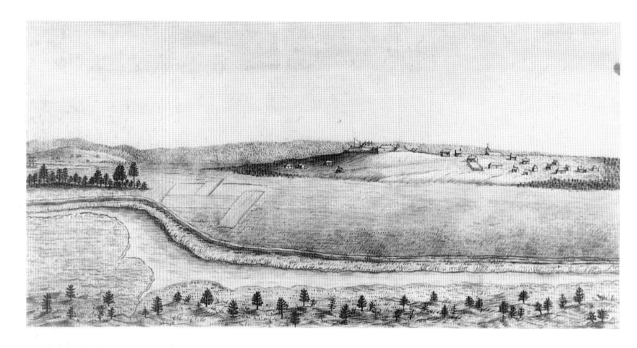

After taking Fort Beauséjour in Nova Scotia in 1755, the British renamed this crucial fortress Fort Cumberland. (National Archives of Canada, C-002707)

New Orleans. Aside from the water route toward Québec, Louisbourg had been utterly cut off by the British action. One lasting, and infamous, legacy of the fighting in Nova Scotia in 1755 was the expulsion of the Acadian population by the British authorities.

FALL INTO WINTER

The overall British strategy for 1755 had not been fully executed. The British had been completely stymied in the Ohio River area and had made limited gains in two other campaigns. Only in Nova Scotia had the strategy borne fruit. The fighting in the New York and western theaters had additionally accelerated the deterioration of relations between regular and provincial troops. Numerous provincial observers were critical of the performance of the regulars with Braddock's expedition, especially after some regulars accidentally mistook Virginian provincials for French troops and fired upon them. The victory at Lake George, also won by provincials, gave further credibility to the colonial belief that British regulars might not be suited to fighting conditions in North America.

Following Monongahela, Colonel Dunbar fell back all the way to Philadelphia, setting up his "winter quarters" there despite it being only August. This led Lieutenant-Governor Dinwiddie to comment that he appeared "to have determined to leave our frontiers as defenseless as possible," and the colonies of Virginia and Maryland took up the challenge. Dinwiddie ordered out the militia,

raised three independent companies and reinforced Fort Cumberland. On August 14, George Washington was commissioned colonel of a new Virginia regiment. The Maryland legislature authorized 80 men to serve on the frontier for four months, and built Fort Frederick, as a second line of defense should Fort Cumberland fall.

Fort Frederick, Maryland, was built after Braddock's defeat to block sizable French expeditions penetrating further east into the heart of the state. A large bastioned fort with stone walls, it served as a base for later British operations. (René Chartrand)

At Fort Duquesne, Dumas succeeded de Contrecoeur as commandant in August. As there were only a few regulars and Canadians in the region, he realized that the American Indians were essential to keep the British at bay. In the absence of a determined enemy, Dumas did all he could to encourage the Indians to mount raids, and for many months the frontiers of the colonies came under attack. That fall was a time of horror for frontier colonists, abandoned to the ravages of French and Indian war-parties, while colonial assemblies argued with their governors. Raids from Fort Duquesne reached almost as far as the coast and even into South Carolina. Washington's Virginia Regiment was virtually the only force covering a 350-mile frontier that winter, and it was quite unable to keep the situation under control, despite the lull in enemy activity which deep winter brought. Organized forces were unable to stop war-parties that could rapidly materialize, strike and disappear into the wilderness with impunity. It was not until December 1755 that the Pennsylvania would turn away from its Shaker background and prepare for war.

RUPERT'S LAND

HUDSON'S BAY COMPANY

NEWFOUNDLA

Gulf of
St Lawrence

St Lawrence

F
R
A
N
C
E

Lake Superior

Île
St Jean

Île Royale
Louisbourg

C A N A D A

ACADIA

Québec

Beauséjour

Michilimackinac

Montréal

Halifax

NOVA
SCOTIA

*Lake
Huron*

Lake Michigan

Frontenac

Ticonderoga

F
R

Niagara

Lake Ontario

William Henry

Detroit

Lake Erie

Albany

Boston

N
E
W

Duquesne

New York

Wabasan

Philadelphia

Chartres

Ohio

BRITISH
13 COLONIES

Vincennes

Alexandria

L
O
U
I
S
I
A
N
A

Williamsburg

ATLANTIC
OCEAN

Mississippi

Mobile
New Orleans

FLORIDA

GULF OF MEXICO

BAHAMA
ISLANDS

Territories in North America early	
	Britain
	France
	Spain
	Disputed

CUBA

0   250 mil

0   400 km

HISPANIOLA

MEXICO

HAITI

PART 2
THE TURNING OF THE TIDE

CHRONOLOGY

1756

April	The Marquis de Montcalm travels to New France to take charge of French forces
May 17	Formal declaration of war between France and Britain
June	Shirley replaced as commander-in-chief of the British army by Lord Loudoun
July	Indecisive naval actions around Louisbourg
August 14	The British forts at Oswego surrender
Winter	The partisan war continues

1757

August	Failed British attempt to take Louisbourg
August 9	Fort William Henry surrenders

1758

March	Abercromby appointed commander-in-chief to replace Loudoun
June 8	Amherst's army lands at Louisbourg
July 5	Abercromby's army sails up Lake George toward Fort Carillon
July 6	Battle of Bernetz Brook
July 8	Battle of Ticonderoga
August 1	Louisbourg capitulates
August 27	Fort Frontenac is sacked
September 14	Grant's battle outside Fort Duquesne
October 12	French repelled at Fort Ligonier
November	Amherst replaces Abercromby as commander-in-chief for North America
November 24	French abandon Fort Duquesne

DECLARATION AND REINFORCEMENT
CAMPAIGNS OF 1756

The French command in Canada in 1756 was largely divided between Marquis de Vaudreuil, who in theory had influence in the deployment of the colonial regulars and militia, and the new commander-in-chief of the French regular forces, Marquis de Montcalm-Gozon de Saint-Véran. The French port of Louisbourg, however, was under the command of neither Montcalm nor Vaudreuil, but that of Chevalier de Augustin Drucour.

Montcalm sailed from France for Québec on April 3, 1756, accompanied by a reinforcement of two battalions of the Royal-Roussillon and La Sarre regiments. His two senior commanders were Brigadier le Chevalier de Lévis and Colonel le Chevalier de Bourlamaque. As Montcalm sailed toward Québec, war between Great Britain and France was formally declared on May 17. For the French forces in North America, this did not mean that France would focus her military might across the Atlantic. On the contrary, strategy in France was divided between colonial and Continental ambitions, and there was strong sentiment at the French court for devoting the largest military effort to the conflict in Europe. By 1758, the French court had shifted almost completely to a strategy of invading and seizing Hanover, in the hope that it could be used as a bargaining chip for the return of New France, should the British succeed in defeating Montcalm.

The British government took the opposite strategic approach following the formal outbreak of war, deciding that seizing New France would be an important strategic advantage in the larger world war that began to develop in the spring of 1756. To this end, two more regiments were sent from Great Britain in 1756, accompanied by senior generals, such as Major-General James Abercromby, Major-General Daniel Webb, and a new commander-in-chief, John Campbell, Earl of Loudoun, with orders to rectify the situation that had developed in 1755.

OSWEGO

Loudoun arrived in Albany in late June, where he assumed overall command of the troops in North America. In preparation for the new season's strategy, a senior officer, Lieutenant-Colonel Burton, was sent to report on the state of the provincial troops stationed at Fort William Henry at the base of Lake George. He soon reported back that the fort was a shambles, with only about two-thirds of the men fit for duty. Clearly the plan for an attack on Fort Carillon would have to be delayed.

The French, however, were unaware of the state of affairs at Fort William Henry, and feared that the main British attack would indeed be at Fort Carillon. Montcalm therefore arrived there in July, with the Royal-Roussillon and some *Compagnies Franches* to reinforce the La Reine and Languedoc battalions already guarding the new fort. He decided to draw off British attention from the fort by applying pressure against Oswego instead. This plan began as a feint attack, but in the end it became the major campaign of the season.

There were three British forts at Oswego – Fort Oswego, Fort Ontario, and Fort George – all under the command of Lieutenant-Colonel James Mercer. Shirley had left two provincial regiments there over the winter, and barely half of these were fit to fight by summer 1756. New Jersey provincials were stationed at the unfinished Fort George. Fort Ontario was a new, star-shaped timber fort which stood on a height on the right bank of River Oswego as it entered the lake, overlooking the other two forts on the opposite bank.

A column of 1,000 French regulars, Canadians, and American Indians under Coulon de Villiers was assembled to cut communications between Oswego and Albany. They arrived in the area in early July, where they encountered a column of about 500 provincial troops under Captain John Bradstreet, who had delivered supplies to Oswego, and were now returning to Albany by boat. The French ambushed Bradstreet on July 3. The skirmish lasted for most of the day, with both sides claiming victory. The encounter was most likely a draw, with prisoners taken, but few casualties on both sides. The ambush did alert the British commanders to the precarious position that Oswego was now in, but a major reinforcement, the 44th Regiment of Foot and a force of provincial troops, was not sent out until August, so arrived too late.

In early July, Montcalm took his leave of Carillon, having satisfied himself of the arrangements there, and leaving it in the command of his deputy, Lévis. He arrived at Fort Frontenac on July 29, and there he mustered his expedition. The La Sarre and Guyenne were already at the fort, and the Béarn soon arrived from Niagara. A detachment of colonial troops, some militia and American Indians brought the total strength to around 3,000 men, with plentiful artillery. Montcalm sent ahead a small detachment to rendezvous with de Villiers near

Pierre de Rigaud, Marquis de Vaudreuil (1698–1767)

Vaudreuil was the governor-general of the colony of Canada from 1755 until the French capitulation. He was of an illustrious French family, and Canadian-born, his father had been governor of the colony early in the 18th century. Vaudreuil was by convention and practice lieutenant-general of all the French forces serving in the colony. Although Vaudreuil had in his youth served as an officer in the colonial forces in Louisiana, he had never before commanded anything much bigger than a company and, so far as is known, had never even been shot at. Of itself this was not necessarily important for, although vain and pompous, he was on the whole a relatively good administrator, untiringly zealous in his efforts to defend his colony. However, as Montcalm's immediate superior, he found himself in constant disagreement over strategy, and Montcalm barely disguised his contempt for his superior. The tension was exacerbated because Montcalm was French-born, and Vaudreuil colonial-born, there was often antagonism between French-born and colonial-born officials. Throughout the campaigns each man accused the other of interfering in issues of strategy. Vaudreuil favored a guerrilla campaign along the frontier while Montcalm continued to believe that the war would ultimately be won by regular troops. In 1759, Montcalm was promoted to the army rank of lieutenant-general as a result of which he at last formally outranked Vaudreuil. (National Archives of Canada)

Oswego, and then transported the rest of the force in 80 gunboats, under cover of darkness. By August 10, the force landed unopposed about a mile from Oswego. The French columns converged on Fort Ontario the next day.

The French had a large contingent of siege artillery for its assault, including the captured guns from Braddock's expedition. After two days and nights of heavy bombardment, Fort Ontario was shattered, and on August 13 Mercer ordered the evacuation of the fort, and withdrawal of the survivors across the river. By the morning of August 14, the French guns were set up on the heights that Fort Ontario had formerly occupied, and started to bombard the two remaining forts. Under cover of fire, a column of French and American Indian troops crossed the river unopposed.

The forts were badly damaged by the bombardment, and despite the spirited defense given by the garrison of the forts, Mercer knew that they were

Louis-Joseph Marquis de Montcalm-Gozon de Saint Véran (1712–59)

With war soon to be declared, and Dieskau still struggling toward recovery in British captivity, France required a new general in the colony. None of the court favorites saw much prospect of glory in such an uncomfortable command, and eventually the choice fell on a 44-year-old brigadier, six times wounded, a front-line colonel in the late wars in Bohemia and Italy. He had no important connections, no wealth, and preferred to spend his time on his estates in the south than circulate with the gilded moths of Versailles.

Born in the family château at Candiac, near Nîmes in 1712, Louis de Montcalm was the son of nobility with land, but little wealth. He joined the Hainault Regiment as an ensign in 1727. In 1729 his father bought him a captaincy, and six years later died, leaving Louis the title and considerable debts. A marriage was arranged which brought him property, some connections, and great happiness. The former Angélique Louise Talon du Boulay bore him ten children, of which five survived him. His surviving letters to his family show him to be a tender husband and a loving father.

In 1741 he fought in Bohemia, and in 1743 became the colonel of the Auxerrois Regiment. Between 1744 and 1746 he saw much hard fighting, including an Italian campaign; in 1746 he was captured after receiving five saber wounds while rallying his men before the walls of Piacenza. Paroled, he returned to active service in time to be hit by a musket-ball before the Peace of Aix-la-Chapelle in 1748. He was appointed to the American command in February 1756, and promoted major-general on his departure. He was given two battalions as reinforcements, and on April 3, 1756, he set sail for New France in the frigate *Licorne*.

Montcalm's subordination to the Marquis de Vaudreuil had been very explicitly set out in his original instructions, but as a professional soldier known for his arrogance, he rather too publicly resented what he saw as civilian primacy

in determining operational matters. By the end of 1758, he was feeling the strain of fighting a long drawn-out losing battle that he was temperamentally unsuited for, and his attempt to force the issue with the French government had been a failure except from solving his problems with Vaudreuil as his promotion gave him superiority over the governor-general in military matters. However, it was too little too late, and despite his best efforts, Montcalm could not halt the British advance. As he said on his deathbed, he was happy not to live to see the surrender of Québec. (National Archives of Canada, C-27665)

outgunned, outnumbered, and isolated. When Mercer was himself killed by a cannon ball, the remaining officers held a council of war, and quickly decided to surrender. The garrison was in no position to negotiate terms, and when the gates were opened the militia and American Indians flooded in. The

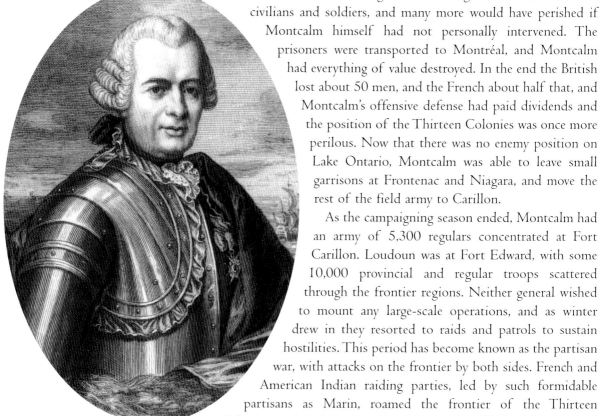

French-allied Indians wrought havoc among the surrendered British civilians and soldiers, and many more would have perished if Montcalm himself had not personally intervened. The prisoners were transported to Montréal, and Montcalm had everything of value destroyed. In the end the British lost about 50 men, and the French about half that, and Montcalm's offensive defense had paid dividends and the position of the Thirteen Colonies was once more perilous. Now that there was no enemy position on Lake Ontario, Montcalm was able to leave small garrisons at Frontenac and Niagara, and move the rest of the field army to Carillon.

As the campaigning season ended, Montcalm had an army of 5,300 regulars concentrated at Fort Carillon. Loudoun was at Fort Edward, with some 10,000 provincial and regular troops scattered through the frontier regions. Neither general wished to mount any large-scale operations, and as winter drew in they resorted to raids and patrols to sustain hostilities. This period has become known as the partisan war, with attacks on the frontier by both sides. French and American Indian raiding parties, led by such formidable partisans as Marin, roamed the frontier of the Thirteen Colonies, and scalp-hunting for bounty was rife. British provincial raiders, particularly Rogers' Rangers, undertook raids deep into French territory, attacking French posts and Indian villages, which caused great distress to those at distant outposts. As well as causing chaos and fear, these raids were aimed at obtaining information by taking prisoners, and disrupting the supply convoys upon which the forts of both sides depended. In the depth of winter, the French army was pulled back from Ticonderoga to the Montréal area where Montcalm and his staff wintered.

French naval Commodore Louis-Joseph Beaussier d'Isle (1701–65), whose squadron in 1756 kept the Royal Navy at bay in a series of engagements off Louisbourg. He was back in Louisbourg in 1758 but was trapped by Boscawen's fleet. He and his men helped Drucour put up a stubborn resistance during the siege. (National Archives of Canada, C-44821)

NAVAL CAMPAIGNS

The Royal Navy engaged in three different forms of strategy during the Seven Years' War. The first was the seizure and destruction of the French trading fleet across the world's oceans, which denied the French government a large percentage of the revenue raised from the colonies, and had the added benefit of increasing British revenue for the war effort. The second was the tying up and emasculating of the French fleet by blockade in its home waters. The third and final strategy was the combined-operations role of the fleet in carrying the war to the colonies and France. The Royal Navy deployed the majority of its fleet in the North American theater and in home waters during the Seven Years' War, intending to disrupt the lucrative trade between France and its colonies as well as protect Britain from a possible French invasion. It is often believed that the Royal Navy dominated the seas unopposed during the French and Indian War and Seven Years' War, but this was not as clear-cut during the first years of the war. Admiral Edward Boscawen's action against the French fleet carrying troops to Canada and Île Royale in 1755 had been deceitful to the last degree as France and Britain were still at peace. When the *Lys* and the *Alcide* asked the nearing British warships if war had been declared, they were answered with broadsides. The rest of the French fleet made it safely to Québec and Louisbourg.

News of Boscawen's action had, by then, long reached Europe and operations had started in the Mediterranean. French commander Vice-Admiral la Galissonière heading the Toulon fleet engaged and drove off Vice-Admiral Byng's British fleet on May 20, 1756. This opened the way for Marshal

French ships-of-the-line, 18th century. (Library of Congress)

Richelieu's army to land on Minorca. After a series of brilliant moves by the French Army and a gallant defense by the British garrison, Port Mahon fell on June 29. The French now dominated the western Mediterranean with the British holding only Gibraltar. All this eventually resulted in the execution of Admiral Byng, "to encourage" the other British admirals as Voltaire put it, but for the present the British mastery of the seas was far from assured.

French commodore Beaussier d'Isle left Brest in April 1756 leading a small squadron which brought the Marquis de Montcalm to Canada with two further army battalions to reinforce its garrison. Unhindered, the French squadron then sailed from Québec to Île Royale and arrived in the vicinity of Louisbourg during the last week of July. The French warships immediately drove off the small British vessels that had been attempting to blockade Louisbourg harbor.

On July 26, part of the Royal Navy's squadron from Halifax came into view. It consisted of HMS *Grafton* (70 guns), HMS *Nottingham* (60 guns), and the frigates HMS *Hornet* and HMS *Jamaica* led by Commodore Charles Holmes. Beaussier's ships were *Le Héros*, normally of 74 guns but now of only 46 because of the amount of space having been taken by troops and supplies, *L'Illustre* (64 guns), and the frigates *La Sirène* (36 guns), and *La Licorne* (30 guns). Beaussier was in a fighting mood, but he restrained himself and first went into Louisbourg to land the supplies, vital for the fortress garrison. The next day, he came out of Louisbourg harbor on board *Le Héros*, reinforced by 200 men in the garrison, and, unsupported by *L'Illustre*, immediately engaged Holmes. A series of "indecisive" actions ensued over the following days, the main result being that the main mast of HMS *Jamaica* was shot away, rendering the frigate useless. The French went back to Louisbourg and the British to Halifax to make repairs and land the wounded. Beaussier stayed in Louisbourg until the middle of August until, satisfied that nothing much would be attempted against Louisbourg that year, he finally sailed for France. His unscathed squadron was joined by the frigate *Concorde*, out from Québec, on the way back. Clearly, in 1756, the French Navy prevailed.

OPPOSITE *French ships-of-the-line going into action. French warships were noted for their good design and elaborate decorations. The great plain white standard was France's naval ensign at this time and was also raised on French forts. It was France's fighting flag, and had no associations with surrender until after the French Revolution. (Print after J. Camoreyt, photo René Chartrand)*

TROUPES DE TERRE
THE FRENCH LINE INFANTRY

In Louis XV's army, the classification of "French" infantry denoted troops recruited from men born and raised in France. These regiments were called *infanterie française* as opposed to the mercenary "foreign" infantry recruited elsewhere from other nationalities. In the French infantry, which made up the bulk of the army, all officers and men were to be of the Roman Catholic faith, the official state religion.

Regimental recruiting parties went to towns and villages looking for young volunteers, inducing them to enlist with the usual promises of money, women, wine, and glory. The enlistment period was for six or eight years, but release from service might not be respected if the unit was short of men.

Many regiments were identified with the provinces that were their particular, but not exclusive, recruiting areas. Similarly, regiments raised by a gentleman tended to include a core of enlisted men from their colonel's fiefdom and its surrounding areas. Thus up to half of the men in a regiment might be from the same province; but many others would come from all over the realm. They were often recruited in Paris, usually near the Pont-Neuf, where the recruiting parties hung around.

Officers of line infantry regiments were generally from a fairly humble background. Most came from provincial noble families which, as brave and loyal as they were, had little money or influence. Serving as officers in the army was their one chance to gain some glory – and a decent pension if they lived to retire. They tended to take the view that army commissions were their birthright, and that *roturiers* (non-noble officers), however worthy and brave, were not in their "rightful place" in society. Up to the mid-18th century, about a third of the officers were *roturiers*. This proportion decreased after this time; from 1750 many officers were admitted to the nobility for their long and distinguished services. Opposition to commissioning *roturiers* grew, and later in the century the nobles finally managed to stop it altogether, which relegated soldiers of talent to the lower ranks and had disastrous consequences for the nobility in the next reign.

During the War of Austrian Succession, there were 98 French infantry regiments, but with a colossal 227 battalions, mustering 164,318 NCOs and men led by 9,323 officers. A few years later, in 1750, France was at peace, and the army was reduced to 84 regiments with 172 battalions, 88,695 NCOs and men led by 5,200 officers. In 1762, this had risen to 88 regiments, 187 battalions, and 110,000 NCOs and men led by 7,737 officers. Senior regiments had more than one battalion, but most only had a single battalion. In 1756, the number of companies per battalion was raised from 13 to 17, although this did not apply to some of the regiments sent to North America.

For most of Louis XV's long reign infantry companies were generally 40 strong for fusiliers, and 45 for grenadiers. Each fusilier company had a captain, a lieutenant, two sergeants, three corporals, three *anspessades* (lance-corporals), one drummer, and the fusilier privates. Grenadier companies were the same, but with the addition of a second-lieutenant. Battalion staff included a lieutenant-colonel (named a "battalion commander" for 2nd, 3rd, etc battalions), a major, an aide-major, and two ensigns (to carry colors). Regimental staff usually included a colonel, a surgeon, a sergeant-major, a drum-major, and a chaplain.

LINE INFANTRY IN NORTH AMERICA

When war first broke out in North America in 1754, no French regular line infantry units were initially deployed to North America – defense of New France was left up to the colonial troops (see page 34). The following year, the French court ordered several battalions of *troupes de terre* to reinforce the colonial garrisons in New France. Despite a British attempt to intercept them, the majority of 2nd battalions of the regiments of La Reine, Languedoc, Béarn, and Guyenne landed in Québec, and the 2nd battalions of Artois and Bourgoyne in Louisbourg. Each battalion had an establishment of 32 officers and 525 NCOs and privates divided into 13 companies, one of grenadiers and 12 of fusiliers. Eight fusilier companies, four of La Reine and four of Languedoc, had been captured by the Royal Navy, so on January 28, 1755, they were recreated by royal order. On February 25 of the same year, the six battalions in Canada had their establishments raised to 50 men per company. To these reinforcements were added a few specialist officers from the army's Royal Artillery and the metropolitan infantry. However, despite this paper increase, recruits were sent to Canada in such small numbers that Montcalm's battalions were slowly decreasing in strength. The increase in companies to 17 per battalion in 1756 was not applied to battalions in Canada, so they remained at 13.

ABOVE LEFT *Soldier with color, Guyenne regiment, c.1757–60. The quarters were light brown and green. (Parks Canada)*

ABOVE RIGHT *Soldier with color, Languedoc regiment. The quarters were buff or light brown and violet. The regiment changed its uniforms in 1761 and again in 1763 when the green collar and lapels shown were adopted. (Parks Canada)*

The 2nd battalions of La Sarre and Royal-Roussillon arrived in Québec with Montcalm in 1756, and the 2nd and 3rd battalions of Berry in 1757. The Berry battalions only had nine companies each because they were originally bound for India and had been organized to be compatible with the troops of the French East India Company. When they left France, they mustered 49 officers and 1,033 NCOs and privates, but epidemic broke out on the voyage, and only 913 men landed at Québec, 200 of whom were very sick. The enlisted men of these battalions were raw recruits with no military experience, and Ticonderoga was their baptism of fire.

So by 1757, only 12 battalions of French regulars, numbering just over 6,000 men, had been shipped to North America. Eight of the battalions saw service with Montcalm in the Canadian and western theaters, and four were sent to Louisbourg to bolster its defenses. The 2nd Battalion of Cambis, of 17 companies, and the 2nd Battalion of *volontaires-étrangers*, reached Louisbourg just before the siege began in 1758.

The French forces in New France suffered interrupted supplies due to the Royal Naval blockade, but more crucially, as the war went on the ability of the French to reinforce their troops in New France was severely jeopardized by British naval dominance. This, in addition to the French focus on the war in Europe, meant that Montcalm was maneuvering ever-smaller forces to defend New France.

Infantry in Canada

These infantrymen wear the special uniform supplied to the battalions sent to Canada in 1755 and used until about September 1757, when their uniform changed to match that of their regiment in France. It was issued by the Ministry of the Navy, so the coats were replaced every two years instead of three as in the metropolitan army. The uniform consisted of the standard grey-white coat, lining and breeches, but the details of the uniform, such as the collar, differed. The sergeant on the left, from the La Reine Regiment, wears the red waistcoat supplied to his regiment in Canada, which differed from the blue worn by the regiment in Europe. He carries the musket that he was issued with shortly after arriving in Canada. The private in the center, of the Languedoc Regiment, wears a relaxed camp dress, including a forage cap and comfortable moccasins, both issue items for undress and campaigning in New France.

In Canada, but not Louisbourg, officers and men were also issued extra equipment when campaigning in the wilderness. In the summer this consisted of a blanket, a *capot*, a forage cap, two cotton shirts, a pair of breeches, a pair of drawers, a pair of *mitasses*, a knife, and a tomahawk. In winter additional equipment was issued consisting of pairs of moccasins, socks, mitts, a vest, thick *mitasses* of blanket cloth, pairs of deerskin shoes, a pair of snowshoes, a deerskin, a bearskin, a portage collar, and two double-edged knives.

The officer on the right is from the Guyenne Regiment and carries the regimental colors, which were carried in battle in Canada, but burned shortly before the surrender of Montréal to avoid handing them over to the British.

Officers soon discovered the wisdom of adapting their dress to the woods, putting aside their jackets to allow movement during actions. In the background is a corporal of the Béarn Regiment. This battalion saw the most notable variation in uniform, its facing changing from red to blue, and buttons from pewter to brass. (Eugène Lelièpvre © Osprey Publishing Ltd)

The fall of Guadeloupe in 1759 revealed to the French court the urgency of reinforcing the West Indian islands. Fifteen companies of royal grenadiers from the royal militia were posted in Martinique from August 1760, but the island nevertheless fell to British forces in January 1762. By then a substantial force had sailed from France to reinforce its islands. It arrived too late to save Martinique, and landed at Saint-Domingue (Haiti) in May 1762. The reinforcements consisted of a battalion each from the regiments of Boulonnois, Foix, Quercy, and Royal-Barrois and the Piquets of St Domingue who joined the local colonial troops, and the royal grenadiers, exchanged from Martinique.

ABOVE LEFT *A 20th-century watercolor depicting a soldier and colors of the Royal-Roussillon Regiment in 1756. (Henri Beau, National Archives of Canada, C-003975)*

ABOVE RIGHT *Uniform and colors of the La Sarre Regiment in 1756. The arms and equipment issued to the troops in Canada were the same as in France, but in Canada the swords of the fusiliers were ordered left in stores, although grenadiers kept their sabers. Sergeants and officers also left their halberds and spontoons in store and were issued with muskets, bayonets, and cartridge boxes.(Henri Beau, National Archives of Canada, C-003974)*

For Louisiana, ten companies of the Angoumois regiment were posted in New Orleans from April 1762 to October 1763. Some 650 men from La Marine, Montrevel, Beauvoisis, and Penthièvre captured and held Saint-Jean/ St John's, Newfoundland, from June 1762 until it was retaken by the British in September.

TACTICS AND PERFORMANCE

French regular soldiers were generally willing to learn some of the woodland warfare techniques used by the Canadian militia and American Indians, and often attached themselves to small raiding parties to learn frontier tactics.

There was some tension between French and Canadian officers, principally on questions of tactics. Some French officers preferred to use linear-style tactics, and believed that the Canadian soldiers and officers were no better than the Indians. The Canadian officers on the other hand did not feel that French

François-Gaston, Chevalier de Lévis (1720–87)

First commissioned in 1735, Lévis fought in Prague during 1741–42, at Dettingen in 1743, and in many engagements in Germany during the War of Austrian Succession, where he distinguished himself as a cool-headed, brave, and competent officer. In 1756, he sailed for New France. As second-in-command of the *troupes de terre* in Canada, he dealt efficiently with purely military matters, earning the appreciation of both officers and enlisted men. Calm, diplomatic, and liberal, he was the very opposite of his commander, which enabled him to stay on good terms with Montcalm and Vaudreuil. He could see the corruption inherent in the colonial administration, but he conceded that the metropolitans, too, could have their faults in colonial eyes. Lévis believed that nothing would be gained by vitriolic comments and bad manners. He felt that patience and understanding could improve most situations, and that the worse offenses were a matter for the law courts. Most of all, this pragmatic officer believed that French leadership in Canada should be united. Lévis' influence and diplomatic behavior helped to restore good relations between the metropolitan and colonial officers during the war.

After Montcalm's death Lévis was commander of the French troops in Canada, and defeated the British at Sainte-Foy, but abandoned his siege of Québec after the arrival of British ships. Later that year he surrendered Montréal to the British. After his return to France he became lieutenant-general, marshal, and in 1784, duke. Here, the Chevalier de Lévis rallies his troops for one last assault at the battle of Sainte-Foy in 1760. (Bombled, National Archives of Canada, C-007700)

troops were suited to frontier warfare. This caused friction, as did the same debate within the British forces.

During the first two years of the war, French regulars performed very well in battle. Discipline was very good, and Montcalm wrote of his approval of the condition and performance of the regular troops. However, as French strategy changed in the wake of the effective British naval blockade, and troops were increasingly left to fend for themselves, discipline and desertion became greater problems. The performance of the French regulars at the battle of the Plains of

This plate shows a variety of French infantry uniforms from the 1750s. The private and officer of the Auvergne Regiment in the background, and the sergeant of the Cambis Regiment on the right, all wear the standard gray-white coat, breeches, and stockings. The Auvergne Regiment, which campaigned in Germany in the 1750s, had distinctive violet facings. The Cambis Regiment was one of the few that had both gold and silver buttons and hat lace. It is unclear whether the battalion sent to Louisbourg in 1757 had red lapels — this may have been an experimental issue. On the left is a drummer of the La Reine Regiment wearing the queen's livery. The 2nd Battalion of the regiment was sent to Canada in 1755. In the center is a private from one of France's elite units, the Grenadiers de France, wearing their distinctive uniform in the red and blue of the king's livery. (Eugène Leliêpvre © Osprey Publishing Ltd)

Abraham indicated that fire discipline had deteriorated noticeably from previous standards. To their credit, they continued to perform very well, particularly considering that they were vastly outnumbered by the British, suffered from unreliable provision of supplies, and increasingly aware that grand strategy in the larger conflict had shifted attention and resources away from them.

COMMANDERS

The French spent almost as much time as the British arguing over strategy and the abilities of their regulars to wage war along the frontier. Montcalm disagreed firmly with the Governor-General of New France, Vaudreuil, on issues of strategy. There was often considerable antagonism between colonial-born and French-born officials; the colonials perceived visitors as high-handed interlopers who did not understand the issues pertinent in the colonial setting. The French government had clearly established the lines of command; Vaudreuil was unquestionably superior to Montcalm, but in practice this had no effect on mitigating tensions or resolving proposals of conflicting strategies. Unlike Loudoun in the British colonies, neither man was removed when tensions flared, and the situation escalated. Each man accused the other of interfering in issues of strategy. Vaudreuil favored a guerrilla campaign along the frontier, and dismissed the ability of the French regulars to adapt to the necessities of wilderness warfare. Montcalm recognized the value of the militia and American Indians in forest operations, but still believed that the war would ultimately be decided by regular troops.

Montcalm did understand the issues of supply and scouting involved in fighting in the woods. A master strategist, he recognized early on that the British were going to outnumber his troops, and decided upon a defensive strategy which would allow him to launch pre-emptive strikes whenever there was an opportunity. His first actions based on this plan were the surprise attacks on the British forts at Oswego and Fort William Henry. He succeeded in overwhelming the troops and forcing a surrender, then destroyed the forts and moved on. This bold strategy knocked the British off balance for a time early on. However, after 1757, when the British were adapting to wilderness warfare and the French were receiving no more reinforcements, Montcalm was forced to guard a vast frontier with a regular force less than a third the size of British resources. He continued to take gambles, some of which paid off, such as Ticonderoga, but from 1758 he was constantly on the defensive.

THE HIGH-WATER MARK
THE CAMPAIGNS OF 1757

Similar to the previous year, 1757 would be marked by only one major engagement between France and Britain. The partisan war continued along the frontier, spreading fear among both French and British settlers.

Over the course of 1757, the British reinforced their war effort with more than 11,000 regular troops shipped out from Great Britain. By the end of 1757, 21 battalions of British regulars and seven independent companies were operating in North America. The British were also able to call upon the colonies for further provincial forces, which were used in increasing numbers to protect lines of communications with forts along the frontier. On the French side, Montcalm received his last major reinforcement in 1757, with the arrival of two battalions of the Berry Regiment. Montcalm had only eight battalions of regulars and 64 companies of colonial regulars, stationed from Louisbourg to New Orleans. He also, like his British counterparts, had a large contingent of militia and a larger number of American Indian allies to draw upon for the campaign.

A change of government in Britain in 1757 caused the Newcastle ministry to be replaced, first by William Pitt and William Cavendish, and then after a short time by a coalition government, the Newcastle-Pitt ministry, in the winter of 1757. The Newcastle-Pitt ministry changed strategy, shifting the British focus to attacking Louisbourg and Québec, the heart of New France. In response to the new strategic plan, Lord Loudoun withdrew a large number of regulars from New York in April and sailed for Halifax. He was further reinforced with newly arrived regular troops from Great Britain, and was ordered to attack the French fortress at Louisbourg, in an attempt to open up Québec to attack.

ATTEMPT AT LOUISBOURG

Loudoun's plan for Louisbourg required that the French be swept from the surrounding seas; therefore additional British ships were sent to Nova Scotia, where

ATLANTIC CANADA, 1713–58

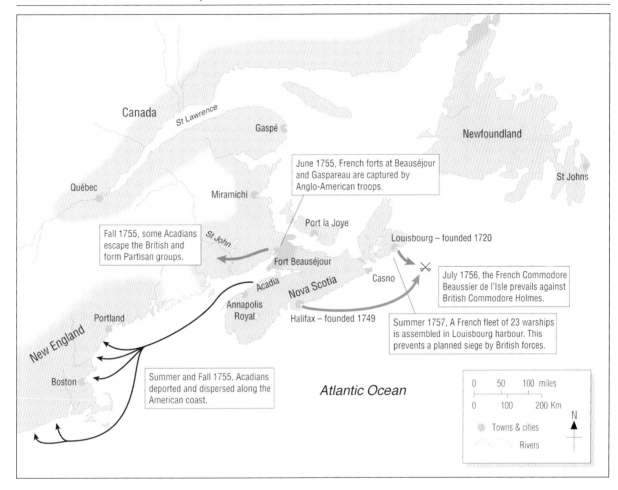

Canada

St Lawrence

Gaspé

Newfoundland

Québec

St Johns

Miramichi

June 1755, French forts at Beauséjour
and Gaspareau are captured by
Anglo-American troops.

Port la Joye

Louisbourg – founded 1720

Fall 1755, some Acadians
escape the British and
form Partisan groups.

St John

Fort Beauséjour

July 1756, the French Commodore
Beaussier de l'Isle prevails against
British Commodore Holmes.

Casno

Acadia

Nova Scotia

Annapolis
Royal

Portland

Halifax – founded 1749

Summer 1757, A French fleet of 23 warships
is assembled in Louisbourg harbour. This
prevents a planned siege by British forces.

New England

Boston

Summer and Fall 1755, Acadians
deported and dispersed along the
American coast.

Atlantic Ocean

0   50   100   miles

0   100   200 Km

N

Towns & cities

Rivers

the regular regiments were assembling. Vice-Admiral Francis Holburne commanded the fleet that was to carry the British army from Halifax to Louisbourg.

The French naval plans for the 1757 campaign in America involved each of the large naval bases, Toulon, Brest, and Rochefort, detaching a number of ships to America which would rendezvous at Louisbourg in mid-June. French spies were reporting persistent rumors that something substantial would be tried by the British against Louisbourg. The presence of a strong squadron, even for a short time, might spoil their plans. Admiral Dubois de la Motte coordinated the effort, which was designed to guarantee Louisbourg's safety.

In January 1757, Commodore de Beauffremont sailed four ships-of-the-line from Brest, arriving in Louisbourg on May 31. In April 1757, four ships -of-the-line sailed from Toulon in the Mediterranean under Commodore du Revest, foiled the attempt of a British squadron to stop them at Gibraltar, and

ATLANTIC CANADA, 1757

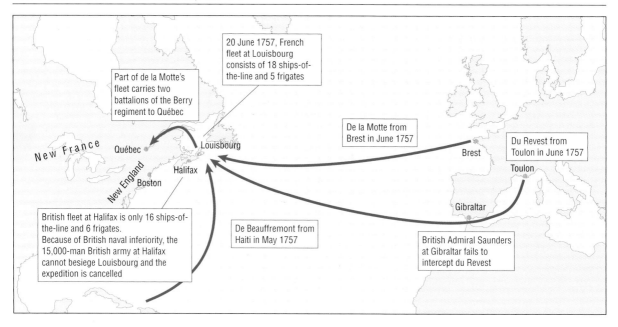

20 June 1757, French fleet at Louisbourg consists of 18 ships-of-the-line and 5 frigates

Part of de la Motte's fleet carries two battalions of the Berry regiment to Québec

De la Motte from Brest in June 1757

Du Revest from Toulon in June 1757

New France

Québec

Louisbourg

Brest

Toulon

New England

Halifax

Boston

Gibraltar

British fleet at Halifax is only 16 ships-of-the-line and 6 frigates.
Because of British naval inferiority, the 15,000-man British army at Halifax cannot besiege Louisbourg and the expedition is cancelled

De Beauffremont from Haiti in May 1757

British Admiral Saunders at Gibraltar fails to intercept du Revest

arrived unscathed at Louisbourg on June 19. Meanwhile, Admiral Dubois de la Motte sailed out of Brest with nine ships-of-the-line and two frigates, with two battalions of the Berry Regiment on board. The squadron was not much hindered by the Royal Navy and dropped anchor at Louisbourg on June 20. In July, the frigates cruised to the north and to the southwest of Cape Breton Island, but did not find any traces of the British. At the end of July, it was learned from various prisoners taken by French and American Indian scouting parties near Halifax that the British fleet had arrived, consisting of 16 ships-of-the-line and six frigates, and the army ready to sail to Louisbourg numbered 12,000–15,000 men.

This intelligence confirmed that the British were planning a large expedition to take the fortress. In the spring, Governor Drucour had asked the officer Charles des Champs de Boishébert, who led the Acadian volunteers on the St John's River, to come closer to Louisbourg with his men. In July, Boishébert arrived on Île Royale with some 400 Acadians and American Indians who positioned themselves in the area of Gabarus Bay, where a landing seemed likely.

Drucour's defense plan called for as much resistance as possible to be waged outside the walls of the city. Admiral Dubois de la Motte detached sailors from his ships to help speed up the repairs to the fortifications. A battalion of 12 temporary companies, each of 50 ships' marines led by two officers, and a further four companies of ships' volunteers intended to serve the guns, were organized to strengthen the garrison, all of which added some 800 men to the garrison besides Boishébert's men.

On the left is a private of the New Jersey Provincial Regiment, wearing their blue uniform faced with red, known as the "Jersey Blues." From 1757, Maryland provincial soldiers, like the private in the center, wore red coats with sleeves turned up with black, red breeches, white shirts and hats. By 1757, the dress of Massachusetts provincials was confirmed as blue with scarlet lapels and cuffs, as worn by the officer on the right. (David Rickman © Osprey Publishing Ltd)

On August 7, the companies of ships' marines and volunteers were marched out of town with three of the garrison's companies and posted in prepared positions and temporary batteries at three coves to the east of the city. Makeshift tents and awnings for these troops were made from old sails and everyone settled down to wait for the British.

On the afternoon of August 19, a British squadron was spotted to the southeast and the next day it came in closer, seemingly to observe if the French fleet was still in Louisbourg harbor. By now the planned expedition was ruined, but to avoid wasting the whole season, Holburne was hoping to lure Dubois de la Motte's squadron out of the harbor to damage, if not defeat it. However, Dubois de la Motte was a wise old sea dog who reasoned that there was nothing to be gained by going out to attack and plenty to gain by waiting for the British. The British no doubt observed that the French fleet and the Louisbourg garrison were ready for a fight and, after an hour or so, Holburne's ships turned and sailed away. Fog covered the departing British and they were not seen again in the following days. On August 27, the ship's marines and volunteer temporary companies were dissolved and everyone went back on board as Admiral Dubois de la Motte felt that his ships should be at full strength if there was to be a battle with the British.

Holburne kept his position off Louisbourg, and the British squadron came back within sight of the town on September 16. Again, the British ships came almost to within cannon range of the fortress guns, loitered for a few days in the area and then left. Dubois de la Motte knew there was nothing to gain by chasing them; Louisbourg was safe as long as his squadron was in the harbor. Besides the British fleet, there was much concern in the French camp concerning the British army in Halifax, which was reputed to be very strong. A French scouting party had just returned from Halifax on September 21. It reported having seen about 1,200 tents with red-coated troops drilling, but there seemed to be many empty tents and it appeared that some of the troops had gone back to New England or Europe. Furthermore, there were very few ships in Halifax harbor. All this seemed to indicate that the attack had been cancelled.

Holburne's squadron remained off Louisbourg. On September 25, gale-force winds sank HMS *Tilbury*, and seriously damaged the other British ships, forcing Holburne to cancel any further attempt to intercept the French fleet. Instead, he had to put into Halifax for repairs. The gale, the worst in many years, also caused some damage to the French fleet in Louisbourg's harbor. After having the damage repaired on the *Tonnant*, Dubois de la Motte and his squadron sailed out of Louisbourg and returned safely to France. The British naval campaign of 1757 had been a failure.

During the summer, Montcalm was kept aware of the developments at Louisbourg, and his scouts reported that the frontier had been stripped of many British regulars. Montcalm decided to take advantage of the situation, and prepared to strike at Fort William Henry, at the southern end of Lake George.

FORT WILLIAM HENRY

By July, Montcalm had amassed a large force in and around Fort Carillon/ Ticonderoga and was planning an attack on Fort William Henry before the end of the month. A previous unsuccessful attack on Fort William Henry had been attempted in March, and had involved a small force attacking the fort from the ice of the frozen lake. This was a much more ambitious plan: the French attack column was to number 7,500 men, including six regular battalions, marines, militia, and American Indians. Montcalm split his force in two; one group of 2,600 men traveled overland, while the other, some 5,000 men, traveled in bateaux over the lake. The two forces met at the southern end of the lake on August 2.

The British force at Fort William Henry comprised just over 2,000 men, half of whom were regulars, under the command of Lieutenant-Colonel George Munro. The fort was now a fairly strong structure, constructed of logs and earth. General Webb was stationed with 1,600 soldiers, mostly provincials, at Fort Edward, 14 miles (22 km) to the south. Webb dispatched a reinforcement of 200 regulars on July 29 to reinforce the garrison at Fort William Henry, and he also alerted the New York and New England colonies of the need for more troops. The message was received, but the reinforcements would arrive too late.

On August 3, the first clashes occurred between scouts of the British and French armies. The road to Fort Edward was cut by a detachment of French and American Indian troops, and British forces and civilians in the area began to withdraw to Fort William Henry, burning the houses and buildings that remained outside the perimeter. The British also held an entrenched camp outside the fort. British artillery fired upon the French build-up outside the fort, but the first French siege trenches were dug under heavy fire on the evening of August 4 and the siege began in earnest.

Both sides exchanged fire as the French trenches crept closer and closer to the British ramparts. Webb was unable to send more reinforcements, fearing that his small force would be decimated trying to reach the besieged British garrison.

Montcalm trying to stop the massacre of British soldiers and civilians at Fort William Henry following the surrender of the British. (Library of Congress)

James Abercromby (1706–81)

James Abercromby was born in Banffshire, Scotland, and entered the army as a young ensign in the 25th Foot in 1717. The next decades saw him rise in the Scottish political hierarchy, thanks to his brother-in-law, Lord Braco. By the late 1730s he was MP for Banffshire, King's Printer for Scotland and lieutenant-governor of Stirling Castle. In 1746 he became colonel of the 1st Foot (Royal Scots) and as deputy quartermaster-general took part in the successful expedition against the French port of Lorient. In Flanders the following year, he was wounded

at Hulst and thereafter retired from active military duty until the eve of the Seven Years' War, when he became colonel of the 52nd (later 50th) Foot. When Lord Loudoun became commander-in-chief in North America in 1756, he appointed his close friend Abercromby his deputy with the rank of major-general and had his colonelcy transferred to the 44th Foot, following Colonel Halket's death at Monongahela.

Abercromby was an efficient second-in-command. He devoted himself to the administrative staff work of the army in North America, as well as to rebuilding his own battered 44th Foot. He found his new regiment "in want of many things" regarding both materials and morale. Abercromby obviously had an engaging and open manner which made him a popular senior staff officer, not only among the British, but also among the American officers and politicians. Governor Alexander Codden of New York and the powerful William Shirley of Massachusetts were charmed by him. When Loudoun was recalled for political reasons, Pitt appointed Abercromby to replace him. In political and diplomatic terms, it was a logical step as he was respected by the colonial leaders. In military terms, Abercromby seemed the best man to continue Loudoun's strategy for the conquest of Canada. However, for all his diplomatic manners, Abercromby's administrative and command record was uninspired if efficient. His personal battle experience was not extensive and was limited to regimental commands. As supreme commander in North America, he now had to prove that he had superior skills in both strategy and tactics as well as being an inspired battlefield commander – a tall order for any officer. (Painting by A. Ramsay, Fort Ligonier Collection, Fort Ligonier, Pennsylvania)

Such a loss would leave the road to Albany open and unprotected, since the provincial reinforcements had not yet arrived. To make matters worse, smallpox broke out inside Fort William Henry.

A few days into the siege, the number of killed and wounded within the fort had reached over 300. Many of the large British cannons and mortars had been blown up or been destroyed. The palisades had been breached in a few locations, and the French continued to pour artillery fire into the fort. Messages sent by Munro had been intercepted by the French and Indians. Munro was advised of

FORT WILLIAM HENRY, 1757

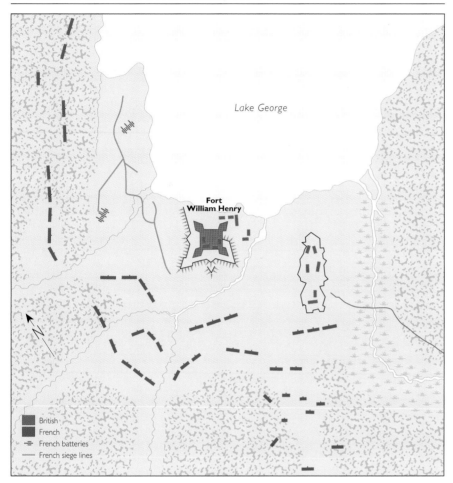

Lake George

Fort
William Henry

British
French
French batteries
French siege lines

this state of affairs by Louis-Antoine de Bougainville, a senior French officer, who warned that the likelihood of reinforcements from Webb was minimal. Munro still refused to surrender, but morale within the fort was sinking.

Following a full night of heavy bombardment Munro at last began to feel that resistance was futile. On the morning of August 9, Lieutenant-Colonel Young was sent to Montcalm's tent to discuss terms of a surrender. The British agreed to a surrender that allowed them to march to Fort Edward with full military honors. They were also required to promise not to serve in the conflict for 18 months. The French prisoners captured since 1754 were to be returned to New France within three months. The stores and artillery of the fort, or what was left of them, were retained as spoils of the French. Montcalm summoned a war council with his Indian allies and called on them to respect the conditions of the surrender. The British evacuated the fort and entrenched camp.

The French-allied Indians, disregarding Montcalm's demands, rushed to the fort as the British evacuated, attacking and killing the wounded left behind. The French guards attempted to stop the killing, but there is debate about how hard they tried. Montcalm was eventually able to restore some level of order, but on the following day, as the British column marched toward Fort Edward, they were attacked again by Indians seeking revenge and prisoners. The French guards again failed to stop the slaughter, and it is estimated that 50 men, women, and children were killed and another 200 taken prisoner by the American Indians. The French finally managed to restore order and escorted the remainder of the column to Fort Edward. Some of the Indians sickened and died of smallpox after their attacks on sick and wounded British.

By August 11, the number of dead and wounded from the British side far exceeded the 300 who had been killed before the surrender of the fort and was well over 700 people killed, wounded, or missing. The French forces had lost fewer than 100 men killed and wounded. It is not known how many French-allied Indians died. However, evidence from some British prisoners of the Indians suggests that the toll on some small Indian villages could have been quite high.

The partisan war on the frontier continued after the British defeat. Montcalm destroyed Fort William Henry and returned to Fort Carillon. He had been ordered to proceed to Fort Edward, but had decided it was not a good idea, as the Canadian militia was nervous about getting back for the harvest.

The year 1757 was actually the high-water mark for the French effort in the French and Indian War, but by the end of 1757 the British were close to despair, and in England a distraught William Pitt reflected the mood of the British public. The 1757 campaign in America had been a shambles. Nothing much had been done in the Ohio Valley. The loss of Fort William Henry and the ensuing massacre of prisoners had enraged public opinion further. Now came the cancellation of the attack on Louisbourg, which had been prepared at great expense. This was too much to bear; politicians and the public demanded a scapegoat. Thus, the commander-in-chief in North America, Lord Loudoun, the architect of the strategy that would ultimately conquer New France, was recalled to England at the end of 1757. Far from discouraged, the British brought in even greater resources for the campaign of 1758. Although he was replaced by Major-General James Abercromby, Lord Loudoun's strategic plan was to be implemented even more fully. A three-pronged attack would be launched against New France: General Abercromby would lead the largest British army ever assembled in North America, take Fort Carillon at Ticonderoga, and secure the Lake Champlain area. Britain's largest commitment in terms of manpower and resources would be concentrated on the expedition against Fortress Louisbourg, commanded by a new and relatively young general, Jeffery Amherst. General Forbes would

Scalping

Scalping was a common occurrence during the French and Indian War, practiced by French, English, and American Indian combatants. Scalping seems to have originated among the American Indian tribes long before the mid-18th century. It was done to enemy dead after a battle, but also, when it was too difficult for Indian warriors to transport their prisoners, they might be killed and scalped instead. Sometimes scalping occurred after the unfortunate soul had suffered torture and a slow death, more likely after a victory where the victors had suffered many losses.

The actual method of scalping by Indian warriors is much documented by soldiers. An incision would be made around the hair from the upper part of the forehead to the back of the neck, and the scalp pulled off. The skin would then be scraped, and stretched over a hoop of wood, and painted. The scalps would then be attached to a stick carried by the proud warrior.

If some Europeans saw scalping as barbarous, others encouraged the spread of scalping in North America through the offering of bounties. This practice was to encourage the collection of as many scalps as possible, to gauge the number of enemy dead. The French paid very little for scalps, preferring to purchase prisoners who could be sold back to their families, but the English offered large sums of money: William Shirley, the governor of Massachusetts, offered £40 for Indian male scalps, and £20 for female scalps in June 1755. After war had been declared, governors offered much higher bounties than these. As bounties for prisoners were often only slightly more than bounties for scalps, warriors often felt it was not worth the hassle of bringing in a prisoner for the small increase in bounty one might receive in return. Even the military commanders who disapproved of scalping did not completely forbid it; at Québec in 1759 Wolfe prohibited the taking of scalps, except when the enemy were Indians, or Canadians dressed as Indians.

Bounties for scalps led to inventiveness, including dividing scalps, or faking scalps from animal skins; and barbarities, such as attacking non-combatants or sleeping warriors to obtain scalps to sell. If not sold for bounty, scalps were used as decoration; the rangers on the St Francis raid were horrified to count the number of scalps on poles. Scalps could replace the dead. Sir William Johnson, for example, would upon return of his warriors present the scalps to the relatives of those killed in combat.

Scalps did not necessarily indicate an enemy death, as there are many recorded instances of soldiers surviving the experience, but generally only because the scalpers believed that the victims were already dead. Although not all survived, some recovered from these horrific maimings. (Library of Congress)

march into the Ohio Valley, take Fort Duquesne (now Pittsburgh) and finally avenge General Braddock's disastrous defeat at Monongahela three years earlier. Some 24,000 British regulars and 22,000 provincials were deployed for these campaigns. The British government also made concessions to the colonial governments on disputes over command and payment, in an effort to resolve past issues of reinforcements and supplies and make the way smoother for Abercromby.

The Last of the Mohicans

James Fenimore Cooper's novel *The Last of the Mohicans* is one of the four "Leatherstocking Tales" about the scout Nathaniel Bumppo, known as Hawkeye. Set during and after the siege of Fort William Henry in 1757, it is one of the most widely read novels in the world, and the story has been adapted to the big screen many times, including the best-known Hollywood version starring Daniel Day-Lewis. It has molded many people's perceptions of the French and Indian War and the warriors involved, particularly of course, the noble Mohicans.

The storyline is one of abduction. The two daughters of Colonel Munro, commander of Fort William Henry, are being escorted to the fort during the siege by Major Heyward. Magua, a Huron Indian, offers to assist them on their way, with the hope that he can betray Heyward and abduct the women, in revenge for humiliation he had suffered at the hands of Munro. However, his plan goes awry when the group meets the scout Hawkeye, and his two close friends, father and son, Chingachgook and Uncas, the last of the Mohican tribe. Hawkeye offers to see the group safely to the fort, but Magua and his Huron Indians give chase, and abduct the girls. Hawkeye rescues them, and kills most of the Hurons, and they reach the fort. However, following the fall of the fort, Magua again abducts the two women during the massacre of the camp followers, and Hawkeye, the Mohicans, Munro, and Major Heyward set out to rescue them again from the Hurons.

Cooper knew the area in which his tale was set, and researched the history before writing his novel, including reading the writings of Munro and Heyward about the siege. Despite this, and the fact that the book was originally well-received, it has gone through a cycle of neglect and insult, and back into critical favor. It has been seen as very unrealistic, with stereotypical characters. The Indians particularly are portrayed as either heroes (the Mohicans), or too villainous (Magua), and the women are simply damsels in distress.

The description of the Indians attacking the baggage train following the surrender of the fort shows the romantic nature of the novel:

At that dangerous moment, Magua placed his hands to his mouth, and raised the fatal and appalling whoop. The scattered Indians started at the well-known cry, as coursers bound at the signal to quit the goal; and directly there arose such a yell along the plain, and through the arches of the wood, as seldom burst from human lips before. They who heard it listened with a curdling horror at the heart, little inferior to that dread which may be expected to attend the blasts of the final summons.

More than two thousand raving savages broke from the forest at the signal, and threw themselves across the fatal plain with instinctive alacrity. We shall not dwell on the revolting horrors that succeeded. Death was everywhere, and in his most terrific and disgusting aspects. Resistance only served to inflame the murderers, who inflicted their furious blows long after their victims were beyond the power of their resentment. The flow of blood might be likened to the outbreaking of a torrent; and as the natives became heated and maddened by the sight, many among them even kneeled to the earth, and drank freely, exultingly, hellishly, of the crimson tide.

Despite the criticisms leveled at it, *The Last of the Mohicans* remains one of the most famous novels in the world, and Cooper is acknowledged as the father of American literature.

AMERICAN COLONIAL RANGERS

Rangers had existed in America since the early 1700s, and were an integral part of the colonies' defenses. They were tough, unconventional, adaptable fighters, often backwoodsmen who were skilled in trapping and hunting. One of the most famous events in early ranger history was the long hard-fought battle of Lovewell's pond in 1724, between Massachusetts' Captain John Lovewell and his "Indian hunters" and Pigwacket Abenakis under the war

A late 19th-century romantic impression of Rogers and some of his men jumping off a height to escape pursuing French and American Indians in March 1758. (Print after Taylor)

chief Paugus. It became a watershed event in New England frontier history, told around hearths for decades, and important in informing future rangers that Indian warriors were not always invincible.

When the War of Austrian Succession broke out in 1744, several veterans of Lovewell's fight raised their own ranger companies and passed on their valuable field knowledge. Among the recruits was the teenage Robert Rogers. The war turned into a largely defensive one for the northern colonies, due to incessant French and American Indian inroads.

By the beginning of the French and Indian War, each newly raised provincial regiment generally included one or two ranger companies: men lightly dressed and equipped to serve as quick-reaction strike forces as well as scouts and intelligence gatherers. The disaster at Monongahela made starkly evident the need to raise more bodies of rangers. The Duke of Cumberland, Captain General of the British Army, not only encouraged their raising but advised that some regular troops were trained in ranger ways. However, it was not until after the shocking fall of Fort William Henry that plans were finally accelerated to counterbalance the large numbers of Canadian and Indian partisans.

Senior British commanders became convinced that the rangers were essential to winning the forest war. Captain Robert Rogers' ranger corps became the primary model for the eventual transformation of the regular and provincial army in the area around Lake George. When Amherst became the new commander-in-chief in 1758, he championed Rogers and his rangers, promising to listen to their advice on scouting and ranging. His faith was rewarded at Ticonderoga in 1759 when during the siege, the rangers were the only unit in the army sufficiently skilled to deal with the enemy's bushfighters.

In 1757, threatened by a possible invasion by Montcalm's forces in the north, and with Rogers' Rangers in Nova Scotia, General Daniel Webb ordered that six temporary ranger companies be drafted from the provincial regiments at Fort Edward. The results were mixed, yet promising enough that Loudoun contemplated raising more such companies later in the year. Provincials prepared to serve under Rogers were offered money over and above their regular pay and those who took up the offer learned fast under Rogers' leadership.

In 1756, rangers started to train regular troops in scouting skills, though early scouting parties of regulars often met with disaster in enemy country. In 1757, Rogers was ordered by Loudoun to write a list of rules for those officers who wanted to learn ranger skills. To ensure the lessons were understood, he organized a special company of 50 volunteers whom he taught himself. The rules included instructions for the organization of small and large scouting parties on the move, routes to take, tactics for battle, and how to arrange camp and discipline. The rangers' example led to innovations in dress, equipment, and tactics, and inspired the formation of the first regiment of British light infantry (see page 149).

Robert Rogers (1731–1795)

Robert Rogers grew up on the frontier in New Hampshire. When just a teenager, he saw service in the New Hampshire militia during the War of Austrian Succession. By the beginning of the French and Indian War, he was acquainted with the British and French colonies, and could speak French. During the French and Indian War he raised, trained, and led ranging units, and in 1758 was given a formal commission as a captain of a ranger company and as "Major of the Rangers in his Majesty's Service." During the war he wrote *Rogers' Rules of Ranging* to enable ranging-type units to successfully campaign in the wilderness. With the end of hostilities, the ranger companies were disbanded, and Rogers became captain of one of the independent companies of regulars stationed in South Carolina. He then moved to a similar appointment in New York, but the company was disbanded in 1763, leaving Rogers on half-pay. Rogers fought his last Indian fight in the sortie from Detroit on July 31, 1763, during Pontiac's War.

By 1765, Rogers was in serious debt, and went to England hoping to get support for plans of western exploration and expansion. He managed to obtain the appointment of commandant of Michilimackinac to allow him to pursue a search for an inland northwest passage. While in London Rogers published at least two books, his *Journals*, an account of his campaigns, and *A Concise Account of North America*, a historical geography of the continent.

Back in North America, Rogers had obtained enemies – both William Johnson and Thomas Gage disliked and distrusted him by this time. Gage was no doubt resentful that Rogers had gone to the authorities over his head to obtain the position he wanted, and wrote to Johnson about the unsuitability of the appointment. Gage soon received an intercepted letter which seemed to indicate that Rogers might be intriguing with the French, which increased his distrust further. Rogers was clearly ambitious and seemed to be aiming at creating a semi-independent fiefdom in the west. His plans in 1767 to create a civil government in Michilimackinac were blocked, and it seems likely that at this point Rogers was considering going over to the French if he did not get his way. On evidence from his secretary, Rogers was arrested by Gage and charged with high treason. He was tried by court martial in 1768, and acquitted. He then went to England on an unsuccessful attempt at obtaining redress and payment of various sums he claimed he was owed.

He returned to America in 1775, where the American Revolution was already raging. He sought a Continental commission, but Washington distrusted and imprisoned him. Escaping, he offered his services to the British, and raised the Queen's American Rangers in 1776. Early the next year, the unit was found to be in poor condition, and Rogers was retired on half pay. Rogers was then commissioned in 1779 to raise a unit to be known as the King's Rangers but the regiment was never completed. Rogers was at this time often drunk and inefficient. At the end of the war, he returned to England, where he spent his last years in debt, poverty, and drunkenness, spending much time in debtors' prisons. His wife had divorced him in 1778, taking their only son with her. Rogers died intestate in London in 1795. His extraordinary career had reached its peak in the French and Indian War, before he was even 30. Though a man of great energy and courage, with a huge talent for frontier warfare, his personality remains a mystery, and his morals were clearly suspect, gaining him enemies, and limiting his ability to carve out a larger niche for himself in American history. (National Archives of Canada, e002140048)

Rangers wearing a variety of clothing and equipment. Camouflage was imperative for bush fighting and scouting, and Rogers' men wore green attire throughout the war. However, ranging units did not have a consistent uniform pattern, as the regulars did. In the foreground is an officer of Rogers' Rangers, wearing green with silver lace, speaking to another ranger. Four of the five ranger companies that Rogers raised in 1758 were uniformed in green with silver lace. Seated in the center is a soldier wearing the black uniform with blue lapels and cuffs, with black leggings and Highland bonnets, worn by some rangers in the later 1750s. In the top left are two of the Stockbridge Indians recruited by Rogers as scouts, dressed in a mixture of European and native dress. In the background are rangers from different units. When in the field, rangers would wear their uniform, or American Indian dress, or a mixture of both depending on the nature of the assignment. When in American Indian dress, rangers could face additional dangers, as nervous provincials and regulars on guard duty sometimes mistook Rogers' white rangers for enemy Indian warriors due to their dress and behavior, and on a few occasions faulty countersign exchanges resulted in returning rangers getting wounded, or even killed. (Gerry Embleton © Osprey Publishing Ltd)

ENLISTMENT

Rogers' Rangers never enjoyed the long-term establishment of a British regular regiment, nor were they classed as a regiment or battalion as the annually raised provincial troops were. In fact, Rogers' command was merely a collection, or corps, of short-term, independently raised ranger companies. Technically, "Rogers' Rangers" were the men in the single company he commanded, but the term was extended to the other ranger companies within the Hudson Valley, Lake George army where he was the senior ranger officer.

Rogers was captain of Ranger Company No.1 of Colonel Joseph Blanhard's New Hampshire Regiment for the Lake George campaign in 1755. He remained

Ranger training

Because the men recruited to the ranger companies were generally frontier-bred, the amount of basic training they had to undergo was not as protracted as that endured by the average regular recruit. Many who joined were already proficient in tracking and hunting, and could shoot amazingly well. Excellent marksmanship was what made the best rangers. Practice firing at marks was very frequent, like the informal session above at Fort William Henry in 1756 attended by (from left) a Mohawk Valley or Albany Dutchman dressed as an American Indian, a member of Hobbs' independent company, an officer of the Stockbridge Indian ranger company, and a Mohawk war captain. A ranger from a provincial regiment shoots at a target in the background. In fact, marksmanship practice was so frequent in ranger training that at least one British commander scolded

Rogers for a waste of ammunition. However, the training paid off, and the issue of rifled carbines to many of the men ensured frequent success against the French and Indians. A good training in hand-to-hand fighting was also important, as engagements were often very close and bloody.

Learning how to operate water craft was another crucial skill for a ranger. Canoes and bateaux were used for Rogers' earliest raids, but in 1756, these were swapped for whaleboats, fast and agile. As well as handle boats, a recruit had to be able to build a raft from scratch, ford a river without a vessel, and portage a whaleboat over a mountain range. Other skills included building temporary fortifications, making moccasins, and imitating animal and bird calls for use as signals in the woods. (Gary Zaboly © Osprey Publishing Ltd)

at Fort William Henry over that winter with 32 hardened volunteers to continue scouting and raiding the enemy forts to the north, regardless of the fact there was no money to pay them salary or bounty. Next spring, Shirley rewarded Rogers with the command of "an independent company of rangers" to consist of 60 privates, three sergeants, an ensign, and two lieutenants. No longer on a provincial footing, the rangers would be paid and fed out of the royal war chest, and answerable to British commanders. Rogers was ordered to recruit brave men used to traveling and hunting, and he soon found many in the frontier towns in New Hampshire. He tempted them with the promise of daily pay, bounties for scalps and prisoners, and help toward clothing and equipment. Equally tempting for many was the chance to help quicken the fall of New France, which would end the American Indian raids on the frontier towns, and open up the vast Abenaki hunting grounds to settlement, including sizable land grants for war veterans. The availability of men in the frontier towns was dependent on the time of year as beaver-hunting season in spring limited the number of men available to Rogers. He managed to recruit 37 men that spring, which along with some re-enlisted rangers from the previous winter, met the company requirement. By July 1756, a second company was commissioned, and Robert became brevet major over both companies, and all the other independent ranger units in the region.

The quality of men in those companies not recruited by Rogers was variable; some companies had few real woodsmen in their ranks. The increasing dearth of true frontiersmen to fill up the ranks of the many new ranger companies

Captain Thomas Davies' A South View of Crown Point, Lake Champlain. In the bottom left can be seen Rangers' huts, and American Indian wigwams. Bark lodges can be seen near the log huts in several forms: wigwam, tent, and lean-to. In the background can be seen Amherst's new fort, marked A, and next to it the ruins of Fort Saint-Frédéric, marked B. (National Archives of Canada, C-013314)

raised during the war became a real problem. A group of Stockbridge Indians arrived at Rogers' Island in summer 1756, and encamped themselves near the huts of the white rangers. They enjoyed the same pay scale as the latter, and to be identifiable as British-allied Indians they had a red garter fixed on the muzzle of their weapons.

With not a little reason, Rogers' rangers considered themselves a breed apart from the redcoats and provincials and roundly resented outside attempts to disturb their special fraternity. As well as pride in their service, they were often linked by other things – many of them had been neighbors on the frontier, and had scouted, traded, or hunted together before the war, which led to very close bonds between the men and their officers. There were virtually no social divisions between Rogers and his men, and he had quite an informal relationship with his men. The rate of ranger desertion was lower than in the regular army, but many regular officers had a low opinion of Ranger discipline, and there were incidents that seemed to vindicate this opinion. When in later campaigns, regular commanders insisted on excessive restraints over the rangers, desertion increased accordingly.

RANGER TACTICS

Rogers' rules laid out the best way to conduct battles and skirmishes, but ranger activities were more often lightning raids, pursuits, and other special operations. Shirley's orders in 1756 had instructed Rogers to distress the French and their allies by destroying property and means of transport, stealing or ruining provisions, slaughtering cattle, observing their movements, and seizing prisoners for interrogation. Rangers would sometimes disguise themselves as fishermen on the lakes, acting as decoys. Rogers was also said to have donned American Indian dress and walked through the village of St Francis the night before he attacked it, and was spoken to, but not discovered. Indian tactics were widely adopted – one such was assigning a pair of rangers to a tree for cover, one to shoot while the other reloaded, thus keeping up a steady, slow fire.

LIFE IN CAMP

Rangers in camp were obliged to bide by Rogers' rules, attending roll-call fully equipped, guard duty at night, and scouting during the day. Rangers did not make camp with tents, but instead made themselves bark shelters or huts from local resources, depending on how long they were to remain there. A bark shelter was swift to erect and camouflage, while huts were much cozier than tents or barracks.

When camped with the main army, their status as a special force usually saved them from drudge work such as fort building, ditch digging, or rowing supply

The St Francis Raid

The raid on the Abenaki mission village of St Francis/Odanak on October 4, 1759, was the most daring coup of Robert Rogers' entire career. The appearance of the village was a surprise to Rogers who had been expecting a small native settlement, but instead the village comprised over sixty well-built houses, many in European style, arranged in a square centered on the mission church. It seems to have resembled a French town in many ways, however the hundreds of human scalps found hung on poles as decoration were a gruesome reminder of Abenaki raids on frontier settlements. On Amherst's order, Rogers, who was known as "White Devil" to the Abenakis, led a disparate group of rangers, Stockbridge and Mohegan Indians, and white volunteers from ten provincial and regular regiments, deep into French and Indian territory to destroy the village. The surprise attack was carried out by three divisions who closed in on the riverside town from three directions. Operating in pairs, the men rushed into the houses, and killed any sleeping warriors they found. They then set the houses and church on fire. A number of the Indians had hidden themselves in attics, where they perished in the flames. Others were killed or captured trying to flee. About 40 Abenakis died. Rogers lost one Stockbridge ranger killed in the raid. However, his force of 200 had been whittled down to 142 by the time of the raid by lameness and sickness. Here Rogers is shouting orders as a New England provincial soldier escorts a freed white captive, and two of the Indian children which were brought

back to Crown Point by the raiders. In the background the rangers mop up the resistance and burn the village. The rangers left the village in flames, with captives in tow and allegedly carrying treasure. The raiders split into small groups to travel back, however the journey was a disaster, and about half the force died on the way. (Gary Zaboly © Osprey Publishing Ltd)

boats, but the regular commanders found ways to use their skills. Rangers would be required to make daily patrols beyond the perimeter, guard workers outside the camp, escort provision wagon trains, and conduct other specialist tasks.

Hunting brought in fresh food and hides, but the mainstays of camp food were salt pork and beef, hard sea biscuits, or rice. These were supplemented with fish, vegetables, cheese, and flour when available. Scurvy was a frequent visitor to ranger camps; it was difficult to keep men supplied with vegetables when they were in camp, but when rangers were on long scouting treks, it was impossible. Rogers himself suffered from the disease for a month in late 1757. Rum was usually doled out to each ranger at a quarter pint a day. Sometimes other types of alcohol were available, otherwise the rangers could brew their own beer from spruce branches and molasses.

On January 21, 1757, Rogers and about 74 rangers, with prisoners in tow, were ambushed at La Barbue Creek by a party of 120 French and American Indians hidden on the crest of a slope. Rogers got the advanced guard back up the small hill they had just descended, while his lieutenant with the main body organized a stand atop the hill in a grove of pine trees. The rangers now numbered just 57, outnumbered two to one, but they held off the enemy for nearly six hours and inflicted severe casualties on the enemy. The rangers used an originally Indian tactic of two men defending a tree, one firing while the other reloaded. The battle became a lethal sniping contest as the French could not get close enough for hand-to-hand combat. When dusk fell, Rogers ordered his men to stay silent and hold their fire — this drew the curious enemy forward into a lethal ranger volley, which inflicted more losses. Overnight, the rangers evaluated their situation and abandoned the field with almost all their wounded, and returned to Lake George next morning. (Gary Zaboly © Osprey Publishing Ltd)

Rangers whiled away their spare time with simple pursuits, chewing tobacco, conversation over clay pipes, snuff, cards or dice, singing or playing the fiddle or jew's harp. Not many of the rangers did much reading or writing – there are very few letters or diaries from rangers. Rangers also had to do their own laundry. Spare time might also be employed adapting or making kit, such as snowshoes, which were produced by the rangers from deer-hide thongs and hickory branches.

Women allowed at the northern outposts consisted of soldiers' wives and camp followers; some rangers may even have taken Indian wives.

CAMPAIGNING

In the demanding environment of North America, the rangers were constantly being pushed to their physical and psychological limits, especially when taken prisoner by the enemy. The Indians would torture prisoners, or burn them at the stake, or sell them to Canadian traders as slaves.

Tasks which might seem extraordinary to most were normal fare for rangers. In July 1756, Rogers and his men chopped open a 6-mile path across the forested mountains between Lake George and Wood Creek, then hauled five armed whaleboats over it to make a raid on French shipping on Lake Champlain. On their way to the St Francis raid, they marched through a bog for nine days, sleeping on rafts they built from saplings. Rogers' four-month mission to Detroit and back in 1760 covered over 1,600 miles, one of the most remarkable expeditions in American history.

This print of the massacre of the American Indians of St Francis by Rogers' Rangers, comes from a 19th-century book entitled The Romance and Tragedy of Pioneer Life. *(Library of Congress)*

Scouting during the winter was perilous, with temperatures in the mountains sometimes 40 degrees below zero, and rangers suffered snowblindness, gangrene, frostbite, and hypothermia. The rangers would wear many layers, and their blankets Indian-style, to keep themselves warm in the cold. Near the frozen lakes the dangers also included falling through the ice. Rogers would routinely send back those who began limping or complaining in the first few days on the trail, as things would only get worse when they got closer to the enemies, with fireless camps and endless sentry parties. When in enemy country the whole detachment would be awoken at dawn, as that was when the Indians preferred to attack. Before setting off in the morning, the area around the camp would be searched for enemy tracks. The men would pull supplies and equipment on hand-sleds to save their strength, and snowshoes allowed them to cover vast distances in the winter. Snowshoes were essential when fighting, and a broken snowshoe could be lethal for a ranger. Ironically their green clothing showed up clearly against the snow, forcing rangers to put aside their jacket during fighting for fear of becoming an easy target.

When preparing to go on the trail, rangers would generally pack beef, pork, rum, sugar, rice, and peas. The rum was carried in canteens, and was stretched with water while on the trail. Rangers might also carry crackers, bread, cheese, or other vegetables if available. Also eaten was the American Indians' favorite trail food, parched corn. It acted as an appetite suppressant; a spoonful of it followed by a drink of water would make it expand in the stomach, making the traveler feel he had consumed a large meal. Obtaining food from the enemy helped sustain the rangers on their way home, whether stolen provisions, or meat from slaughtered cattle. Provisions could of course be added to with game. On the return from the St Francis raid, food was very scarce, and the men ended up eating acorns, their own shoes, belts, and powder horns, and eventually, the Abenaki bounty scalps they were carrying. One small party of rangers and light infantry was ambushed and almost entirely destroyed by the French and Indians. When other rangers discovered the bodies, they resorted to cannibalism, devouring parts of the bodies raw. One ranger later confessed that he and his starving comrades "hardly deserved the name of human beings."

BATTLE

Rangers are widely recorded as having been ruthless and savage in battle, taking scalps, and killing prisoners. As well as their invaluable tasks of raiding, scouting, and intelligence gathering, rangers took part in many of the large battles of the war. At Montmorency in 1759, they formed a reserve during Wolfe's disastrous assault. At the beginning of Abercromby's attack on the French lines at Ticonderoga, Rogers' Rangers drew first blood, driving in advanced enemy pickets. At sunset, they formed a rearguard to cover the retreating British army. In 1759, Rogers was tasked with heading off the French garrison of Ticonderoga as they evacuated by boat. The rangers in their whaleboats managed to corral ten enemy boats loaded with ammunition, official papers, and prisoners.

The behavior of John Stark's rangers was deemed very courageous during the battle of Fort William Henry in 1757. Rangers spearheaded the landing of Amherst's invasion of Cape Breton island in June 1758, fighting units of French soldiers and Micmac Indians at the summit long enough to allow Wolfe's main brigade to land and sweep the enemy island. Their service was exemplary at Île aux Noix in 1760, and during the battle of Sainte-Foy against the Chevalier de Lévis outside Québec in the same year.

Rogers' Rangers helped to shorten the war by neutralizing the power of the enemy's partisans, defeating them in dozens of engagements large and small. Despite criticism from many sides, they proved themselves warriors who achieved success against the odds, and often exceeded all expectations. Some of the rangers who fought in the French and Indian War became generals or colonels in the American army of the Revolution, while others became loyalist officers. By clearly demonstrating the futility of linear tactics in the wilderness, the rangers also inspired reforms in the regular British Army, and the creation of the first light infantry units. *Rogers' Rules for Ranging* are still issued to United States Special Forces, and remain posted at Ranger battalion headquarters at Fort Benning, Georgia.

MONTCALM'S VICTORY
TICONDEROGA, 1758

Ticonderoga is the American Indian name of the area which was controlled by the Mohawk nation of the Iroquois confederation. Its French name of Carillon is said to have been given because of the nearby waterfalls of La Chute river, the sound of which was reminiscent of church bells. The first European party to explore the area was led by Samuel de Champlain in 1609. In 1731, the Marquis de Beauharnois, Governor-General of New France, ordered the construction of a fort at Pointe-à-la-Chevelure (Scalp Point, or Crown Point to the British and New Englanders). Over the next few years, an imposing stone structure went up known as Fort Saint-Frédéric which secured Lake Champlain. Following the battle of Lake George and building of Fort William Henry in 1755, Governor-General Vaudreuil of New France ordered the construction of a fort at Ticonderoga to guard the northern tip of Lake George: Fort Carillon. By mid-1756, some 30 cannons were mounted in the bastioned fort and work continued for the next two years. The completed fort was the most forward base on the vital Richelieu River–Lake Champlain–Lake George waterway. Therefore taking the fort was crucial to Loudoun's invasion strategy for the conquest of Canada.

INTO POSITION

On March 7, 1758, the instruction for the promotion of Abercromby, signed by William Pitt on December 30, 1757, arrived at Albany. The regulars now knew Abercromby was confirmed in command, and he knew he was to attack Ticonderoga. Couriers went out in the following days to the governors of New York, Massachusetts, Connecticut, New Jersey, New Hampshire and Rhode Island calling for some 20,000 provincial troops to be recruited and put on active service. The six northern colonies voted to raise 17,480 men,

NORTH AMERICA IN 1758

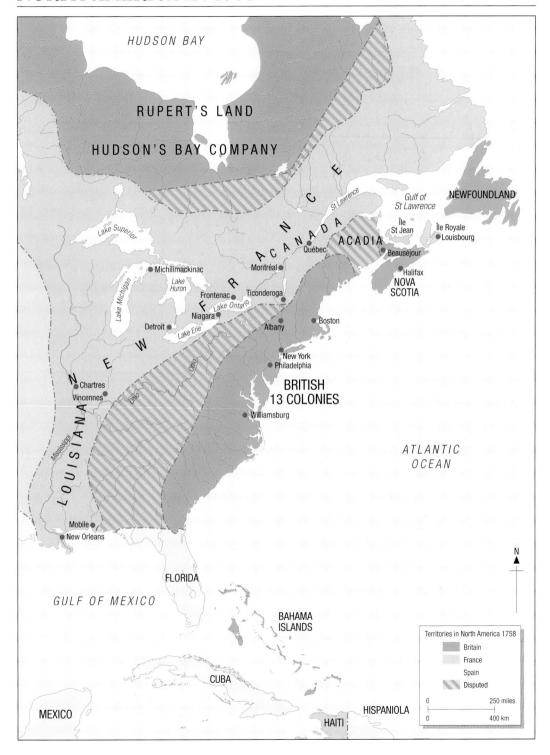

HUDSON BAY

RUPERT'S LAND

HUDSON'S BAY COMPANY

Lake Superior

F R A N C E

St Lawrence

Gulf of
St Lawrence

NEWFOUNDLAND

C A N A D A

Île
St Jean

Île Royale
Louisbourg

ACADIA

Québec

Beauséjour

Michilimackinac

*Lake
Huron*

Montréal

Halifax

NOVA
SCOTIA

Frontenac

Ticonderoga

Lake Ontario

Lake Michigan

Niagara

Detroit

Lake Erie

Albany

Boston

Ohio

New York
Philadelphia

N E W

Chartres

Vincennes

Ohio

BRITISH
13 COLONIES

L O U I S I A N A

Williamsburg

ATLANTIC
OCEAN

Mississippi

Mobile
New Orleans

N

FLORIDA

GULF OF MEXICO

BAHAMA
ISLANDS

CUBA

Territories in North America 1758

Britain
France
Spain
Disputed

0   250 miles
0   400 km

MEXICO

HISPANIOLA

HAITI

which of course took some weeks; there were recruiting shortfalls in spite of decent bounties, and several colonies eventually resorted to compulsory drafts to fill the ranks.

The concentration point was Albany. British regular regiments gathered there, and from late May when the first contingents arrived from New York, they were joined by the provincials who would form the bulk of the army. By then, the gathering site had been moved closer to the southern tip of Lake George, to the site of Fort William Henry destroyed by Montcalm the previous summer. Camp was set up from June 19 by the 42nd, 44th and 55th regiments, the New Jersey Regiment and the rangers led by Lord Howe. The logistical problems were substantial, with a lack of arms and camp equipage for the provincials being especially worrisome; it was only when 10,000 muskets and camp equipage for 4,000 men arrived in Albany from Britain that most provincials moved on to Lake George. Abercromby arrived in the last week of June, by which time the operation was finally coming together. Masses of supplies were being stockpiled, and about 1,000 bateaux and 200 whaleboats sent by Massachusetts were on the spot; Bradstreet's boatmen were preparing rafts for the artillery.

Montcalm followed his eight metropolitan army battalions to Fort Carillon, arriving on June 30. He knew that he would have to stop what was obviously a large force gathering at the south end of Lake George, and on his arrival, scouts confirmed his suspicions. On receiving a letter from Montcalm, Vaudreuil sent to Ticonderoga a force of 400 men under Lévis, which left Montréal on July 1. The French spent the next week preparing for whatever lay ahead. Montcalm put guards on the portage road, the west bank of the La Chute river and in the heights of Ticonderoga. Montcalm was nervous at facing such a powerful enemy. He had the soldiers start to work on an entrenched camp with *abbatis* (obstacles made of logs with sharpened branches) built on Ticonderoga heights. Further entrenchments were also planned, but in the event little was done with those plans. The lines really hemmed in the French defenders, but with the number of men available to Montcalm, there was not much choice. A French attack would have been suicidal, but in an entrenched, raised position, they might stand a chance. However, if they lost, it would be the end for Canada, as most of its defenders would probably be killed, wounded, or prisoners. Montcalm wished for a day or two to finish the entrenchments, and hoped that Abercromby would attack without waiting for his artillery to bombard the French positions.

By the beginning of July, in spite of the substantial supply difficulties associated with assembling so many men, Abercromby and Lord Howe stood at the head of some 17,000 men, the largest army ever assembled in North America. The British regiments were divided into three brigades under

Lieutenant-Colonel William Haviland, Lieutenant-Colonel Francis Grant, and Lieutenant-Colonel John Donaldson. Scout reports indicated a much smaller number of French troops at Fort Carillon.

On July 5, Abercromby's army, encamped at the south end of Lake George, was in high spirits and ready to proceed. The troops and supplies were loaded onto some 900 bateaux and 135 barges. The artillery was loaded on to a number of large flat-bottomed craft. In order to prevent confusion and to provide enough rowing space, the boats were arrayed in rows in an orderly fashion. The fleet of innumerable boats with their little white sails must have made an awesome sight: the armada moving up the lake was about a mile wide (which was nearly the width of Lake George), and stretched for about seven miles in length.

At the head of the fleet the rangers and the 80th Light Infantry formed the advance guard, followed by the British regular regiments which formed the center, the New England provincial troops on each side, and the army's stores and supplies behind, with the artillery bringing up the rear. More light infantry formed a rearguard.

This extraordinary sight soon came into view of French scouts under Ensign de Langy, who went back at once to Ticonderoga to report to Montcalm. On the hills and mountains further north were two other large detachments of French troops: on the west side of the lake, 150 men mostly from La Reine with 100 volunteers from various regiments were at Roger's Rock under the command of Captain de Trépezec. They kept the flotilla under surveillance from a safe distance and counted at least 700 boats. Another party of 300 men under Captain Bernard was further back along Bernetz Brook to watch for enemy ranger parties which might try to outflank the French positions from the northwest.

At the top of Lake George, French sentry posts were dotted from the present Cook's Mountain to a camp at the beginning of the portage road. The agreed signal was to raise and lower a white flag when the British were fully in view. The sentries relayed the signal from post to post until Montcalm received word of the sightings and ordered the troops at the head of the portage road to withdraw to the lines near the fort.

The vast fleet of British boats went as far as Sabbath Day Point, some 25 miles to the north. The first division landed there in the late afternoon, while rangers and light infantry secured the landing area about two miles above. Tents and supplies were brought out of the bateaux and the army set up camp as darkness fell. Many fires were lit as the men cooked dinner and settled down for the night – or so it seemed to the French scouts who watched the glow of hundreds of camp fires in the darkness. However, the British had a surprise for the French. Late in the evening, the whole British force was re-embarked, and by midnight, in strict silence, the fleet sailed past the French scouts undetected.

By early light on July 6, the leading bateaux were near the north end of Lake George at the "French Narrows" (Coate's Point and Black Point). Trépezec's detachment had been totally bypassed. However, a French canoe now came upon the British lead boats, quickly turned about and hurried back to shore. There were French advance posts in the area and, as the light became stronger, the small French detachments saw the multitude of bateaux before them. Resistance was out of the question and they rapidly retreated, carrying this latest news of the advance of Abercromby's army.

First ashore were parties of rangers, followed by American provincials, the light infantrymen of the 80th and the grenadiers from the six regular regiments who had been formed into a temporary shock battalion. They landed in the area now known as Howe's Landing. A hundred men of the 80th advanced, followed by the grenadiers, and found the area deserted. They were elated as resistance had been expected; instead, they found the outpost, a "strong entrenched camp" that had been set on fire and destroyed by the French who "retired very precipitately." The beach of the left bank and its immediate area was soon secured as more troops were landed. The beginning of a portage road on the right bank was also occupied by rangers, its entrenched camp also evacuated by the French. The whole army landed on the left bank without almost any opposition. So far, everything was going wonderfully well for Abercromby and Howe. The British army was now only two miles from its objective. The French offered no resistance and seemed to be in retreat; they might even be trapped into Fort Carillon and would surely soon be vanquished by such a powerful army. Abercromby and Howe and their whole army must have felt that victory was within their grasp. In a matter of days, the fate of Canada might be sealed.

BERNETZ BROOK

By 10.00am on the morning of July 6, with the whole army safely ashore and the French seemingly on the run, an enthusiastic Lord Howe decided to press ahead immediately. His plan called for the army to march in columns to take possession of the west side of the La Chute River which connected Lake George to Ticonderoga. The river was unnavigable, with five rapids dropping by some 200ft over a two-mile stretch. With the British army coming this way, the French would not be able to resist along the portage road, nor at the saw mills at the end of it, as their position would be turned. Thus, they would be trapped in the peninsula of Ticonderoga. At 2.00pm, the army was formed into three main columns. The left flank column was made up of American provincial troops mostly from Massachusetts. The center column had the 44th, 55th, 46th, and 42nd regiments. The right column consisted of the 27th, the 4th, and the six companies of the 1st Battalion of the 60th. These three faced a difficult march through the woods.

A fourth column was headed by Lord Howe himself and mainly consisted of American provincial units: Putnam's Connecticut Rangers, Lyman's 1st Connecticut, Fitch's 3rd Connecticut, the New York and New Jersey regiments. A party of the 80th acted as forward skirmishers, following a trail edging the river. Rogers' Rangers had been sent ahead a couple of hours earlier to secure a stream the French called Bernetz Brook (now Trout Brook) so the whole army could cross it.

It was at this time that the good luck of the British turned bad. The trail near the river was clear and Howe sent the 1st and 3rd Connecticut regiments ahead to join Rogers at the brook. When they got there, Rogers was able to report that his scouts had found the French army camped only half a mile away at the saw mills. It was about four in the afternoon. What happened next, judging from the accounts of various participants and observers on both sides, was one of the more confused bush fights of the war. The British decimated the French scouting party of Trépezec, but at the cost of Lord Howe, whose death was a huge shock to the army and devastated Abercromby.

The effect of this 20-minute fiercely fought skirmish in the forest created profoundly disruptive commotion within the columns of the British army. The sound of gunfire had produced considerable confusion in the various British columns struggling through the wood, more or less lost. Many soldiers now

Bernetz Brook, July 6, 1758. Trépezec's French scouting party had lost its way in the forest when the Indian guides departed after seeing the British armada. While they were trying to return to Ticonderoga, Abercromby's army had landed and got ahead of them. On reaching Bernetz Brook, one of the advance party saw something in the brush and challenged it. Realizing it was an enemy, but not that it was the entire British army, they fired. A fierce forest fight ensued. Lord Howe decided to counterattack and sweep off the French so as not to delay the march of the army. Hurrying to the scene, he reached the top of a hill where the firing was, and was shot dead. The French were pushed back, fighting from tree to tree, and the left column of the army then cut off their retreat. Overwhelmed, the French lost 150 men killed, wounded, or drowned, and another 150 surrendered. All in all about 100 managed to escape, including the badly wounded Trépezec, who died a few hours later. (Patrice Courcelle © Osprey Publishing Ltd)

thought it was Montcalm's army attacking them in the woods – and many must have remembered Braddock's disastrous defeat three years earlier in an equally alien environment at Monongahela. Panic was widespread.

It took hours to sort out the confusion, and as dusk fell the uncertainty brought fears that the French and Indians were lurking nearby. The worst now happened as two columns mistook each other for the enemy and fired on each other through the wood. By the time the situation became clear, the columns were dispersed and Abercromby put a stop to everything for the night. The advance on Fort Carillon was totally ruined. The spirit of the army, so optimistic that morning, was now very gloomy and fearful; many men did not sleep that night. British losses for the day are curiously not given, all the attention being devoted to Lord Howe, but might be estimated at about a hundred or so casualties between the fight and the incidents of "friendly fire" later on.

BRADSTREET ADVANCES

The French do not seem to have been aware of Lord Howe's death at this point, though they sensed something was wrong in the British camp as their advance had stopped. They expected the British to rally and advance on July 7, so that the French field fortifications, already started on the 6th, had to be made ready in all haste. Every battalion was put to work on building up the line on the heights as soon as the sun was up on the 7th. Scouts were sent out to watch the British.

The dawn of July 7 found Abercromby's force spread all over the area in gloom and disorder. The regulars of the 44th and 55th regiments had returned to the landing place with some provincial units to regroup, probably the best thing to do under the circumstances. Abercromby called his officers to an early morning council of war to determine what to do next. There was little choice but to make the best of it, regroup and advance once again. After some tense discussions, Abercromby finally agreed to Bradstreet's proposal to march directly along the portage road to the saw mills. Bradstreet was given some 5,000 men, and Stark's company of rangers and some Stockbridge Indians would provide the advance parties. Bradstreet's column met no opposition, and by early afternoon was at the saw mills, which had been mostly destroyed by the retreating French troops. Bradstreet sent word back to Abercromby that the burned-down saw mills had been occupied without any opposition and that the carpenters were already repairing the bridge which had been partly destroyed by the French. Obviously, after securing a good bridgehead on the north side of the La Chute River, Bradstreet was much tempted to push on ahead with his men, perhaps catch the French unprepared, and proceed toward the fort. Abercromby ignored his request and instead ordered the remaining troops to join Bradstreet's column. During the late afternoon, Abercromby and the rest

CANADIAN INDIAN.

Some 400 Mohawk warriors led by William Johnson finally arrived at Ticonderoga on July 8. They chose to sit out the contest and watched the battle from the slopes of Mount Defiance. (Print after Benjamin West, photo by René Chartrand)

of the British army arrived at the saw mills. They were eventually joined by another column made up of Rogers' Rangers, the 80th Light Infantry, and Bagley's Massachusetts Regiment, who arrived by trailing the west bank of the La Chute River.

One may wonder what might have happened if Bradstreet had been allowed to press ahead. In the best scenario he might have come upon Montcalm's regiments still busy constructing their field fortifications and driven them into the fort. On the other hand, Montcalm had parties of lookouts watching the British. They had been instructed to warn him immediately of any suspicious moves so that the battalions could put down their axes, prime their muskets, and man their entrenchments. Their field fortifications, it is true, would not have been as good in mid-afternoon as they were to be subsequently, but they were advanced enough in most places that the men had camouflaged part of them. Another consideration, no doubt much in the mind of Abercromby and some of his officers, was that there might be an ambush set up by the French and Canadians, the past masters at this type of warfare. At this point, the British had no intelligence of what was ahead so General Abercromby's caution was certainly proper.

The French worked on the entrenchments all day and into the night, as everyone knew that the chances of success against the forthcoming British attack depended on the earthworks. By the evening, the entrenched position on the heights, with its protective *abbatis* in front, was built up and about ready. Reasonably secure, the French were further encouraged by the arrival of General Lévis and his 400 men, who provided a much needed reinforcement, and a great morale boost.

That same evening, the senior engineer, Lieutenant Clerk, and his assistant with an escort climbed Rattlesnake Mountain to view the fort. Once they moved high up they could see not only the fort, but the thousands of French soldiers working on fortifications west of the fort. They judged the fortifications to be rather unimpressive, and far from finished, and reported them as such to Abercromby, who was heartened by the news. None of them had any idea that the main entrenchments and *abbatis* were almost completely finished, as they had been carefully camouflaged by the French, and were invisible from the engineers' viewpoint.

BATTLE AT TICONDEROGA

The next morning, July 8, 1758, Bradstreet scouted the area for a second time, and concurred with the engineers that the fortifications were not elaborate. Abercromby called a council of war, and using the engineers' report, and Bradstreet's confirmation, along with plans of the grounds, the decision was made to attack that very day, before the fortifications could be finished. Reports from deserters and prisoners led Abercromby to believe that Montcalm had about 6,000 soldiers at the fort, who would soon be joined by another force of 3,000, and therefore he encouraged an attack as soon as possible. Montcalm's second-in-command, Gage, was absent from the council. However, encouraged by the daring Bradstreet, Abercromby was anxious to move fast. Victory seemed ensured as the French were obviously unprepared.

The 80th Light Infantry, rangers, river boatmen, and provincial units were formed into a skirmish line that could only cover the main French entrenchments on the heights. Behind this forward line were the British regiments, formed three deep, and divided into their usual three brigades of 2,100, 1,500, and 1,600 men respectively. The six grenadier companies, about 600 strong, were brigaded together into a temporary unit. Behind the regulars was a rearguard of provincial troops. Abercromby's plan was a sound one for a classic frontal assault. Skirmishers would go in first, followed by the provincials who would test the

TICONDEROGA, 1758

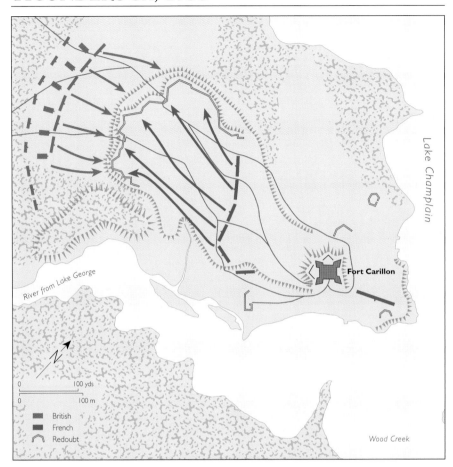

defenses; the regular columns would then come up simultaneously to storm and take the defenses. As long as the formation held, and the attack was coordinated, this had a good chance of success.

The French had been carefully arranged overnight to ensure advance warning of a British attack, and long before dawn on July 8, the army was roused, and deployed along the entrenchments on the heights, and the fort itself. Once the battalions had taken up their positions, they continued raising the height of the entrenchments and building an earthen embankment on the southern side in case the British put a battery on Rattlesnake Mountain. A battery and redoubt were also being erected to secure this area, but they were a long way from ready. On the northern side work continued to link the main entrenchments to the lake, but the 350-yard distance made it impossible to erect anything like finished fortifications here. A battery was planned near Lake Champlain, but construction had hardly started. This was definitely the weak point in the

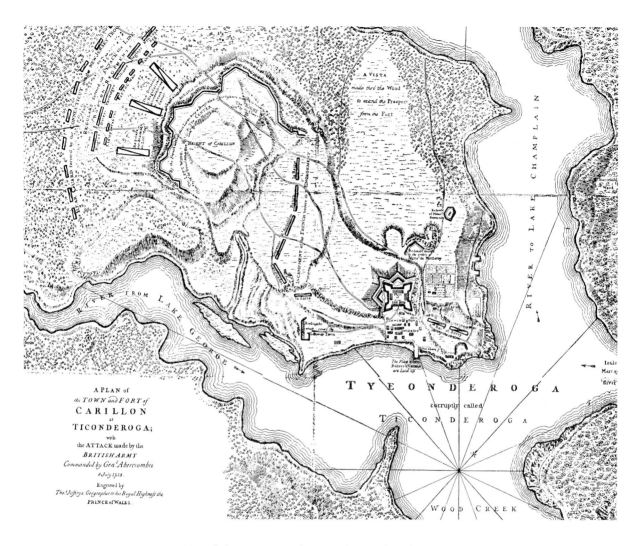

A PLAN of
the TOWN and FORT of
CARILLON
at
TICONDEROGA;
with
the ATTACK made by the
BRITISH ARMY
Commanded by Gen.ˡ Abercrombie
8 July 1758.
Engraved by
Tho.ˢ Jeffreys. Geographer to his Royal Highness the
PRINCE of WALES.

Plan of Fort Carillon and the attack on Ticonderoga, by Thomas Jeffreys. This plan is the best-known and most widely published of the various maps of the battle. It is said to have been based on the map made by Lobtinière which was found in Québec following its capture in 1759, but the trench line north and south of the height has been left out, and the island in the La Chute River is smaller. (National Archives of Canada)

French line, its one advantage being that the artillery in the fort had a clear field of vision in this direction, which would be crucial if a British force attempted to overcome it.

Montcalm arranged a reserve of grenadiers behind each battalion on the heights, and had the most proficient marksmen of the fusiliers at the wall ready to make aimed shots at close range, using loaded muskets passed on by their comrades.

During the middle of the morning, the French noticed a lot of movement on the flank of Rattlesnake Mountain. These were the 400 American Indians, mostly Mohawks, of Sir William Johnson. Although they were out of musket range, they made a considerable show of themselves with a great deal of shooting. After a while, they settled down. Linear-style warfare and all-out assaults on fortified positions were completely unlike their way of war, so they decided to watch the oncoming battle from the first-class viewpoint of the mountain.

The first attack

At around 10.00am, the skirmishing line moved out cautiously. The lead unit was Captain Stark's rangers closely followed by the rest of the rangers. Stark's rangers understandably made first contact, with a party of French sentries posted ahead of the *abbatis* to warn of the British advance, but the sentries retreated when the rest of the rangers arrived to assist.

Shortly after, at about 12.30pm, de Lancey's New York Regiment had formed on the extreme left and were advancing. Because Rogers' Rangers had veered somewhat to the right, they were not protected by the skirmish line that was supposed to be in front of them. They were surprised by the enemy about 300 yards from the breastworks, but reacted swiftly, forming up, firing back and, with a cheer, charged the French who were driven back into their trenches.

These first contacts were most encouraging, with the French already on the run and part of their entrenchments breached, or so it seemed to the rangers and the New Yorkers. The shooting on the left drew the attention of Lieutenant-Colonel Haviland who was coming up from behind with his brigade. Haldiman's grenadier brigade was also nearby, as was a body of detached regular piquets under Major Proby of the 55th. At this point, Haviland made a momentous decision which was to profoundly influence the subsequent events: believing the French entrenchments to be breached, he decided that his regular brigade should advance and attack the French. He therefore instructed Rogers to provide cover with his rangers until his regulars had bypassed them and assaulted the French. Formed into columns, Haviland's brigade, with Proby's men in the vanguard, charged ahead.

However, as they surged forward they found that the French had disappeared, and that they were charging into a hidden *abbatis*. As the soldiers struggled over and around the obstacles, their formation disintegrated. They were now being fired upon quite heavily from beyond the *abbatis*. The British at last realized the true position of the French entrenchments: what the rangers and New York Regiment had taken was simply parts of the fence-like line in front of the *abbatis* held by Montcalm's advance parties. Haviland's men tried to push on, but with losses mounting they retreated to regroup. Haldiman's grenadiers had also advanced, and been almost completely destroyed. The remaining men were ordered to retreat.

At this point Abercromby went up with the 42nd to the line of the *abbatis*. He first believed that only the skirmish line had been engaged. He was hugely surprised to find out that the regulars had attacked, without orders. Instead of the coordinated attack he had planned, the left of his army was now involved in a premature, unplanned attack, and the result was disastrous confusion. Once again in this campaign, the command discipline of the army fell short in spite of his orders to observe stricter discipline. Whatever control he had had over

Inside the French entrenchments at Ticonderoga

The log walls protected the French fusiliers firing on the attacking British troops. They were selected from the better shots; loaded muskets were passed to them or they might load with only ball and powder when rapid fire was required; at other times, they took aimed shots at enemy sharpshooters in the *abbatis*. One French officer noted "our musketry fire was so well aimed that the enemy was destroyed as soon as they appeared." (Sautai) The French soldiers at the log wall probably took their waistcoats off, but kept wearing their gray-white coats to avoid confusion as had been experienced during the Fort William Henry campaign the previous summer. Behind in reserve were the battalion's grenadiers and piquets ready to intervene should the attackers manage to break in. The battalion's HQ was to be marked by the two battalion colors, but at least one of these was at the log wall. The three sectors of the French position were commanded by Bourlamaque on the right, Lévis on the left and

Montcalm at the center. The sector that came under the most intense assault by the 42nd Highlanders in the late afternoon of July 8 was defended by the Royal-Roussillon. Montcalm went there with some reserves to check any breach in the position and encourage his soldiers, making sure that detachments of grenadiers and piquets were sent to reinforce and give heart to the men in the line wherever they seemed threatened. He was at his best at the front line, a brave and energetic battlefield commander who had a quick eye for any crisis, who loved sharing the dangers with his men, who managed to keep control, and who could lead coolly in the heat of battle. An officer of the metropolitan army engineers is at Montcalm's right and an officer of Royal-Roussillon on his left. A drummer would have been nearby and possibly a Canadian militiaman for communication with the colonial troops and militias posted on the northern flank. (Patrice Courcelle © Osprey Publishing Ltd)

the army was now gone, and impossible to regain. With coordination now lost, the British attack was now being implemented by the individual commanding officers. Haviland's and Haldiman's survivors were regrouping at the edge of the *abbatis*, while assorted men of the skirmish line returned fire using the *abbatis* as cover. Meanwhile, the regiments of the center brigade were getting ready to go into the *abbatis*, and the right brigade, having been stopped from outflanking the entrenchments, were hurrying toward the left as this seemed to be where the attack was being pursued. The order of attack was now totally muddled, but Abercromby does not seem to have attempted to correct the situation. Things had gone wrong from the start of the advance and it would appear that, considering the difficulties of communications on a battlefield, everything was left to area commanders. They, in turn, could do little besides trying to overcome the French lines by the sheer courage and determination of their men.

Abercromby appears to have had no alternate plans, such as trying to outflank the French entrenchments, or to retreat and wait for the artillery. He thus seems to have been overcome by events, a serious fault for a commander-in-chief. His second-in-command, Gage, had novel tactical concepts and might have come up with a new plan of attack; however he seems to have been absent, as on previous days. Of course, ultimate responsibility must rest with Abercromby, but he was certainly left to himself by Gage. As for Bradstreet, who had filled in the previous day as an unofficial second-in-command, he was back in the line with his men. The British senior command was thus most deficient for the task ahead.

The situation was very different behind the French entrenchments. Each man was in his designated spot, the battalion commanders were in the vicinity of the colors, and the brigade commanders would have moved around their respective sectors. The forward parties had given ample warning of the British advance, and then retreated in an orderly fashion taking no casualties. The commanders reassigned men when they realized the British were attacking the French right. There was panic amongst some of the Canadian militiamen on the right, which was controlled by the colonial gunners, but overall, the troops held their positions and repulsed the British attacks. By 2.00pm, it became clear that all the British assaults were failing.

Also at about 2.00pm, the French spotted to their left about 20 barges full of men and two cannon on rafts on the La Chute river, approaching the north shore. The gunners in the fort, thinking this another attempt to outflank them, opened fire, sinking two barges. At this point, the other barges started to back away and eventually vanished from view. Contrary to the French perception, this was not a flanking movement, but in fact a failed operation, led by the engineer Clerk, to install artillery batteries at the foot of Rattlesnake Mountain. The barges set off about the same time as the first attack, but, either due to fast currents or human error, drifted closer to the northern shore rather than the

This widely distributed mid-19th-century engraving of the battle of Ticonderoga is a spirited impression of the British attack, but is full of anachronisms, such as cannon on the French entrenchments, and horses and colors for the attacking British. (National Archives of Canada, C-4664)

southern shore, and ended up in full view of the fort. With some of the equipment lost, and the men confused, the idea of the battery was abandoned. With retrospect it was a serious omission not to try again, but in the heat of the assault, priorities must have altered.

In the line of fire

On the heights of Ticonderoga, the British were not giving up. Repeatedly repulsed, they kept re-forming and went back in with great courage and stubbornness. The French were coping well with the onslaughts, though many of the men were worried that they might be outflanked from either side. The most stubborn attacks were usually at the center, but the British soldiers' outstanding bravery did not waver. Time after time, units went up, struggled over the *abbatis*, now strewn with bodies, and were shot at close range. The French soldiers were just as resolute. The British casualties were already high, but the French too were being shot at by the rangers and light infantrymen who had taken cover between the attacking columns. As some of these men were armed with rifles, their marksmanship must have been especially effective and Bougainville told of "their light troops and better marksmen who, protected by the trees, delivered a most murderous fire on us." Another cause of casualties was the masses of British bullets that arched over the men in the entrenchments, and hit those further back in reserve.

The rearguard of provincial troops was marched up at about 2.00pm to support the British regulars. They seemed to have formed themselves between the regular brigades, and they also suffered severe casualties. They had no more luck storming the entrenchments than the regulars, but acted with courage.

From about 2.30pm, the British attacks decreased as Abercromby called back his mauled regiments to regroup and recuperate. Once again his instructions were badly relayed, or ignored, and Grant's brigade, for example, continued to stage new attacks. It seems that others joined them, and the shooting kept on, punctuated by various surges through the afternoon. Sometime before 5.00pm, a massive attack was launched by two columns united, including the 42nd and the grenadiers, of which a few Highlanders managed to get beyond the *abbatis* and into the entrenchment, but the attack was eventually repulsed with horrific casualties.

Throughout the attacks, the British had also been plagued with parties of colonial skirmishers from the French right. The column of the 42nd and 46th reacted, but the skirmishers retreated, and kept harassing from a distance, which must have had an effect on the tiring British.

At about 6.00pm the British columns tried again to storm the French right, then the center, then the left, without any further success. Indeed the attacks were slackening as they finally realized they could not overcome Montcalm's position. Captain Lee summarized the reasons for defeat with his account of how the unevenness and ruggedness of the ground and height of the breastwork

> ...rendered it an absolute impossibility ... no order given to change attack ... but every officer led at the head of his division, company or squadron to fall a sacrifice to his own good behavior and stupidity of his commander ... the fire was prodigiously hot and the slaughter of the officers was great; almost all wounded, the men still furiously rushing forward almost without leaders, five hours persisted in this diabolical attempt and at length obliged to retire. (Journal of Charles Lee)

Around 7.00pm, the columns retreated, covered by the light troops. Some of the dead and wounded were left behind as the army retreated. Luckily for the British, Montcalm's men were exhausted and did not pursue them. They were aware that Abercromby might try again at dawn the next day, and the whole French army stayed in the entrenchments overnight.

Next morning, the French soldiers refurbished their entrenchments and finished off the lines and batteries. A party of volunteers went toward the British army's positions and found them abandoned and the army gone. Word was brought back to the French lines upon which the soldiers went into the

Of the many courageous charges made against the French entrenchments on July 8, 1758, the most determined and ferocious was made by the brave Highlanders of the 42nd Regiment (The Black Watch) sometime before 5.00pm. They attacked the French right and then the center, and seemed almost unstoppable, despite grievous losses. Time and again, they persisted in their attacks. Some were seen in a rage hacking away at the abbatis; the wounded encouraged their comrades to attack rather than help them; some few even managed to climb up the log wall and jump into the French position wielding their broadswords, meeting their end on a bayonet. The casualties resulting from such outstanding conduct under fire were terrible: some 647 were reported killed, wounded, or lost, well over half of the regiment. (Patrice Courcelle © Osprey Publishing Ltd)

abbatis and carried out the remaining wounded British soldiers. There was no further intelligence on the British, so the French continued to work on the fortifications. They believed Abercromby had suffered about 4,000 casualties, but with 16,000–21,000 men remaining, he might try again, with artillery. By evening the works had progressed considerably.

The following day, there was still no sign of Abercromby and groups were sent out as far as 7½ miles south, finding only abandoned British wounded, so confirming that the enemy force was gone.

AFTER THE BATTLE

It is difficult to estimate British casualties at Ticonderoga, as Abercromby seems to have considerably minimized losses when reporting them. Working from the reported figures, and the number that the French buried, a reasonable figure might be 1,000 killed or missing, and 1,500 wounded, a total of 2,500 casualties for the battle on July 8. When added to the casualties of July 6, the total would seem to be about 2,600. The French casualties were naturally considerably less, but nevertheless quite high for an army that could ill afford any losses. The action on July 6 had lost Montcalm six officers and about 300 men killed, wounded, or made prisoner. Lévis reported the casualties of July 8 as a total of 372, including 14 officers killed and 18 wounded. These figures were later revised to a total of 377. In all, the total for the campaign was around 550.

The battle had been a tremendous pounding match of frontal assaults, all of which had failed. There was no serious British attempt to outflank or even create a diversion, and the artillery was not deployed at all except for one timid and failed attempt. The British could have built strong counter lines of entrenchments to seal in the peninsula. Instead, the considerable four-to-one advantage enjoyed by Abercromby was gambled on the assaults in a matter of hours.

The French defense, while gallant, was hardly innovative. Again there was no thought to creating a diversion other than Lévis' attempt to send out skirmishers. Montcalm could have used his colonial troops and militia to harass the flanks and rear of the enemy force. However, he was never very keen on the

Montcalm cheered by his troops following the final repulse of the British assaults on July 8, 1758. Many of the uniform details are erroneous in this early 20th-century painting by Henry Ogden, but it does capture the elation in the French camp after the battle. (Fort Ticonderoga Museum)

Canadian tactics of woodland warfare, and he knew the British had a large force of light infantry to oppose such a move. Leaving daring moves aside, he decided to keep those colonial troops to cover his own flank.

Subsequent letters show that Abercromby decided to shoulder the blame, while claiming he had been badly advised by his engineer, Clerk, who had been conveniently killed in the field on July 8. This was a worthy covering operation as it whitewashed Bradstreet, who had provided similar erroneous information, protected Rogers, who did not create the screen he was supposed to, and absolved Haviland, who had independently decided to engage his column. Grant was not above reproach either, as he had stubbornly maintained his Highlanders' attacks after Abercromby had ordered a withdrawal. Finally Gage, the absent second-in-command, seems to have contributed very little. The subterfuge worked, with most of the officers going on to promotions and distinguished careers, especially Gage.

Montcalm's day of glory was widely publicized in France, but his reports of victory gave no credit to the colonial troops. Indeed he minimized their numbers and role. As a result, Vaudreuil wrote in August to the minister of the navy that the Colonial troops had "nearly blown up and if the worst [mutiny] did not happen, it was due to their spirit of moderation. And their mortification was great when they saw that M. de Montcalm, instead of reporting their services, attributed them to the metropolitan troops." It is unfortunate that Montcalm did not use this remarkable victory as an opportunity to bind the two rival camps in his army together, instead doing exactly the opposite. It was only after his death at Québec in 1759, when Lévis assumed command, that an attempt was made to unify the army.

THE LIGHT BOBS
THE TRANSFORMATION OF THE BRITISH ARMY

By 1757, 14,000 regulars had been posted to the Thirteen Colonies to fight, and by the peak of the regular establishment in North America in 1759, nearly 24,000 men were under arms. However, the harrowing experiences of 1755 had illustrated to the British that numbers alone would not win this war. Commanders in the North American theater needed a highly trained army of experts, light troops, rangers, friendly American Indians for scouting and skirmishing, bateaux men to move the armies along the waterways, and artillerymen and engineers to lay siege to the French forts once the army had reached its objectives. Between 1757 and 1764, the army in America underwent a dramatic period of transformation. This transition was started and overseen by the commander-in-chief for 1756–57, Lieutenant-General John Campbell, Earl Loudoun. While Loudoun was not as successful in battle as Amherst, his innovations laid the foundations for victory in the campaigns of 1758–60.

LOUDOUN'S INNOVATIONS

Firstly, Loudoun centralized the system of supplies for British regular and provincial soldiers to a degree previously unheard of in the Thirteen Colonies. Main storehouses were created at Halifax, New York, and Albany. Because of this restructuring, soldiers reporting for duty in North America were consistently able to receive adequate uniforms and arms.

Loudoun realized that transportation was an important factor in the success of his army, and that transportation in the North American theater posed a unique problem, as was clear from the difficulties Braddock and other commanders had experienced. A reform of the system was necessary. Previously the army had depended upon local wagoners to move supplies; this was an

Thomas Gage, (c.1720–87) having acted as Lord Albemarle's ADC in the 1740s and seen action at Fontenoy and Culloden, became lieutenant-colonel of the 44th Foot, and arrived in America in 1755. Gage was noted as a good regimental commander insisting on strict discipline. While serving under Lord Loudoun, Gage felt that a repeat of Monongahela could be avoided if the British Army had light infantry, and Loudoun instructed him to recruit the new 80th Light Infantry, a regiment Gage would command as colonel. In 1758, Gage was third in command, and second after Lord Howe's death. However his location on July 6–8, when he should have been with his commander at Ticonderoga, are shrouded in mystery. He became commander-in-chief of all British forces in North America after the French and Indian War, and was instrumental in shaping the Coercive/Intolerable Acts following the Boston Tea Party. Engraving after a portrait of c.1770. (National Archives of Canada, C-1347)

unsatisfactory system, and so Loudoun replaced it with a corps of army wagons, and a road improvement program. He also appreciated the importance of waterways for the movement of armies, and he delegated John Bradstreet to investigate alternative plans for moving materiel. This led to the building of a fleet of standardized supply boats piloted by experienced and armed boatmen. A program of creating portages accompanied this scheme, and the army and navy also built sloops to move supplies from coastal cities upriver to the army's major staging areas.

The most important of the changes brought in under Loudoun were the plans to make the soldier of the British Army more effective in the North American theater. It was realized that the men had to be clothed and equipped for the forest, but more importantly, trained to enable them to move and fight in the wilderness. The regular soldiers received training in wooded conditions, including newly developed firing sequences and tactics, to dispel their fear of the woodlands, and allow them to fight back successfully. Following the success of the light infantry units, all regular and provincial troops at Ticonderoga had their coats cut short like the light infantry, and were allocated a bearskin to use as a mattress, blanket, or backpack. Lord Howe also had hats cut down, and had officers leave their sashes behind. All of this acted to ease the movement of regular troops in the woods. These innovations did not make the British invincible, but made them the equal of their French equivalent, and most importantly, meant that by 1759 the average British soldier had lost his fear of fighting in the forest, having received the training required to deal with most situations.

Retraining and equipping the regular soldiers was not enough; Loudoun recognized that there needed to be groups of soldiers specifically trained for skirmishing, scouting, and woodland fighting. Rangers were an important part of this process, (see page 119) but could not be the only solution, partly as many of the commanders saw them as undisciplined, even savage fighters. Loudoun decided to create units comprising regulars who would receive ranger-type training, as well as instruction in linear methods, therefore supplying commanders with soldiers who could adapt to any situation, but who operated under the discipline that was lacking from the rangers. Loudoun's scheme took two shapes. The 62nd (later 60th) Regiment of Foot was raised initially from the frontier peoples of Virginia and Pennsylvania, with the intent that the regiment would embody the spirit and abilities of the frontiersmen, but

Light Infantry Uniform, 1758

This light infantryman wears the uniform of the 55th Regiment, 1758. Under the leadership of Lord Howe, the soldier's appearance has changed drastically from official regulations. The coat has been shortened, and the lace removed. Though still seen here, in some cases the facing was removed. His tricorn has been cut down to a "round hat" and he wears *mitasses* for campaigning. Many of the light infantry also adopted moccasins for campaigning. During the Ticonderoga campaign, the light infantry's clothing was affected by Lord Howe's reforms as they too were issued with just one bearskin to use as bedding, blanket, and backpack. In this reform, commanding officers were left to decide on the color of leggings their light infantry soldiers would wear and were directed to ensure that the barrels of the firearms the men carried were camouflaged, and jackets plain, to avoid detection in the woods. The final development and standardization of light infantry dress came in 1759, when Amherst issued a dress policy. All the light infantry of the army in North America were now to be uniform in appearance, wearing a long-sleeved waistcoat and a coat with grenadier-style "wings." The coat had no lace, but extra pockets for ball and flints. Hats were caps with ear-flaps that kept the head warm. During winter, the light infantrymen would adopt greatcoats, under-waistcoats, warm socks, and leggings, and later the white blanket coat, the *capot*, not only warm, but also useful camouflage in the snow. From the rangers and American Indian auxiliaries they learnt the art of using snowshoes. (Steve Noon © Osprey Publishing Ltd)

with the discipline of the regular soldier. Although not all of the recruits for this four-battalion regiment originated from the frontier population, the development marked a significant change in policy. The ultimate stage in this policy was the raising of regiments of light infantry.

THE LIGHT INFANTRY

In 1757, British commanders introduced an experimental, temporary corps that stemmed from the nature of the terrain as well as the tactics of the enemy. These troops were called "light troops," or "light infantry," and sometimes "light bobs," to distinguish them from the heavy infantry in marching regiments.

Light infantrymen were selected and recruited internally from the fusilier companies of British line infantry battalions. The type of man required for the light infantry had to be a cut above the ordinary soldier – officers were looking for physically fit marksmen prepared to be detached on independent service. Those who had been in North America for a time were useful, as they were accustomed to the woods. Invariably, the men recruited for the light companies looked upon themselves as "chosen men."

Training and tactics

Just as dress differed from theater to theater, so did the standard, quality, and amount of training. No two light infantry corps were trained the same because no written doctrine existed.

The first light infantry in the British Army was the 80th Foot, or Gage's Light Infantry, raised in December 1757. It consisted of experienced officers and men from the regimental light companies, some of whom had trained or served as volunteers with Rogers' Rangers. Some recruiting was done in the colonies as well, but most men inclined to join had already done so, and preferred the ranger companies that offered better pay and less discipline. Gage's light infantrymen underwent extensive training under experienced officers and NCOs.

The men formed into light companies for the abortive 1757 Louisbourg campaign under Loudoun experienced a very strenuous training regime, spending days alternately attacking and defending mock fortifications. Musketry and target practice became a top training priority for all light infantry soldiers, so that all were expert marksmen.

To ensure that his light infantry were led by fit officers capable of woodland warfare, Loudoun arranged for 55 handpicked "gentleman" officers serving in the ranks to be trained by Rogers for seven weeks, to then serve as ensigns in their own regimental light companies, or the rangers, as vacancies occurred.

Other officers were formulating training and tactics for their light infantry. Henri Bouquet, the second-in-command on the 1758 expedition to take Fort Duquesne, was a Swiss officer who had seen irregular warfare on European service. He started to arm and clothe his men like American Indians, and trained them by sending them into the thick forest in small columns, and accustoming them to swift deployment into line. He later identified certain traits of American Indian warfare which he then used to instruct his light infantrymen in the best way to fight them. Eventually his training program developed to encompass clothing, arms, training, camp construction, logistics, and tactical maneuvers. Under his supervision, the company replaced the battalion as the unit of maneuver, and troops were taught to snapshoot, wheel on the run over broken terrain, swim rivers, and march on snowshoes.

By the 1758 Louisbourg campaign, there were a large number of established light infantry tactics and techniques, which companies had mastered and could put into use in woodland warfare. However, training alone could never replace experience. Only time in the wilderness could build up the expertise that a light infantryman needed to be able to confidently take on his adversaries.

Light infantry were issued carbines rather than firelocks, as they were lighter and more accurate. The best marksmen were issued rifled carbines, which were more accurate still. The men used cartridge boxes which were lighter than a leather cartouche box, and carried more rounds, and were covered in tin to guard against the wet. They carried a powder horn for pistol powder, finer and more combustible. Ready to hand, slung off the left shoulder under the right armpit, the horn was a quicker and more convenient way of priming a musket. Light infantry were also equipped with tomahawks that could be wielded from a distance or in close engagements with the enemy, and a short knife used for dressing game or eating meals. The tomahawk was an important backup to the musket in close-quarter fighting if the user was skilled in its use.

Campaigning and battle

Battle experiences could vary considerably for the light infantry, from desperate hand-to-hand comabt in the forest, through heading amphibious assaults to skirmishing or fighting in line as part of a linear battle. The adaptability of the light infantryman meant he could be sent into any situation and expected to fight appropriately.

Like the rangers, and often with the rangers, the light infantry would be sent out on patrol, or on expeditions in any weather or conditions. They soon learned how to adapt their clothing to the weather, and how to cope with the many flies, ticks, and parasites which made their home in the American woodlands, and preyed on the unsuspecting British soldier. Snakes were also a common hazard. The light infantry were encouraged to break up the whiteness of their faces before going on operations by growing a beard, or smutting it with charcoal.

In addition to the dangers of campaigning in snow and ice in the winter, the light infantry were exposed to perils on the waterways of North America. Sudden thunderstorms on the Great Lakes meant certain death for men in small whaleboats or other small craft. Equally dangerous was the practice of shooting

Lieutenant-Colonel William Howe (1729–1814), commander of the light infantry at Québec. He led the light infantry up the cliffs at Foulon to the Plains of Abraham. His light infantry were extremely successful in skirmishing and patrolling against the American Indians and French irregulars that constantly harassed the British siege camps. He later became commander-in-chief of the British forces during the American Revolution. (National Archives of Canada, C-96946)

Daily life in camp at Crown Point, 1761

In the foreground are three members of the 27th (Inniskilling) Regiment cleaning their rifles, while a corporal of the 42nd (Royal Highland) Regiment inspects one of his men. The soldiers of the 26th wear fatigue caps and flap caps. For greater versatility the light infantry companies in existing regiments removed the sleeves from their regimental coats and sewed them to their waistcoats, giving them a sleeved waistcoat and a sleeveless regimental coat which could be worn in various combinations depending on the weather. Both standard military shoes and moccasins were worn. The Highlanders have also adapted their clothing to the theater, with leather pockets sewn onto their coats, and the lacing removed. When in camp like this, the light infantry would sleep in tents like the regulars, and in more established camps they might build huts, while on campaign they might build shelters from branches and pine boughs like the rangers and American Indians, or sleep in the open.

While in camp, the weekly rations could be subsidized with fresh vegetables from the camp gardens, and fresh meat from livestock kept by the regiment. The men could also obtain luxuries from the sutlers and camp followers. As many of the light infantry were accomplished at hunting and fishing, they could supplement the salted meat ration with fresh game or fish. A ration of "spruce beer" per man was a useful weapon against the constant enemy of scurvy.

For some off-duty light infantrymen, singing and music were a pleasant way of passing the time; others coped with the stress of the army with drinking. Drinking became a serious problem for commanders in some outposts as drunkenness in the troops led to insolence, violence, theft, and even murder. Incidents of violence and theft would be answered with the severe punishments of the British Army. Even minor transgressions would be punished with flogging, and the worst crimes, including murder and desertion, would have been punished with death. There would have been camp followers and women at the camp, and like the rangers some light bobs may even have taken Indian wives. (Steve Noon © Osprey Publishing Ltd)

A mixed group of light infantrymen from the 80th (Gage's) and 42nd (Royal Highland) regiments are preparing to ambush a party of French-allied American Indians who have just landed their canoes on the shore of Lake George. (Steve Noon © Osprey Publishing Ltd)

rapids rather than portaging, which some men were prepared to risk because portaging was a long and laborious process of unloading the boats and transporting them and their cargoes overland.

On campaign the light infantryman was expected to carry his own provisions – salted meat, parched Indian corn, peas, rice, biscuits, and perhaps some sugar or chocolate. Sometimes on campaign they could supplement this fare with hunting and fishing, but not always when raiding. As with the rangers, campaigning in winter could lead to terrible hardships, and there are several documented incidents of desperate acts, including cannibalism.

Light bobs were often taken prisoner by the American Indians and suffered torture and scalping like their ranger comrades. Many soldiers preferred to try and kill themselves rather than submit to a painful, slow, and undignified death by torture. Whether true or apocryphal, the story of Private Allan Macpherson demonstrates the fear of torture by the Indians. Macpherson was of the 77th Foot, and was taken prisoner by the Indians at Fort Duquesne in 1758. He

This well-known print after a sketch by Hervey Smyth gives a very good impression of the difficulties facing the light infantry when they landed at the Foulon. The road by which the majority of the troops reached the Plains is visible, as is the cliff face scaled by the light infantry.

tried to kill himself before capture, but was disarmed and taken prisoner. After seeing his comrades tortured in agony, he decided to take action. He told the Indians, through an interpreter, that he wished to show them a very powerful medicine, that if applied to the skin, would stop the strongest blow of a tomahawk. He persuaded them to allow him to go and gather herbs in the forest to make the potion for a demonstration. On his return, Macpherson boiled the herbs, made a paste, and spread it over his neck. He lay his neck over a log, and dared their stronger warrior to take up his weapon, boasting that his potion would prevent even a scratch. The challenge was taken up, and the Indian put all his strength behind the blow, and Macpherson was beheaded. The Indians were amazed at their own credulity. Macpherson's ingenuity enabled him to avoid the lingering death they had planned for him, but instead of being enraged at the actions of their victim, they were so impressed that they did not torture the remaining prisoners.

If wounded at one of the large battles like Louisbourg or Ticonderoga, a soldier could reasonably expect some form of medical care, however rudimentary. However, the detached nature of the majority of their service, where fast and light travel was essential, meant that any seriously wounded light infantryman had to be left behind, and was often never seen again. If a light bob could keep up with the group, he might receive treatment when he got back to camp in a field hospital, or possibly he might be left with the inhabitants of a colony in the campaign area until he had recuperated. If he did not recuperate sufficiently to serve, like other British regulars, he would be discharged and sent home, many abandoned to fend for themselves.

The light infantry had a strong *esprit de corps*, fostered by their shared experiences and hardship. The strongest sense of community and group loyalty was among the Highland units, who were further distinguished from the redcoats by their dress and language. The light infantry were very proud of their skills and self-sufficiency, looking down their noses at newly arrived redcoats in their bright, clean uniforms. The light infantry met their biggest challenge just after the official end of the French and Indian War at the battle of Bushy Run. Bushy Run is said to have been the fiercest battle ever fought against American Indians, and it proved to be the turning point in Pontiac's War. The victory of the British line and light infantry over the force of Indians was proof that the light infantry had evolved over the course of the war into a well-respected force, resilient and adaptable in any battle, and were quickly becoming an essential part of the British battle line.

THE GATEWAY TO NEW FRANCE
LOUISBOURG, 1758

HISTORY OF LOUISBOURG

Louisbourg, the capital of the French colony of Île Royale, was pivotal in the great contest for the domination of North America: whoever controlled the island and the fortress of Louisbourg had the key to New France.

The history of the French on Île Royale or Cape Breton Island is interlinked with that of the early French settlements in Acadia and Placentia. The first French settlements were established by the French explorer Samuel de Champlain in 1603. From that time further settlements were formed in what the French called Acadia. Over the years, Acadia was subject to various attacks and invasions by New Englanders, and also suffered occasional civil strife. During the 1660s and 1670s, Louis XIV took some measures to consolidate the French positions in Acadia and installed a permanent station on the southern coast of Newfoundland to protect French interests in the Grand Bank fisheries. By the 1680s, permanent garrisons of colonial troops were being established, both in Acadia and Placentia, and ships going back and forth from Europe to North America and the West Indies made frequent stopovers. The wars between the French and English during the 1690s and early 1700s brought much military activity to the area. Eventually, Port Royal, the capital of Acadia, was captured by a large combined British and New England force in 1710 and renamed Annapolis Royal.

The Treaty of Utrecht, signed in 1713 between Britain and France, conceded Acadia and Newfoundland to Britain. France, however, kept Île Royale and Île Saint-Jean. In July 1713, French colonists sailed from Placentia to Île Royale and resettled at Port Saint-Louis. In 1719, Port Saint-Louis was renamed

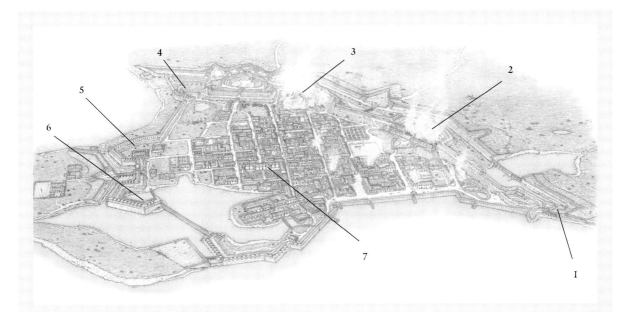

The defenses of Louisbourg

The main features of Louisbourg during its second siege in 1758 were broadly similar to those in 1745. The walls and buildings were much the same except for improvements in the Dauphin Demi-bastion (1), which had been rebuilt with a cavalier so as to cover the land side with artillery fire. Despite the spirited counterfire by the French gunners, the relentless bombardment of the fortress by General Amherst's and Admiral Boscawen's gunners had inflicted heavy damage on the fortifications by the last week of July 1758. By July 24–25, the top of the cavalier and the walls of the Dauphin Demi-bastion and the King's Bastion (2) had been reduced to rubble; part of the King's Bastion and the barracks in the Queen's Bastion (3) were burning, as were some houses in the town. The hospital was mercifully unscathed (7). The bastions on the seaward side of

Louisbourg were also undamaged: Princess Bastion (4), Brouillon Bastion (5), and Maurepas Bastion (6).

Even more critical than the damage to the bastions was the breach in the curtain wall between the Dauphin Demi-bastion and the King's Bastion. This gave the British the option of attempting an assault into the town. In spite of its partially filled moat, storming the town via this large breach had every chance of success. The consequences of such assaults were costly in lives for both sides and likely meant a dire fate for the civilians at the hands of enemy soldiers half-crazed from the fighting. When fortresses reached the point of being partly destroyed and breached, further fighting was considered useless and negotiations leading to surrender were held, as at Louisbourg. (Donato Spedaliere © Osprey Publishing Ltd)

Louisbourg and a fortress and naval base erected. They were inaugurated in 1720 and, for the next 23 years at considerable expense, a town surrounded by substantial fortifications arose. True, Louisbourg did not come cheap, but on the other hand, it was a commercial success. It provided French Grand Banks fishermen with a secure harbor, and this became the scene of intense maritime traffic from France, Canada, the West Indies, and the Thirteen Colonies.

By the 1740s, the town had grown to about 4,000 souls and had, according to some accounts, become the fourth busiest harbor in North America. The

New Englanders hated the outright competition, and one suspects the Bible-quoting volunteers who, almost incredibly, took Louisbourg in 1745 also wanted to appropriate this exceptionally good commercial port. The town's population was deported to France while Britain immediately posted a strong garrison there. France wanted Louisbourg back, but the fleet sent in 1746 under the Duc d'Anville was cursed by bad luck and failed. By the 1748 Treaty of Aix-la-Chapelle, Fortress Louisbourg was returned to France, leaving the New Englanders very bitter. This transfer reaffirmed that Louisbourg was more than just a successful commercial port, it was a strategic naval base which could command the North Atlantic if a strong enough fleet was posted there. It was the sentry to Canada and the vast expanses of North America. The French doubled the garrison and, from then on, sizable French warships patrolled the waters around Île Royale. However, Louisbourg's fortifications benefited from only summary repairs. The emphasis was on rebuilding trade and commerce and, within a few years, the town was flourishing.

On its side, Britain also had to act if it was to challenge the French forces in that area. In 1749, Halifax was founded to act as a naval base, and rapidly grew to be a substantial town and the capital of Nova Scotia. During the 1750s, Halifax was the assembly point for large combined operations of sea and land forces. There were always several ships-of-the-line in its harbor or in the area, and two or three infantry regiments in garrison besides auxiliary troops.

The problem of Nova Scotia was not solved for the British with the deportation of the Acadians in 1755. Some Acadians managed to escape and bitterly sought vengeance. Raids on British outposts multiplied and entire regiments had to be posted to them. The soldiers hardly dared leave their forts, and even wood-cutting parties required heavy escorts. Some of the Acadians had become experts at partisan warfare and were assisted by Abenakis and Micmac Indians. Arms and supplies were sent, while from Canada, officers well versed in bush warfare arrived to train these aggrieved men. The guerrilla activity had immediate repercussions in the whole area. If the Acadian raiders could maintain a permanent threat on the frontier, and if a sufficient French naval force could be kept in Louisbourg to threaten the western coast of Nova Scotia, the British colony would be hemmed in, just like the western frontiers of Massachusetts and other New England colonies had been for half a century by the French and American Indians.

Loudoun's strategy for taking New France depended upon near-complete control of the seas, especially the North Atlantic (see page 96). Such was essential for the plan that called for the invasion of Canada via the St Lawrence. This plan was impossible without securing Louisbourg, the most powerful naval base in North America. First, it was crucial to neutralize local naval opposition, before executing an amphibious landing on the rocky island. Amherst and

Boscawen planned to land their force of 14 line infantry battalions, 500 rangers, and artillery, supported by marines and sailors, on the same beach as the New Englanders had in 1745. After this they would attempt to take the Royal Battery and Lighthouse Point, enabling them to besiege the town.

The officers at Louisbourg were well aware that they were a target. They knew that strategists in Versailles were concerned with Germany, not naval matters, and that the best efforts of the senior officials of the French Navy would not protect them forever. Following the aborted British attempt to take Louisbourg in 1757, the officers continued to repair the town fortifications, and built field fortifications to try and prevent the British securing a beachhead. Should the British manage to land, the French could only hope to destroy and deny them everything that might be useful, and hold out for as long as possible. The ships in the harbor would be outclassed by the British ships outside, but could be used as floating batteries to hinder fieldworks. Basically the French plan was to use all their resources and forces, the *Compagnies Franches*, the *Canonniers-Bombardiers*, and four regular battalions, to delay the capture of Louisbourg for as long as possible.

THE LANDING

The British armada under Admiral Boscawen sailed from Halifax on May 28. By June 2, it was in the Louisbourg area. French detachments were posted all along the coast and reported to Governor Drucour that the British ships had sailed past "in two files." The winds, which had been strong, were lessening, but fog and drizzling rain set in as the fleet gathered in Gabarus Bay and weighed anchor the next day. HMS *Namur*'s boats were hoisted out and the generals went to reconnoiter the coast. Amherst decided to try landing the next day. The

Major George Scott's Composite Light Infantry Battalion storm ashore in a crashing surf on June 8, 1758. In the foreground are boatloads of light infantrymen from the 60th (Royal American) Regiment just hitting the beach. Beyond them, light infantrymen of the 35th (Otway's) Regiment have already landed and are charging up a small brush-covered hill. (Steve Noon © Osprey Publishing Ltd)

landing troops would be divided into three groups under brigadiers Wolfe, Lawrence, and Whitmore. However, bad weather over the next few days made landing attempts impossible. During this time, the garrison of Louisbourg was strengthened with more sailors, and ten companies of the Cambis Regiment. On the evening of June 7, the weather calmed a bit and Amherst ordered a landing attempt early the next morning.

At 4.00am on June 8, the weather being at last rather good, the British decided to attempt a general landing at Cormorandière Cove, now Kennington Cove, and a rocket was fired as a signal. The boats were filled with soldiers and rowed toward the shore, while warships bombarded the shore defenses. The initial attempt at landing was repulsed by the French, who waited until the boats were in the cove to open a crossfire with guns and musketry. To make matters worse, the wind rose again and made "the surf so great that the troops could not get on shore," noted Amherst. Things were going badly, with boats full of troops all over the bay caught in a rough surf, being fired upon, and unable to land.

In one of the boats was young Brigadier Wolfe leading the left division, consisting of the grenadier companies, the light infantry, the rangers, and the 78th. Searching for a solution, he ordered his boats to row further left of the cove. It worked, and a boatload of light infantry under lieutenants Brown and Hopkins landed in spite of the surf and scrambled up the rocks at Anse aux Sables, a small cove full of rocks overlooked by a steep bluff. Wolfe directed as many boats to it as fast as possible to support the men already on shore, then, armed only with a cane, he jumped into the surf and waded to shore with the Highlanders and grenadiers. They were fired at by a few French soldiers in the area, but the British soon consolidated their position.

The French had not considered a landing likely at Anse aux Sables and had not built extensive defenses or posted many men in that area, due not to negligence, but to the simple fact that they did not have enough men to guard the entire Gabarus Bay. Instead, grenadier companies were stationed as reserves and it was hoped they could push back to the sea the small parties that might land. The French saw Wolfe's men land and the grenadier companies of Artois and Bourgogne arrived to reinforce the piquet, but it was already too late. Hundreds of British troops had landed within minutes. When Wolfe saw the French arriving, he coolly formed his men in rank to return a withering fire, killing the captain and the sub-lieutenant of Bourgogne's grenadier company. The French grenadiers retreated with their wounded. Meanwhile,

Louisbourg seen in the distance from about halfway up the hills to the northwest. This would be what British scouts and Wolfe first saw of Louisbourg in June 1758. (René Chartrand)

Whitmore's and Lawrence's divisions went to Wolfe's landing place, and the beachhead was soon totally secured.

The French position had been turned and their retreat was inevitable. Wolfe's men engaged further French troops, and stormed and took a shore battery at bayonet point, while other British brigades were rushing to join them. Within half an hour, some 4,000–5,000 men had stepped ashore. Pressed by Wolfe's troops, Drucour and de la Houlière ordered the withdrawal of their men back to Louisbourg. They now rightly feared that the French troops still posted at Cormorandière Cove might be cut off. The retreat was effected in good order, although they had to abandon the guns at the shore batteries, which were now useless anyway. British parties followed them but stopped when they got within artillery range of the town's bastions, which opened up a tremendous fire. By noon, the action was over. The landing had been successful, but it was clear that a full-scale siege would have to be undertaken.

The British reported two officers and 37 men killed and 18 men wounded. They thought they had killed over 100 French, which seems a considerable exaggeration, as a French source reports a loss of only 18 men. In the evening, the rest of the Cambis Regiment arrived in town. Over the next two days, despite the weather, the British established a large camp at Gabarus with a perimeter of fieldworks to consolidate their beachhead. French scouts reported to Drucour and his officers that the British were solidly entrenched in great numbers, perhaps as many as 12,000 men having landed, which was remarkably accurate intelligence.

LIGHTHOUSE POINT

With a strong force of about 1,400 men, including four companies of grenadiers, Wolfe left the camp on June 12 to capture Lighthouse Point on the other side of the town. This required a long march through unfamiliar terrain with the possibility of being ambushed. Major Ross was posted with 400 men at the far end of the harbor with orders to entrench. Wolfe and the rest of his force went on, and established a camp near Lighthouse Point in the early afternoon. The small French battery near the lighthouse had previously been abandoned and its cannons thrown over the cliff.

In the afternoon, French volunteers skirmished with British light infantrymen south of the town and spiked two cannons at a battery near White Point. The next day, Ross warned Wolfe that parties of French troops were advancing toward him, but the French did not attack, and retired after burning down a few buildings in the area to prevent the British using them. The next day French gunners in the Island Battery trained some of their guns on Wolfe's position and the tents were struck and moved away to a covered position.

Over the next few days, the troops in the main British camp erected magazines and field hospitals. Supplies were still being landed but the heavy surf made this difficult, and supply ships were attacked by the French gunners on several occasions. General Amherst wanted to secure the heights overlooking the landing site with three redoubts. A strong detachment went out to carry out the order, but ran into a force of some 300 French troops posted in the area and much shooting ensued. The British were reinforced from the camp, and the French were forced to retreat. On June 14, Amherst moved more troops closer to the town, compelling the French volunteer company on the heights overlooking the Dauphin Gate to retreat.

Governor Drucour's sensible decision to demolish the Royal Battery before a siege began meant that the British now had to build siege works to bombard the French ships. They started putting gun positions on Lighthouse Point and at other positions at the far end of the harbor on June 15. French warships fired upon the British positions, but were mainly ineffectual, though they did cause a few casualties. Amherst and his engineers wanted to take Green Hill, west of the town. The Royal Navy could not enter the harbor to eliminate the French ships, so it was necessary to reinforce the battery at Lighthouse Point with the aim of destroying the Island Battery.

From June 19, the siege entered a bombardment phase, which it maintained until the end. The British harbor batteries were now just about ready, and as the evening set in Wolfe ordered the new batteries to return the French ships' fire, causing considerable damage. The following evening the British battery at Lighthouse Point started shelling the French on Battery Island. Furious artillery fire continued through the next day, mainly between Battery Island and Lighthouse Point, as the two were almost face to face. The British commanders saw that to succeed, Battery Island had to be silenced and, on the 22nd, some 400 men were sent to Lighthouse Point to build up the existing gun positions into a large battery. This took three days and nights, with the soldiers constantly menaced by the French artillery fire. They were finished by June 25, and that day managed to destroy the guns of Battery Island.

Over the next few days Amherst received more supplies and artillery, though over 100 boats were lost to bad weather. On June 23, Drucour received word that Boishébert was marching toward Louisbourg with a mixed force of colonial troops, militiamen, and Micmac Indians.

WOLFE TAKES GREEN HILL

The next step for the British was to occupy the heights around the harbor, particularly Green Hill, which was just 1,000 yards west of the Dauphin Bastion and gate. On June 26, Wolfe led four companies of grenadiers and 200 fusiliers

One of the most energetic and engaging figures in the French garrison of Louisbourg was Madame Drucour, the wife of the governor. It was observed that "this lady performed, during the siege, actions which will insure her a place amongst the illustrious persons of her sex; she fired herself three cannons every day to encourage the artillerymen." General Amherst too was impressed by her bravery during the siege and this led to a charming episode of the "lace wars" in the New World. During a truce, Amherst had two pineapples, then a rare delicacy, sent to her as a present. Madame de Drucour returned the courtesy by sending him bottles of wine, and went on firing her three cannons a day. Here Madame de Drucour, in a green dress and white cape-shawl, is holding a portfire stick, helped by an officer of the colonial artillery. (Patrice Courcelle © Osprey Publishing Ltd)

to occupy a height evacuated by the French. Pressing their advantage, the British took Green Hill in the evening. The occupation of Green Hill by the British was bad news for the French. They reasoned that eventually Green Hill would be transformed into a strong British position that would threaten the town's west side. On June 27, the heavy guns in the Dauphin Bastion opened up a brisk fire at the British on Green Hill. The British soldiers sheltered themselves as best they could while trying to build up the works. The next day, a French frigate fired on workers attempting to create a covert-way from Green Hill to the city's Dauphin Gate. The work was interrupted, and the men withdrew to Green Hill. The next couple of days were very dangerous for the British pioneers and soldiers working on the batteries. The French warships in the harbor and the town's batteries poured on a relentless fire, which often caused considerable disturbances, as Drucour noted. But the British were not about to be discouraged, and the work went on. Slowly but surely the British batteries were erected and gradually provided better and better protection as time passed.

With the Island Battery out of action, the possibility that the British squadron might break into the harbor was very real. To prevent this, Drucour and the Marquis Desgouttes agreed to scuttle four ships at the entrance on the night of June 28, leaving them six operational ships in the harbor.

In the early morning of July 1, a force of about 200 men slipped out of the town to gather wood to the north. The British saw the move and engaged them. Turning the situation to their advantage, the British gained possession of two small heights nearer to the town.

The next day, the British decided to build a large semicircular defense on the height they had just taken near the Dauphin Gate, and called it Grenadiers' Redoubt. It was in an excellent position from which to batter down the fortifications on the west side of the city. The French knew it, and also realized that they were in no position to recapture it. Drucour reported that his parties of volunteers could hardly operate outside the city any longer. Given their resources, the best they could do was to cannonade the British troops working on this new redoubt both from the town and from the warships in the harbor. On the British side, work went on in earnest, and almost incredibly, the Grenadier's Redoubt was ready by the evening of July 3, and batteries were built nearby at the same time. Despite heavy French artillery fire, the batteries were soon operational.

On July 3, Boishébert's detachment reached the vicinity of Louisbourg, but this mixed body of Canadians, Acadians, and American Indians was in a miserable state. The supplies they had expected Drucour to send to Miramichi were not there and the force, which was smaller than the 500 men expected, was too short of food and equipment to be fully effective.

That evening, the British started bombarding the French ships with hot shot. The Marquis Desgouttes ordered that only 50 men remain on each ship in case the ships caught fire and exploded, and sent the seamen to serve the guns and repair the works in the bastions, while the marines joined the garrison — this soon became a permanent arrangement. The next day, the bombardment from the new battery at Green Hill continued, returned by cannon fire from the French. A planned French sortie was canceled when French scouts reported that many British troops were nearby.

On July 6, another battery near Grenadier's Redoubt now opened fire specifically on the French ships. It was joined by other batteries in the nearby hills and the mortar battery. The cannonade exchange was very heavy throughout the day. Every once in a while, the British would also fire mortar shells, which burst into Louisbourg. In the evening, one of the British batteries managed to enfilade the frigate *L'Aréthuse*, which withdrew nearer to the town. This meant that the British siege works between Green Hill and the town would be much safer. The British batteries concentrated their fire mostly on the ships in the harbor during July 6 and 7. Wolfe proposed to build another large battery and install the 32-pdr cannons with which to ruin the Dauphin and the King's bastions, and this was approved by Amherst on July 7. Elsewhere, there was a good deal of skirmishing between the French and British advanced posts.

By now, the British bombardment of the town was regular. The women and children, with other civilians unable to bear arms, were huddled into the town's casemates, as these were the safest places. The British gunners tried to avoid the town's hospital, easily plotted because of its chapel's spire, although it was on the trajectory of guns firing on the eastern part of the town's fortifications. As the hospital overflowed, a field hospital was set up under canvas, and was also

James Wolfe (1727–59)

James Wolfe was by any standards a very professional soldier, from a family of professional soldiers. He had risen very quickly through a combination of his own not inconsiderable talents, the assistance of an "Old Army" mafia, and ultimately the patronage of the Duke of Cumberland. His first battle was Dettingen, in the 12th Foot; by 1744 he was a captain in the 4th Foot and was serving on the staff in the following year. Promoted to major, he served as an aide-de-camp to Henry Hawley at Culloden in 1746. On January 5, 1749, after some very complicated maneuvering, he was appointed major of the 20th Foot and then as a result of determined string-pulling became its lieutenant-colonel a year later. He cared deeply about his duty, tried to live on his pay, and suffered an endless run of ill health. Most of his pre-American career was spent in Scotland, where he never ceased trying to improve himself, even hiring a mathematics tutor. He went to America as the quartermaster-general of the abortive Rochefort expedition and emerged from the debacle with sufficient credit to win first a brevet promotion to full colonel and then, on January 23, 1758, an appointment as brigadier-general in North America for the expedition against Louisbourg.

His actions during this campaign demonstrated his ruthlessness and naked ambition. First he attempted to hijack the Louisbourg expeditionary force before its actual commander arrived, then engineered what was in effect a separate command during the siege. Afterwards, in blatant defiance of orders, he went home and arranged his appointment to command the Québec expedition. The command was accompanied by promotion to major-general, at the age of 31. Notwithstanding some very real and unattractive flaws in his character, there is no doubt that Wolfe was the right man for the job. However, it was also his first independent command and, as is often the case, the unaccustomed responsibility sometimes had a paralyzing effect on his decision-making. Furthermore, the ruthless way in which he habitually dealt with both superiors and rivals won him few real friends and ensured that relations with his colleagues would be far from easy. (Topfoto/British Library/HIP)

exposed to the fire of British guns. Drucour sent a drummer under a flag of truce with a letter about this, but nothing was formally resolved. As for the able French soldiers, they were "borne down with fatigue" and preferred sleeping in the streets where they were only exposed to shells, rather than in their barracks where they could be killed by both shot and shell.

On the evening of July 8, Drucour and his officers decided to make a sortie during the night. Between 1.00am and 2.00am on the 9th, a force of about 720 French, under Lieutenant-Colonel Marin of the Bourgogne Regiment, made a sortie to the west of the town. They were divided into two columns and moved in the dark until they came up to a working party, which they captured, then moved against the first British advanced post. It seems that most of the British grenadiers of Forbes' 17th Foot were asleep. The French attacked at bayonet point and carried the advanced post. Some of the British soldiers managed to escape to the second line to give the alarm, but were closely followed by French troops. In the British camp, the drums were beating the general alarm. It was clear to Marin and his men that they would not get much further, and they did not have much time. The workmen with the French soldiers set about demolishing the works as quickly as possible, then the force withdrew to the city with two captured British officers and 28 grenadiers. After a truce to bury the dead, the artillery duels continued through the day, with the French ships particularly targeting Wolfe's batteries on the west side of town. In the evening, the British started building a six-gun battery near Grenadier's Redoubt.

ARTILLERY DUELS

The French ships and town batteries opened up intense fire on the new six-gun battery on July 11. Wolfe's request for seven more 24-pdrs was acted upon, and two additional 32-pdrs were also landed from Boscawen's ships. Considerable damage was caused to the battery by the ships' fire, and work continued on the following days under French fire. It was completed a couple of days later and became operational.

On the outskirts of the British camp, Boishébert's American Indians captured a wagoner to gain information. He managed to escape the next day and reported to Amherst that he had seen about 250 Canadians and American Indians about four miles into the woods. In fact, Boishébert's forces were diminishing fast. His Acadian militiamen from Port Toulouse mostly deserted, as did all the Indians; over 60 men were sick and he reported having only 140 men left by mid-July. There were several more skirmishes between Boishébert's forces and the British in the coming days, but nothing significant was achieved by these run-ins in the woods.

LOUISBOURG, 1758

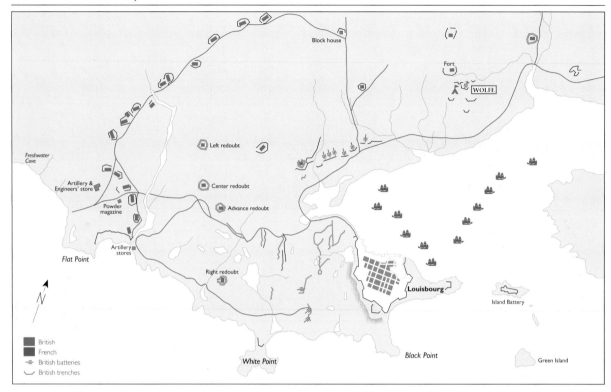

July 14 saw the renewal of a vigorous artillery duel. A new British battery, "Warburton's Battery," of two guns was begun near the six-gun battery at the Grenadier's Redoubt. On the British right, the siege works were slowly approaching the city, and two new batteries were started.

The French work at Black Rock Point which had been started on July 8 was completed on July 15 and mounted two 12-pdrs. Although the weather was again very bad, Amherst reconnoitered the positions to the west of the town and doubled the number of men in the area. The number of men camping further back was the same as the number of troops posted in the trenches between the harbor and Green Hill. This reduced the amount of marching needed, as they could quickly support each other if attacked.

Since July 9, the British had concentrated part of their fire on the ships in the harbor, damaging masts, riggings, and hulls. During the night, the frigate *L'Aréthuse* managed to slip out of the harbor. She was spotted by the British at Lighthouse Point who fired rockets to warn the fleet of her departure. The Lighthouse battery fired at her in the dark and Sir Charles Hardy's squadron gave chase, but the wily and lucky Captain Vauquelin slipped through and got away in the last French ship to leave Louisbourg.

That evening Wolfe ordered a force of rangers and light infantry to capture a French advanced post at Barachois, only 250 yards from the Dauphin Gate. They did so briskly and the French retired into the city. Wolfe sent in reinforcements, and within minutes they were entrenching themselves to secure the position, as well as two nearby hills to their right. French bullets did not hit much in the dark and by morning the British had dug in enough to have good cover.

July 17 saw the British continue their bombardment of the ships in the harbor while strengthening their positions. A communications trench was started to reach the parallel in front of Green Hill, and construction of a mortar battery was begun. Next day, work continued strengthening the British entrenchments. The parapet was made cannon-proof and the development of a parallel trench progressed briskly. Meanwhile, the British batteries on the west side of the city at White Point were getting stronger and more effective. Their main target was now the Dauphin Bastion's cavalier and the spur. The next day, it became clear that on the west side, the British were gaining the upper hand. They managed to enfilade an end of the cavalier on the Dauphin Bastion, and British fire destroyed the carriages of two French guns. A day later, the Dauphin

As the British forces secured positions that enclosed the town and the harbor of Louisbourg, General Amherst made sure that logistics for large and substantial batteries would be available to bombard the city and the ships in the harbor. In spite of persistent difficulties due to the weather, this was accomplished largely thanks to the efforts of Admiral Boscawen's Royal Navy officers and sailors. In this respect, given the complexity of the operation, one of the first of this scale to be attempted by British forces, it stands as a model of what can be achieved by harmonious relations between the army and the navy. Amherst is shown accompanied by several officers inspecting a battery of heavy siege guns manned by personnel of the Royal Artillery. (Patrice Courcelle © Osprey Publishing Ltd)

Bastion's spur was reduced to silence and its cavalier was seriously damaged, with several embrasures destroyed. The damage to the bastion was severe and the British reported that its fire considerably slackened. At night, however, the French made repairs and opened up "a great fire" from the bastion, but only inflicted light casualties on the British.

LOSS OF THREE FRENCH SHIPS

On July 21 the British gunners firing at the French ships had a great stroke of luck. One of their mortar shells squarely hit the poop deck of *L'Entreprenant*, setting fire to the ship. The fire was impossible to put out, and the flames spread to *Le Célèbre* and *Le Capricieux*. *L'Entreprenant* blew up and the two other ships were almost totally consumed by 7.00pm. It was a heavy loss for the French, and Wolfe's batteries could now fire almost unhindered. Bombardment of the Dauphin Bastion was accordingly very heavy, and embrasures were badly damaged. Drucour noted that its cavalier was so weakened that it could crumble at any time.

Two new British batteries south of the town, consisting of 13 24-pdr cannons and seven mortars, went into action on July 22 and fired on the Queen's Bastion. A British battery of four 24-pdr guns was started on the left side of the King's Bastion. The British bombardments finally set on fire the large building housing the barracks, the chapel, and the governor's quarters, which the British called the citadel. There were also fires in the town, so part of the garrison was occupied with firefighting. Many French guns in batteries all over the town were knocked out of action.

On July 23, on the British left, a second parallel was started, which crept ever closer to the Dauphin Bastion, while a small redoubt was begun on the right. Again, the British gunnery was very effective, starting many fires in the town. Some 400 sailors finished the battery to the left of the King's Bastion. At 10.00pm, the wooden barracks originally built by the British and New Englanders in 1745–46 went up in flames. Amherst commented that perhaps they should not have done this, no doubt already wondering how he would lodge his troops once the town surrendered.

After inspecting the Dauphin Bastion at dawn on July 24, Drucour concluded that it would "soon be out of use," and that the French batteries were generally "in a sad state." The British continued to pour a heavy fire into the town and "silenced the guns" in the Queen's Bastion. The British battery on the right side of the King's Bastion was completed and opened fire in the afternoon. Another battery containing five guns was started next to the four-gun battery at the left of the King's Bastion. The French maintained a heavy fire against them, but the British were now so close that they could fire muskets into the embrasures and stop the French from firing their guns.

CAPITULATION

On July 25, the British batteries again successfully bombarded their various targets. The fortifications were crumbling faster than they could be repaired, and a breach was reported in the Dauphin Bastion. As a French officer described,

> as our batteries and ramparts had been very much damaged these three days, and as the fire of the enemy's small arms made it impracticable for us to maintain ourselves on those ramparts which we were endeavoring to repair ... a breech had been [made] in the Dauphin Bastion." (Knox, *Historical Journals*, vol.3)

Scaling ladders were sent to the trenches in preparation for an assault. By now, the town offered a pitiful sight. Many of its buildings were burned and others partly demolished by the intense bombardments of the last few weeks. There was hardly a structure which did not have pieces of shells or cannonballs embedded in its walls. The town's population was shell-shocked, having been traumatized by the intense bombardments and from huddling in casemates day and night for weeks on end.

The following night, captains John Laforey and George Balfour led 600 sailors and marines into the harbor in longboats under cover of fog to attack the two remaining French warships. *Le Prudent* went up in flames, and *Le Bienfaisant* was quickly towed to the other end of the harbor.

By the time the sun rose on July 26, the day had already been disastrous for the garrison of Louisbourg. The capture of the ships was the *coup de grâce* for the defenders' morale. The bombardments had caused a breach in the Dauphin Bastion and another would soon be apparent in the King's Bastion. Of the 52 cannons opposed to the British batteries, 40 had been knocked out of action. Drucour bowed to the inevitable and sent a message to Amherst proposing terms for a capitulation.

At 8.00am, Boishébert noted that the cannon fire constantly heard in the distance for weeks, night and day, had ceased. Negotiations were under way. The French garrison hoped to obtain the "honors of war," but Amherst and Boscawen decreed that the garrison was to surrender as prisoners-of-war. The conditions proposed insulted Drucour and his senior officers. After such a valiant defense they felt they and their men deserved the honors of war. Drucour asked for better terms, but Amherst was adamant. Mortified, Drucour and his officers resolved to die fighting. However, Commissaire-Ordonnateur Jacques Prévost begged the military officers to reconsider, as their sacrifice would not alter the military outcome of the siege, and would put the civilians and wounded at great risk. Their first duty was to afford some protection to the

A view of the siege of Louisbourg from near Lighthouse Point. The French ships can be seen corralled in the harbor, and the British ships are ranged outside. The British soldiers and marines are busy working, while their officers watch the city closely through a telescope. (National Archives of Canada, C-005907)

civilians and the weak, Prévost argued, rather than save their pride. Bowing to this inexorable logic, and perhaps remembering the horrific aftermath at Fort William Henry the previous year, they reluctantly agreed except for the commanders of the Artois, Bourgogne, and Cambis Regiments. Drucour sent word to Amherst that the garrison would surrender on his terms.

The men of the Cambis Regiment, outraged at having to surrender their muskets and the battalion's colors to the hated British, mutinied, broke their muskets, seized the colors, and burned them. The other troops were calmer, although some looting and theft was reported. Some French officers even feared that the British might take revenge for the American Indian attack on the prisoners at Fort William Henry the preceding year.

On the morning of July 27, the three senior British grenadier companies took over the Dauphin Gate from the French sentries. At 12 noon, the garrison laid down their arms and 11 remaining colors. In terms of casualties, the French reported 102 killed and 303 wounded of their land forces at the time of the surrender. The British reported 172 killed and 355 wounded of their land forces, a total of 527. These figures vary little from one account to the other. Most of the casualties occurred during the daily artillery duels and the French gunners did remarkably well under adverse circumstances. There were more losses among sailors, marines, and civilians on both sides, but no figures are given of their casualties, except that the French had 1,347 sailors and marines

sick and wounded on July 26. Overall, it would appear that the French inflicted five casualties to every four they sustained.

The differences between Abercromby's failure at Ticonderoga and Amherst's conduct of the campaign at Louisbourg in the same month are striking. The patient and methodical Amherst used every advantage at his disposal and wasted none of them; he used his subordinates to the best of their varied talents; he never lost control of the operations and his relations with Admiral Boscawen were exemplary. Amherst was not a brilliant tactician with a genius for battlefield moves like Marlborough or Frederick the Great; he always enjoyed superior numbers to his enemies in all his campaigns and his great quality was that he never wasted that superiority.

Upon receiving the news of the fall of Louisbourg, some in Québec expected the British to attack the capital of New France by late August. In fact, it was

Captains Laforey and Balfour's attack with sailors and marines on Le Prudent *and* Le Bienfaisant *in Louisbourg harbor on the night of July 25–26, 1758.* Le Prudent *ran aground and was set on fire, while* Le Bienfaisant *was captured. This painting is probably the large work submitted to the Royal Academy exhibition of 1779 by Richard Paton. This and his other paintings of the events are based on sketches by a Midshipman Young who was one of the boarding party in the action. (National Archives of Canada, C-143388)*

already too late in the year to mount such an expedition because of the difficult sailing conditions of the St Lawrence River and the short season of good weather. As it was, Montcalm's incredible victory at Ticonderoga against Abercromby's army, and Drucour's stubborn resistance until the end of July, had given Canada another year under the French flag.

SECURING ATLANTIC CANADA

Once in possession of Louisbourg, Amherst wished to consolidate his position. He began by sending the French garrison and Louisbourg's civilian population back to Europe in August. Lieutenant-Colonel Lord Rollo was sent to Île Saint-Jean, (renamed by the British as St John's island, and later Prince Edward Island) as it was included in the capitulation. As in Nova Scotia three years earlier, the island's Acadian population was deported and their dwellings destroyed. Over 2,400 Acadians were reported embarked for France by November.

Now enjoying total naval control of the area, Boscawen and Amherst quickly resolved to send a squadron and troops to the Gaspé Peninsula, to destroy a number of French fishing establishments there that could supply Acadian partisans. The force arrived at Gaspé Bay on September 4. As there were no French military forces in the area, the troops landed unopposed, rounded up anybody they found, leveled to the ground whatever stood, and sank fishing boats. These actions were repeated further to the southwest of the peninsula's coast at Grande-Rivière, and Pabos. But Wolfe wished to strike much closer to the St Lawrence, and sent Major John Dalling with some 300 men by land from Gaspé Bay to Mont-Louis, on top of the peninsula, at about 93 miles east of Matane. After a difficult five-day march edging the shore, they reached Mont-Louis on September 19, razed the place and came back, manning the boats seized there. Some fishermen and their families escaped into the woods, but hundreds were rounded up by the British and deported to France. Wolfe sent another party under Colonel James Murray as far south as Miramichi with orders to destroy it. Some resistance was expected here, but on September 15 Murray's force reached the settlement, found it abandoned, and razed it.

With Louisbourg fallen, the British were now able to deal with the persistent aggravation from the French and Indian raiding parties based to the west of Nova Scotia. A 2,000-man force under Brigadier-General Robert Monckton sailed from Louisbourg on August 28, and landed at the mouth of the St John River on September 20, at the site of the modern city of St John, New Brunswick. A fort was immediately built and named Fort Frederick. As the British had received exaggerated reports that Boishébert was lurking in the area with hundreds of men, Monckton sent rangers up the river to find them. They traveled some 80 miles up the river without finding the rumored force of 500

men and 200 Indians which was, in fact, imaginary. However, the area was now securely in British hands, and the force spent the rest of the fall burning isolated dwellings and rounding up hapless civilians for deportation. Some Acadian partisans remained hidden, and the hazardous situation in that area was never really resolved until the end of the war in North America.

The 22nd, 28th, 40th, and 45th regiments were left in garrison at Louisbourg with a company of rangers over the winter of 1758–59. In 1759, the 28th and the rangers went to Québec with Wolfe, along with the grenadier companies of the three other regiments, forming the famous "Louisbourg Grenadiers" during that campaign. The 28th was replaced by Colonel Jonathan Bagley's Massachusetts Provincial Regiment.

Although the fortress was badly damaged and the town partly in ruins from the 1758 siege, there was still anxiety in Britain and in New England that Louisbourg might be recaptured by the French or, as in 1748, returned to France at the end of the war. Thus in February 1760, it was "His Majesty's orders and Mr. Pitt's," that "all the Fortifications, Works and Deffences whatever shall be totally demolished and Razed." The demolition was hard work, and a company of miners was raised in England especially for the purpose. By the late fall, all the works had become piles of rubble and Louisbourg was a fortress no more. Thereafter, only small detachments of regulars were posted to the town, whose population consisted mostly of dependents from the garrison and various naval establishments. In 1768, its small garrison was withdrawn and what remained of the town's site was eventually abandoned.

TAKING BACK THE OHIO
FORT DUQUESNE, 1758

The season had so far been a mixed one for the British, the success of Louisbourg tainted by the failure at Ticonderoga. However, late summer brought more good news for the British. Since the previous year Lieutenant-Colonel Bradstreet had been eager to attack Fort Frontenac on Lake Ontario, the supply base for the French western outposts. He got his chance in August 1758, leading a force of over 2,500 men, provincials, militia, and Royal Americans. They passed the ruins of Oswego, and sailed across Lake Ontario, avoiding contact with three French ships, and arrived at Fort Frontenac on August 25 to find only 110 men there, plus nine ships and 60 cannon. All fell easily into Bradstreet's hands before Vaudreuil could rush reinforcements to the fort, which was then destroyed. This major provincial triumph lost the French control of Lake Ontario, and cut communications between Canada and Fort Duquesne at a time when that post needed all the support possible, as the British were aiming to reverse old wrongs.

FORT DUQUESNE

The expedition to take Fort Duquesne was led by Brigadier John Forbes, the Scottish colonel of the 17th Foot, who was a fine soldier with many years experience, and who believed in studying the art of war from all sources to enable him to command effectively in the terrain. He reached Philadelphia in April 1758, and soon ran into the same difficulties that had earlier afflicted Braddock. He finally mustered a force over 6,000 men, comprising provincials from all the central colonies, Montgomery's Highlanders, and a battalion of Royal Americans, as well as many southern American Indians.

His expedition toward the fort was different to Braddock's in several ways. For a start the route was shorter, originating in Philadelphia. Forbes went against the advice of land-hungry Americans of the Ohio Company who

Here a senior officer of the Royal Regiment of Foot, and an officer of the Grenadier Company, 46th Regiment of Foot who is wearing parade dress, listen to an infantry officer. The infantry officer is wearing field dress, a plain red "frock," and carrying his sporting gun, powder flask, and shot bag. In the background are a fifer and drummer of the 35th Foot. They wear coats of facing color, in this case orange, with cuffs, lapels, and linings of red, with decoration of regimental pattern lace. (Gerry Embleton © Osprey Publishing Ltd)

wanted to use Braddock's old road, repair it, and turn it into a free short-cut to their would-be possessions. One of those who urged this was Washington, whose motives may or may not have been disinterested. He had endured several years of frontier warfare, still without a regular commission, but he served Forbes loyally with his Virginian provincials.

Forbes' highly motivated and trained second-in-command, Lieutenant-Colonel Henri Bouquet of the 60th Foot, was actively involved in drawing up battle plans and devising tactics for wilderness fighting. His plan of marching in the woods focused on constant scouting and destruction of any ambush met. The plan formulated for the expedition was to construct forts and maintain a secure line of communications as they advanced, a very different approach to that of Braddock.

The forward elements of the column began to move out in late June. The march was slow, and halted for several weeks at a time to build first Fort Bedford, at Raystown, and then Fort Ligonier at Loyalhannon Creek. By September 6, the forward elements under Bouquet were within 40 miles of Fort Duquesne. Forbes, with the larger part of the force, remained further back, hampered by discipline and supply problems. The autumn rains delayed progress still further. Forbes had been hit with severe dysentery, which gradually wrecked his health altogether, and he was being carried on a litter between two horses.

The French position at Fort Duquesne was still fairly formidable, with a garrison of some 1,200 militia and marines, supported by some 1,000 American Indian warriors. The garrison did not have a large contingent of regulars, as Vaudreuil was confident in the support of the American Indians in the area. As the march progressed however, the British were negotiating with the

Louis-Antoine de Bougainville (1729–1811)

Born north of Paris in 1729, Bougainville joined the military in 1750, and in 1753 became an adjutant in the Picardie Regiment. In 1754, he left the army and traveled to London to serve on the staff of the French ambassador. In 1756, Bougainville received his commission as captain, and sailed to New France as Montcalm's aide-de-camp. Bougainville's first experience of warfare was in August 1756 when he was part of the assault on Fort Oswego. While in North America he met Celuta, the daughter of one of the Iroquois chiefs, and they had a child together in 1758. He was a valuable asset to Montcalm, both assisting him directly, and carrying out detached assignments. Sent to France in late 1758 to try and obtain reinforcements, he failed to persuade the French authorities to help New France. Nevertheless the trip was a personal success for Bougainville since, perhaps as a consolation as well as a compliment to his general, he was promoted from captain to colonel. In the final stages of the Québec campaign, he was given an important independent command. His failure in this undoubtedly stemmed in the first instance from being over-promoted. After the surrender of Montréal, Bougainville, along with the other French officers, was transported back to France aboard British ships. He was placed under parole, and could not participate in the war continuing in Europe until 1762, instead cultivating a hedonistic lifestyle in Paris. Following the end of the war, he was a successful scientist and explorer. (National Archives of Canada, C-010601)

local tribes. They wished particularly to win over the Delawares, who had sided with the French. Ligneris, the commandant at Fort Duquesne, had neglected relations with the local tribes over recent months, and after a series of meetings many of the tribes, including some previously allied with the French, decided to side with the British.

At Fort Ligonier, Bouquet made a major operational error and allowed a disaster to occur. Major James Grant got permission from Bouquet, leading the vanguard, to take 800 regulars and provincials, push toward Fort Duquesne, make a reconnaissance, and harrass the fort. As he believed the fort to be garrisoned by only 600 men, Bouquet agreed to the plan, and the men set off, and were within five miles of the fort by September 13. The next day, Grant divided the force into three columns, sending one column toward the fort, setting another up in an ambush position, and remaining with the third behind. The French attacked out of the fort, killing the officer in charge of the front column, and scattering the others. As Grant reported to Bouquet, the plan went badly wrong:

Advancing through the wilderness are, from front, a light infantryman, an officer of the 40th Foot, a grenadier of the 60th Regiment of Foot, a private of Gage's Light Infantry, and soldiers of the 55th Foot. (Gerry Embleton © Osprey Publishing Ltd)

For about half an hour after the enemy came from the fort, in different parties, without much order and getting behind forces they advanced briskly, and attacked our left where there were 250 men. Captain MacDonald was soon killed ... our people being overpowered, gave way, where those officers had been killed ... the 100 Pennsylvanians who were posted on the right at the greatest distance from the enemy, went off without orders and without firing a shot. In short in less than half an hour all was in confusion ... we were fired upon from every quarter

An engraving of Washington raising a flag at Fort Duquesne following its abandonment by the French. (Library of Congress)

> ... Orders were to no purpose, fear had then got the better of every other passion and I hope I shall never see again such pannick among troops. (Bouquet, *Papers II*)

Although 400 men and officers were able to escape, some 200 were killed or captured, and Grant was forced to surrender. A panic-stricken rout was only halted by Bouquet at the base camp. British morale was now very low, and was also depressed by the wet autumn weather and early snows.

Following this action, the French tried to build on their advantage with an attack by 500 French and American Indians on Fort Ligonier on October 12. The French managed to push two British forward reconnaissance units back toward the fort before a British counterattack under the British commander Burd forced the French to withdraw. Though relatively minor, this failed skirmish further lowered morale at Fort Duquesne, where the troops had been suffering from lack of supplies since the fall of Fort Frontenac in August.

By early November, the main British force was established at Fort Ligonier, and reports were coming in of low morale at Fort Duquesne. On November 18, a strong British force headed out to try and exploit the situation. They arrived at the fort on November 24, just in time to see the French blowing up their own fort. Ligneris and his garrison withdrew to Presqu'Île and Le Boeuf. The next day the British marched in and took control of the remains of the fort that had started the war three years previously. Returning to Philadelphia, where he died a hero, Forbes left Bouquet in charge of building an outpost on the site, named Fort Pittsborough, which was soon shortened to "Pitt." He also ordered that the grisly debris of Braddock's column in the nearby forest was finally given a decent burial.

PREPARATIONS FOR 1759

The campaign having been successful, the regulars were sent back to Philadelphia to winter, while the provincial troops were stationed along the newly built road and its protecting forts. After a successful season, Pitt made some changes in preparation for the following year's onslaught. Abercromby was sacked, and Amherst appointed to replace him. The young James Wolfe left America and returned to Britain suffering ill health. He was received at home as a hero. His actions would be revealed as a shrewd and ruthless political move by the following spring.

The campaigns of 1758 had definitely shifted the momentum of the war in Britain's favor. With Fort Duquesne in the south, Fort Frontenac in the center, and Louisbourg in the north all taken by the British, and the American Indian alliance crumbling, the French faced the ruin of the defensive strategy which they had pursued with such success, despite feeble resources, for five years. It seemed inevitable that the British would attack again, and stronger, the following year. It was characteristic of Vaudreuil that he should hunt for a scapegoat. His correspondence with France now demanded Montcalm's recall on every pretext from outrageous comments in public, to military incompetence; the reply was that he should defer to Montcalm in all things military. Montcalm meanwhile, was in despair over the corruption and mismanagement that was in large part responsible for the loss of Fort Duquesne. He would have liked nothing better than an honorable recall; however, he was determined to see his duty out to the end. The Canadian civilian population was becoming uneasy, having suffered wild inflation, the shortage of every necessity due to the blockade by the Royal Navy, and a poor harvest. It seemed that Old France, preoccupied with disasters in Europe, had abandoned the colony to its fate.

In desperation, Montcalm sent his principal aide-de-camp, Captain de Bougainville, home to France to appeal for support in the defense of the colony and with Montcalm's resignation letter. If it was an ultimatum it failed, for Bougainville's audience with the king and la Pompadour only achieved the confirmation of Montcalm's position, and promotion of Bougainville, Montcalm, Lévis, and Bourlamaque by one rank each. Vaudreuil was formally instructed to defer to Montcalm on all military matters. In reality nothing changed, for this merely reflected the existing position and all that the new orders really achieved was to further embitter an already sour relationship. The only practical help that Bougainville could wring from France was a few hundred replacements and a few shiploads of supplies to meet immediate needs.

RUPERT'S LAND

HUDSON'S BAY COMPANY

Lake Superior

Michilimackinac

Lake Michigan

Lake Huron

Frontenac

Niagara

Detroit

Lake Ontario

Lake Erie

Ohio

N E W

F R A N C E

C A N A D A

St Lawrence

Québec

Montréal

Ticonderoga

Albany

Boston

New York

Philadelphia

Gulf of St Lawrence

NEWFOUNDL

Île St Jean

Île Royale

Louisbourg

ACADIA

Beauséjour

Halifax

NOVA SCOTIA

BRITISH 13 COLONIES

Williamsburg

L O U I S I A N A

Chartres

Vincennes

Ohio

Mississippi

Mobile

New Orleans

FLORIDA

GULF OF MEXICO

ATLANTIC OCEAN

BAHAMA ISLANDS

CUBA

MEXICO

HISPANIOLA

HAITI

Territories in North America

Britain

France

Spain

Disputed

0   250

0   400

PART 3
SIEGES AND SURRENDER

CHRONOLOGY

1759

July 26	French Fort Niagara capitulates
July 26	French Fort Carillon abandoned
July 31	French Fort Saint-Frédéric abandoned
July 31	British attack Montmorency Falls
September 13	Battle of the Plains of Abraham
September 17	Surrender of Québec

1760

April 28	Battle of Sainte-Foy
May 9	French siege of Québec lifted
September 8/9	Montréal surrenders

1763

February 10	Treaty of Paris
February 15	Treaty of Hubertusburg
May 10–October 15	Siege of Fort Detroit, Pontiac's War
July 31	Battle of Bloody Run
August 5/6	Battle of Bushy Run
August 10	Fort Pitt relieved
October 7	Royal Proclamation of 1763

1764

December	End of Indian Uprising

THE YEAR OF MIRACLES
CAMPAIGNS OF 1759

Given their success the previous year, it was natural that the British adopt a similar multi-pronged strategy for the campaign for 1759. General Amherst, the new commander-in-chief, would lead a mixed force of provincials and regulars against Fort Carillon and Fort Saint-Frédéric, moving gradually towards their final destination of Montréal. Brigadier John Prideaux would campaign from the rebuilt Fort Oswego, striking towards Fort Niagara. A small force was tasked with reopening communications between Fort Pitt and Fort Ligonier in the Ohio Valley, and then establishing a force at Fort Pitt to attack forts Presqu'Île and Venango. The main thrust of the year however, would forge farther into Canada, aiming to take Québec.

Montcalm was aware of the importance of Québec to the British strategy for the year, and early in the year he had to make some hard decisions about his strategic priorities. Thus far he had successfully and indeed very aggressively defended the New York frontier, but the fall of Louisbourg clearly pointed to a direct assault on Québec in the summer of 1759. When Bougainville returned to New France in the spring, he had brought with him the instruction that Montcalm was to defend the capital with all his paltry resources.

THE OHIO VALLEY

The regulars of 1/60th Foot marched for Lancaster in Pennsylvania on May 31. They spent a month effecting repairs and mounting security along the road before they reached Fort Bedford, one of the sites built the previous year. June and early July were then employed fighting skirmishes whilst moving supplies and reinforcements to Fort Pitt. The 1/60th Foot received orders to march from Fort Pitt toward Fort Ligonier, but as they were moving out they received the news that the French had abandoned both Venango and Presqu'Île as well as several other outposts following

the fall of Fort Niagara to the British. The 1/60th marched to the forts anyway, to confirm that they had been abandoned. While the regulars returned to Fort Pitt where five companies remained for the winter, the provincials were sent north to winter at the newly British forts. The rest of the battalion was sent along the road to Lancaster to maintain lines of communication over the winter.

Captain Thomas Davies' View of the Lines at Lake George, 1759. Amherst's camp is in the middle distance, with the no-man's land of Lake George beyond it. In the foreground are a Stockbridge Indian and a Ranger. (Fort Ticonderoga Museum)

NIAGARA

Brigadier Prideaux was tasked with taking Fort Niagara, and then heading eastwards down the St Lawrence. His second-in-command was Sir William Johnson, which gained the expedition Iroquois allies. This campaign was to cut communications between Canada's outposts in the west, and stop any plans to retake Fort Pitt. Prideaux had two regular regiments, a battalion of Royal Americans, over 3,000 provincials, and 900 previously neutral Iroquois. By

In May 1758, General Forbes ordered that all new levies be clothed in green cloth, and subsequently the Pennsylvania Regiment changed its uniform from standard coats with red facing to the more practical green short jacket, as worn by the center private. The weapons carried by the Pennsylvania provincials were varied, since recruited men were encouraged by cash payments to bring their own blankets and muskets. Many of those of German origin and frontiersmen brought their long Pennsylvania rifles. The government provided cartridge boxes and tomahawks. On the left is a private of the Pennsylvania Regiment wearing the blue provincial uniform adopted in 1760. Blue was the color seen in most other colonies. The private on the right from the Delaware (Lower Counties) Companies, wears the same green uniform ordered in 1758, which the Delaware troops seem to have retained, unlike Pennsylvania. (David Rickman © Osprey Publishing Ltd)

early spring the forward elements of his force had reached Oswego, where they began to fortify the area. When news of the British force reached the commander of Fort Niagara, he began to repair the fort after winter damages. He had a garrison about 400 strong, and the fortifications at the fort were reasonable, but he continued improvements to the defenses in preparation for the inevitable attack.

Prideaux left some of his force at Oswego, and sailed for Niagara in early July. They arrived on July 7, and prepared to invest the fort. Skirmishes were frequent

FORT NIAGARA, 1759

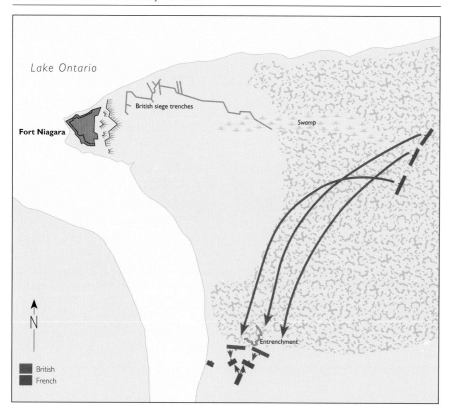

as the British advanced. By mid-July they had surrounded the fort, and the formal siege began with artillery. Prideaux was killed early in the siege, when he walked in front of one of his own mortars as it was being fired, and Johnson took control. Hearing that a relieving force was on its way, Johnson called for reinforcements from Oswego. The French relief force came from French posts on Lake Erie, and included many of the hardiest and most dreaded of the partisans and *coureurs de bois*. The two forces met on July 24. The British were outnumbered two to one, but managed to rout the French and take prisoners. The commander of the British force, Lieutenant-Colonel Eyre Massy commented: "the men received the enemy with vast resolution, and never fired one shot, until we could almost reach them with our bayonets." The following day the Niagara commander attempted a raid on the British trenches which failed, and the day after he surrendered. The surrender of Fort Niagara secured Lake Ontario, and the elimination of the relief force made it a double victory securing Lake Erie as well. Overall, the campaign had effectively destroyed the French presence on the western frontier. Though a little-remembered battle, it was quite as crucial to the British war effort as Québec.

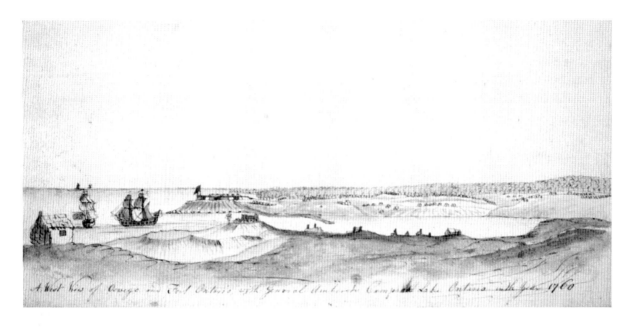

AMHERST'S PROGRESS

Amherst's advance was slow but successful. In March he sent a large raiding party of regulars, rangers, and American Indians to observe and assess the French and the area around Fort Ticonderoga. The force destroyed French supplies outside the fort, captured French soldiers, and drew maps of the defenses.

Amherst gathered troops at the southern end of Lake George in June and prepared for the coming operation. Whilst there, he built Fort George on the entrenchment constructed in 1757, and ensured that forts were built between forts Edward and George to protect his rear. By late July, sufficient reinforcements for his regulars had arrived, and his provincial forces were fully mustered. On July 21, the army sailed north on Lake George, and then started to advance against Fort Ticonderoga. The fort had been reinforced with 4,000 troops in mid-May, but due to the expected attack on Québec, the commander Chevalier de Bourlamaque was ordered to withdraw and attempt to hold the line at the north end of Lake Champlain. However, he decided to hamper the approaching British before withdrawing, so a small but strong force of 400 men was left at the fort to repel the British advance, while the rest of the troops moved to Fort Saint-Frédéric. The rearguard held off Amherst for four days with artillery fire, and Amherst only managed to take the fort after bringing his heavy artillery into range. The rearguard withdrew, and met up with Bourlamaque at Saint-Frédéric, which they blew up a few days later, fearing the British artillery train would soon be upon them. The force then withdrew further to Île aux Noix. Amherst, however, did not follow immediately, but

settled down to rebuild forts Ticonderoga and Saint-Frédéric (Crown Point), and construct ships to dominate Lake Champlain. His scouts were sent out to observe the French on Lake Champlain, and Rogers and his rangers were dispatched on the famous St Francis raid. Amherst began his advance again on October 11, but after an unsuccessful attempt to destroy the French shipping, he decided to winter at Ticonderoga and Crown Point, and advance north on Lake Champlain the following year.

Captain Thomas Davies' A South West View of the Lines and Fort of Tyconderoga, as drawn in 1759 after its capture by Amherst. The view is from the summit of Rattlesnake Mountain, the same vantage point that Rogers' Rangers had used to study enemy activity at the fort over the previous four years. (National Archives of Canada, C-010653)

191

Jeffery Amherst (1717–97)

Jeffrey Amherst was born in Kent, England, to a family of successful lawyers. The choice of military careers for three of the Amherst sons was influenced by a close friend of the family, Lionel Sackville, Duke of Dorset. In 1735, Jeffery was commissioned as an ensign in the 1st Foot Guards. In 1741, the regiment went to Flanders and the following year Major-General John Ligonier noticed him and appointed him as his aide-de-camp. In this role, Amherst was exposed to general staff duties, work for which his methodical character was ideally suited. His first battle was Dettingen in 1743, followed by Fontenoy in 1745. In 1747, no doubt on Ligonier's recommendation, Amherst became ADC to the Duke of Cumberland, King George II's son, and commander-in-chief of the British contingent on the Continent. Amherst campaigned with the duke throughout the war, and following the end of hostilities in 1748 he remained attached to the duke's personal staff. With the outbreak of war in 1756, he was sent to Germany to perform staff work, and the following year was again working for the Duke of Cumberland. He also obtained the colonelcy of the 15th Foot. The duke was, however, totally outmaneuvered by the French and practically had to sign away Hanover. A furious George II recalled his disgraced son and repudiated the agreement. Ligonier was appointed commander-in-chief of the British Army. In January 1758, Amherst was recalled to England. Pitt had heard of the competent and experienced colonel and presented Amherst with a great opportunity: to command the army that would attack Louisbourg, with the rank of major-general in America. Although no doubt influenced by Ligonier's recommendations and Amherst's own qualities, the appointment was a remarkable act of faith on Pitt's part. Amherst had never held any previous field commands and was inexperienced in the coordination of military and naval forces. As it turned out, the stolid and unemotional Amherst was an excellent choice. He was a methodical soldier, shrewdly calculating the elements in his favor without ever losing sight of the ultimate goal which must be victory.

His conduct at Louisbourg fully revealed his capacity as an effective senior commander. He quickly saw that his keenest and best brigadier was Wolfe, and used him to

the fullest. In spite of his dour personality, it was Amherst's ability to communicate efficiently, delegate, and maintain good relations with staff that made him commander-in-chief in North America in 1759. That year, he carried Ticonderoga, and the following year he received the surrender of Montréal. He had, by then, coordinated the approach of three British armies to meet in Montréal, thus achieving the final objective of Loudoun's strategic plan. After the war he went on to become commander-in-chief of the British Army and was elevated to the peerage. As a last honor he was made field marshal in 1795. (Topfoto/ARPL/HIP)

DEPRIVATION, MASSACRE, AND EXILE
THE CIVILIAN FATE

The civilians living in North America during the French and Indian War were affected by the conflict in many and varied ways. Both French and British colonists on the frontier were fearful for their lives and property during the winters when raiding parties roamed unchecked aiming to cause maximum damage to enemy settlements, while civilians living in the French fortresses were wary of their fate if the fortress fell. Rural populations of the hinterland of the French fortresses like Québec suffered raids and destruction during the sieges in the later years of the war, while the Acadian population suffered expulsion from their homeland.

A late 18th-century painting of Québec from Point Levis. The civilians living near Québec during the siege of 1759 were subject to Wolfe's policy of devastation to the surrounding area. Though this campaign did have some military reasoning behind it, many historians feel that this civilian suffering was inflicted simply because of Wolfe's extreme frustration during the siege. (National Archives of Canada, C-012746)

CIVILIANS IN BATTLE

Camp followers often fulfilled valuable roles during campaign, and were susceptible to attack during or after a battle. Braddock sent the camp followers back in 1755, mainly as they were slowing his progress. As the baggage train was destroyed during the battle, his actions probably saved many of the women who were following their husbands into battle. It is difficult to judge how many women and children were killed in the aftermath of battles during the French and Indian War, as they were not included in the official counts and casualty reports.

When the battle was a siege, of course, it was much more difficult to protect the non-combatants after the fall or surrender, of a fort or settlement. Even when an agreement laying out the terms of surrender had been made, commanders could not always force all their troops to comply with the terms. The aftermath of Fort William Henry in 1757 is the most infamous incident of this type, when militia and allied American Indians, possibly drunk on captured rum, massacred all the camp followers as they marched out of the fort. Fort William Henry was not only a tragedy, but shaped interaction between the French and British later in the war. Montcalm was always wary during later actions that similar regrettable acts might occur, while for British forces the atrocity provided a reason for raids and reprisals against French civilians whenever possible. This trend was continuing when the British came into contact with large numbers of civilians later in the war as they made inroads on the territory of New France. Concern for the civilians' fate was consequently a deciding factor in the surrender of Louisbourg in 1758.

DEPRIVATIONS IN NEW FRANCE

Many of the settlers of the Thirteen Colonies were not much affected by the war. The colonies not directly threatened by the conflict did not provide many troops, so civilian life was not disrupted by recruitment, food and supplies were not restricted, and the major British towns were not occupied at any point during the war. The frontier colonies like Pennsylvania and Virginia supplied more troops for the war, and during the early period of the war the frontier settlers suffered constant brutal raids. However, it was the civilians of New France who were most adversely affected, though of course experiences differed between communities.

The most widespread deprivation suffered by the civilians of New France was food shortages. The colonists produced enough food for themselves during peacetime, but they could not also supply the 6,000 regular soldiers shipped

Man reasoning with American Indian warriors who are about to burn a bound captive, possibly during the French and Indian War. Many captives taken by American Indian warriors were subject to a slow, painful death. (Library of Congress)

over during the war. It was planned that the soldiers would therefore be shipped with their own provisions, and that a large supply convoy each year from France would support operations during the season. However, as the war progressed, and the Royal Navy blockade continued, the food supplies slowly dwindled, and the situation hit crisis point in 1757. Although a large flotilla arrived with stores, it was not enough to support both soldiers and civilians. Rationing was imposed to try and stretch the food further. Bad harvests in 1756 and 1757, and a severe winter in 1757–58, worsened the situation, as the population was forced to consume the seed crop of wheat for the following year. Luckily the ships sent from France with replacement seed did reach their destination.

As many of the militia were farmers, the continuation of the war meant a dilemma for the commanders. If the militia were kept out over the harvest, then the yield would be affected, causing food shortages. There was also a good risk that many of the militia would desert during the harvest season to return to their farms. However any allowance made for the harvest could

Human scalp from North America, 18th century. Stretched on a wooden hoop, and painted red with a face. Analysis of the hair has indicated that the victim came from an agricultural village, so may have been taken from a farmer fighting in the militia, or a civilian. (Topfoto/British Museum/HIP)

endanger the security of the entire colony. The two conflicting priorities caused an insoluble dilemma.

By 1758, the British blockade, and the shifting priorities of the French authorities, caused New France to be almost totally abandoned, with supplies, soldiers, and currency diverted to other regions. Not only were civilians suffering a lack of food and essential supplies, but as the war turned in favor of the British, the population of New France had to contend with the presence of first the British-allied American Indians and rangers, and later British Army regulars. French civilians suffered greatly during the siege of Québec when Wolfe had the countryside around the city destroyed, ruining crops and burning villages. Journal entries by British soldiers give insight into these raids. A sergeant-major from a grenadier company wrote that "on the 20th [August] the Louisbourg Grenadiers began their march down the main land of Quebec, in order to burn and destroy all the houses on that side ... [on] the 25th began to destroy the country, burning houses, cutting down corn and the like." However the following year, there is evidence that some units were ordered not to abuse the population as they marched to Montréal.

FRONTIER WARFARE

Warfare along the frontier was brutal, with many settlers taken prisoner or killed by raiding parties. This was not a new phenomenon – raiding and random violence had occurred since the mid-1600s – but the French and Indian War caused a dramatic increase in the efforts to spread fear among the isolated frontier settlements. The development of long raiding by the rangers meant that settlements in the heartland of New France were targeted more and more in the later years of the war.

Living with the American Indians

Mary Jemison was the daughter of Scottish-Irish settlers, who lived near the Pennsylvanian frontier. On April 5, 1758 a raiding party of French soldiers and Shawnee came to the family farm. Almost the whole family was taken captive, and the rest of the family was killed. Mary was forced to walk to Fort Duquesne, where she was given to two Seneca women. The Seneca women adopted her as a sister. She learned Seneca ways and married a Lenape warrior. They had a baby together, but he died while their child was still young. Several years later the British offered money to anyone who returned white captives to them. Mary did not want to leave her American Indian family. Other people in her town wanted to turn her in for the money, so she had to run away and hide twice. Eventually the chiefs decided that she could stay as long as she wanted. She lived her whole life with the Seneca, becoming a member of Seneca society.

James Smith was captured in 1755 by American Indians while working on a road in the Ohio Valley. The warriors took Smith to Fort Duquesne, where he was forced to run the gauntlet between two lines of warriors, who hit him with sticks. Captives were often forced to run the gauntlet. If they acted with strength and courage, they would be kept. James' wounds were bad, but healed quickly and he was soon taken to a village where he underwent a complicated adoption ceremony. At the time, he did not understand the ceremony, and feared that he was to be put to death. After his adoption he was a full member of the village, and hunted and trapped with the men. James lived with the American Indians for four years. In 1759 he left the American Indians to return home.

Jean Lowry's homestead was attacked by a raiding party of American Indians in April 1755. Jean and her five children were taken captive. After marching for four days they were rescued, but a larger American Indian party returned and attacked the group, taking all survivors prisoner. Despite being pregnant, Jean was beaten and tortured many times, and all of her children were taken away from her. Jean may have received such treatment because she refused to cooperate in any way. After she had lost all her children she moderated her behavior in the hope of surviving. She was taken to Fort Venango under the ownership of another warrior. While at the fort, she gave birth to a child who died the same day. She remained at Venango as a servant of the French commanding officer, and was eventually exchanged for French captives in Montréal. There is no indication that she saw any of her children again.

Civilians captured during raids by American Indians allied to the enemy force could experience very different fates. Often it was a terrifying experience, being dragged away from a burning homestead and dead or dying relatives. As they were marched through the wilderness, settlers or troops might try to rescue them, initiating battles and reprisals during which the captives were often wounded or killed. The treatment that a captive received could often depend on their cooperation. Torture or death might be the outcome for a prisoner determined not to accept anything from their captives or do as bidden. On the other hand, compliant captives, and children, might be adopted by Indian families. Male captives were sometimes treated better than female captives. Males could be adopted by families who had lost warriors in battle, and as such they were of greater value to the American Indian tribes.

If lucky, those taken prisoner might be exchanged and eventually return home. Alternatively, they might settle into their new way of life – there are examples of men and women remaining in an American Indian village with a family, taking a full part in community life for many years.

EXILE

The strategically important area of Acadian Nova Scotia had long been a problem area for the British, as the Acadians were subjects of the British Crown, but only as a result of treaty agreements. They were French-speaking, and naturally sympathetic to the French. As well as building forts, including Beauséjour, to defend their interests in the region, the French authorities deliberately stirred Acadian aspirations to independence. Therefore, after the British had captured Fort Beauséjour in 1755, they had to deal with the Acadians who posed a risk to the security of Nova Scotia. The British solution was an oath of allegiance to the British Crown, which the Acadians were required to adhere to. Many of the population, however, had no desire to swear allegiance, they wished to remain neutral, and exempt from military duty. British commanders reported that their mood changed from neutral to hostile when rumors began to circulate of a French fleet arriving in the Bay of Fundy. The British were in a difficult position. The area needed to be secure, and there were also British land speculators waiting to cash in on the excellent lands occupied by the Acadian farms.

British military and colonial officials met in Halifax, and determined that the Acadians should be forcibly removed from their homes and transported to the Thirteen Colonies. They decided against sending them to Québec or Louisbourg because in either place they would provide valuable reinforcements for the militia. The Acadian villages were emptied and the settlers marshaled toward the Bay of Fundy where, over the course of the fall of 1755, ships arrived from the Thirteen Colonies to transport the people. In the end more than 6,000 men, women, and children were transported. Some Acadians, upon receiving word of the British plan, escaped to Québec. Other groups of people withdrew into the woods of Nova Scotia. Some of the men in these groups carried out a guerrilla campaign against the British over the coming years. Many of the Acadian homes and farms were burned to prevent escaped refugees returning to their homes. The British government also hoped that people would surrender to British authorities once they realized their position was hopeless. Many of the Acadians who were sent to the Thirteen Colonies eventually made their way to Louisiana. Some returned to Acadia after the Treaty of Paris and their descendants continue to live in the same districts today. The story of the Acadians was later made famous in Longfellow's poem *Evangeline*.

The British continued their policy of evacuation for most of the war. Following the seizure of Louisbourg in 1758, General Amherst decided to round up and transport the civilian populations in and around Louisbourg, as well as the French colonists on Île Saint-Jean (Prince Edward Island).

A depiction of the exile of the Acadians. (National Archives of Canada)

Evangeline

Longfellow's poem tells the story of a young woman who, along with her fellow Acadians, is torn away from her home and family, and who travels west across America looking for her lover. The following extract, in a rather romantic manner, describes how the people from small close-knit farming communities were dispersed through the Thirteen Colonies:

> Many a weary year had passed since the burning of Grand-Pré,
> When on the falling tide the freighted vessels departed,
> Bearing a nation, with all its household gods, into exile,
> Exile without an end, and without an example in story.
> Far asunder, on separate coasts, the Acadians landed;
> Scattered were they, like flakes of snow, when the wind from the northeast
> Strikes aslant through the fogs that darken the Banks of Newfoundland.
> Friendless, homeless, hopeless, they wandered from city to city,
> From the cold lakes of the North to sultry Southern savannas, –
> From the bleak shores of the sea to the lands where the Father of Waters
> Seizes the hills in his hands, and drags them down to the ocean,
> Deep in their sands to bury the scattered bones of the mammoth.
> Friends they sought and homes; and many, despairing, heart-broken,
> Asked of the earth but a grave, and no longer a friend nor a fireside.
>
> (Henry Wadsworth Longfellow, *Evangeline*, Part 2)

All colonists who took up arms were considered prisoners of war and were subsequently transported to Great Britain along with the French soldiers. Colonists who did not take up arms were sent to France. More than 8,000 people were transported from Cape Breton and Île Saint-Jean. It seems that Amherst decided on this policy after the killings at Fort William Henry, and felt that such treatment was duly deserved.

THE ARMIES OF 1759

WOLFE'S ARMY

At the beginning of 1759, Amherst was commander-in-chief of 23 under-strength battalions of regulars, and many promises of provincial troops, whose numbers finally reached 12,000 in all. These men were divided between the four prongs of the attack for 1759.

Wolfe's army at Québec was smaller than the force that had attacked Louisbourg, since a garrison was required to remain there in case of counter-attacks. Wolfe's planned army was to have numbered 12,000. Sickness, desertions, and other causes, however, reduced the force to 8,500. The army was, rather unusually, almost wholly comprised of infantrymen with a few gunners. There were no cavalrymen and indeed there is no real evidence of even the staff officers being mounted. Even more unusually, with the exception of the rangers, there were no provincial troops. Almost the entire force was regulars.

The army was organized into three brigades, under brigadier-generals Monckton, Murray, and Townshend. Robert Monckton was the most senior and an experienced and dependable officer. He had been in Nova Scotia since 1752, had taken Fort Beauséjour in 1755 and since then served as lieutenant-governor of the colony. James Murray was a prickly character, and he and Wolfe did not get on from the outset. George Townshend obtained his position through his political connections and was completely unqualified for the job. Wolfe was unimpressed at this imposition and his letter of welcome, while polite, contained a barbed reference to his unwanted subordinate's lack of experience. It was hardly a good start, but at least relations between the French senior officers were no better and in some cases rather worse.

There was a provisional battalion of marines under Lieutenant-Colonel Boisrond, and also a considerable number of marines were landed from the

British officers and men wearing winter dress. On the left is a sergeant of the 58th Regiment of Foot wearing a capot, with his equipment belted over it. British soldiers were not issued overcoats, although a small number of "watch coats" were issued to each battalion for use by sentries, so it is certain that thick winter coats must have been improvised for the severe American winter. In the center is a grenadier of the 28th Regiment wearing his uniform coat buttoned over a second coat, and "ice-creepers" are strapped to his feet to stop him slipping. Some of the British garrison of Québec over the winter of 1759 were issued French uniform coats as part of their winter clothing — the private on the right, of the 17th Regiment, wears his over his own red coat. (Gerry Embleton © Osprey Publishing Ltd)

ships. In theory as many as 1,945 rank and file would have been carried as part of the various ships' complements at Québec, although not all of them may have been available for service on land and none will have been commanded by anyone senior to Boisrond, since field officers of marines did not serve afloat.

Included among the marines were a fair number of regular infantrymen. The four companies of the 62nd had been embarked as marines on board the

fleet in January 1758, and sailed with Boscawen for Halifax and Louisbourg, where they took part in various actions usually ascribed to "marines." One company was carried home in September 1758 but the other three remained, together with the companies of the 69th Foot, and fought in various land operations during the siege and took part in the demonstration off Beauport on September 13. Both they and the 69th companies were eventually drafted into the ranks of the infantry when the fleet sailed for home before the winter.

Print by Richard Short of British infantry parading on the Place d'Armes in Québec in 1759 after its capture. In the background can be seen the bombed-out houses and buildings in which British troops were quartered during the harsh winter of 1759—60, and subsequently were looted as a result. (National Archives of Canada, C-361)

The Louisbourg Grenadiers, three companies taken from the garrison there, and the light infantry battalion of 200 rank and file under Major Dalling, together received orders from Colonel Guy Carleton. The ten companies of grenadiers of the line were to be commanded by Lieutenant-Colonel Burton as one corps. Major Dalling's little battalion was not the only regular light infantry corps serving with the army. Following Amherst's order of April 14, 1759, each regular battalion serving in North America had its own light company and when the light infantry acted in one corps, they were under the command of Lieutenant-Colonel Howe.

The figure on the left is a light infantry officer of the 40th Regiment of Foot, 1758, wearing dress adapted for duty in the wilderness. The hat has become a packed skull cap; the gold lace has been taken off the coat, and the tails are cut short. The breeches would probably have been exchanged for mitasses when in the forest. The center figure is a private of Gage's 80th (Light Armed) Regiment of Foot in the brown uniform they wore from the time they were raised until 1761 or 1762, when they were issued with a more colorful uniform. On the right is a grenadier from Burton's 95th Regiment of Foot, wearing the red uniform faced with light gray that they were issued in 1761. (David Rickman © Osprey Publishing Ltd)

At the outset of the expedition Wolfe disparagingly dismissed his rangers as "six new raised companies of North American Rangers – not complete, and the worst soldiers in the universe." While these comments have predictably enough been held against him, they were only too accurate, for while Captain Joseph Gorham had a solid core of veterans, the best of the available men were already serving on the New York frontier. All too many of the provincials who were now enlisting in the ranger companies were the scrapings, attracted by the higher pay of the ranging service, the supposed easy discipline, and the opportunities for plunder. Most of their service during the coming campaign against Québec was

to consist of plundering and burning, and terrorizing the civilian population. Notwithstanding Gorham's long experience and solid ability, it is perhaps unsurprising that Wolfe insisted on placing the rangers under the overall command of a regular officer.

British infantry uniforms of the 1750s. From left, a corporal, 45th Foot; grenadier, 15th Foot; private, 43rd Regiment of Foot, marching order; sergeant, 27th (Inniskilling) Regiment of Foot. (Gerry Embleton © Osprey Publishing Ltd)

Preparation

Wolfe sailed from Spithead on February 14, arrived at Halifax on April 30, and was at Louisbourg two weeks later. There he found rather fewer troops waiting for him than he had expected. A certain level of wastage had always been anticipated, but the assumption that this could be made good through local recruiting in North America had proved, according to Amherst at least, to be a mistake. Nor had any reinforcements come from the West Indies – quite the reverse as it happened, since the available recruits were actually sent there, or to Germany, rather than to North America. Consequently, instead of the 12,000 men discussed in London, Wolfe found himself at the head of only around 400 officers and just over 7,000 regular infantry, besides 300 gunners and a battalion of marines.

Wolfe expected to supplement his force with an additional three companies of grenadiers and at least one company of light infantry from the Louisbourg garrison. Unfortunately, the orders which the governor of Louisbourg had received from London directed him to give up the three grenadier companies but made no mention of any other troops. Consequently, when Wolfe asked for the grenadiers and for one or more of the companies of light infantry, the governor quite flatly refused to part with the light infantry, despite Wolfe's hopeful offer of some of his New England rangers in their place.

Wolfe's orders for May 1759 are taken up with instructions for his officers to check the condition of both men and arms, and to ensure that each soldier was provided ammunition. Time was also employed practicing landings from a selection of flat-bottomed boats, whaleboats and cutters, and also maneuvering on land. Such rehearsals seem to have been successful, as Wolfe was said to be well pleased with the performance of the men upon inspection.

MONTCALM'S ARMY

Following his instructions from France, Montcalm marched the bulk of his regulars north to defend Québec. The remainder, the La Reine Regiment and the two battalions of the Berry Regiment, under Brigadier Bourlamaque, eventually evacuated forts Carillon and Saint-Frédéric under pressure from Amherst and retired to a new defensive position at Île aux Noix at the bottom of Lake Champlain. In theory, by stripping the southern front Montcalm was leaving Montréal vulnerable to a determined offensive, but in the event he judged both the New York army and Amherst correctly. Far from rolling straight over Bourlamaque, Amherst opted for a slow and methodical advance and wasted the summer in building a fleet and a new fort – Crown Point – on the site of the destroyed Fort Saint-Frédéric.

The core of Montcalm's army at Québec was a force of eight regular infantry battalions (mostly the 2nd battalions of their regiments) from metropolitan France. Although well experienced, and with a good history of success, they were badly worn down by constant campaigning and through being milked of piquets to serve in various garrisons or even in provisional battalions for specific operations. They would also be further weakened by the ill-advised attempt to make up for these losses by drafting undisciplined militiamen into their ranks. None of the eight battalions was at full strength at the beginning of the Québec campaign.

In addition to the regular army troops, Montcalm also exercised operational control over the various *Compagnies Franches de la Marine*, of which there seem to have been two companies at Québec in 1759. Posted on either flank of Montcalm's battleline they would return with the other regulars under Lévis six

months later. The militia played a very prominent role in the defense of the colony. They were primarily organized by parish on a regional basis under the auspices of the colony's three governments; Québec, Montréal, and Trois-Rivières, but actually were employed in a variety of ways. The older men served in transport brigades, usually as bateaux men or carters. In theory the younger men were then formed into battalions for fighting, but in practice a further distinction was made whereby in June 1759 about 600 were drafted into the depleted ranks of the regulars. The criteria for deciding which men were to be drafted are unclear, but when the first of the provisional Marine battalions was formed back in 1757, it was supposed to be led by those officers "least fit" for operations in the woods, and the same may well have been the case with the militia. In other words, the bush-fighters remained in the ranks of the militia, while those less able were moved to the regulars. At any rate those militiamen who were drafted gradually assumed an increasing importance as time went on and of the 1,297 men mustered in the Berry Regiment for Levis' ill-fated attempt to recapture Québec in April 1760, almost half were actually Canadian militia.

Those actually serving as militia soldiers took the field under the overall direction of professional officers such as Captain Louis de Vergor, seconded from the *Compagnies Franches*. Once again they were in theory organized in battalions corresponding to their government of origin; one each from Trois-Rivières and Québec and two from Montréal, plus another of refugee Acadians. They also appear to have followed the regular practice of forming piquets or ad hoc detachments for particular operations. In September 1759, for example, de Vergor's men at the Anse au Foulon were apparently a mixture of militiamen

French infantry practicing the platoon exercise as depicted by Le Blond in 1758. Note they are deployed in three ranks in accordance with the Instruction of May 14, 1754. Only the front row is now kneeling. So far as is known, this formation was used by Montcalm's regulars. Their British opponents meanwhile had reduced their ranks to two.

Rangers 1758–61

All the rangers with Wolfe at Québec wore the same uniform, black lapelled and cuffed in blue, comprising a waistcoat with sleeves, a short jacket with wings instead of sleeves, white metal buttons, canvas drawers, and a pair of leggings. On the left is one of Rogers' Rangers, wearing the green short coat with green collar and cuffs, and buckskin breeches that they were issued from January 1758. Lapels were added in 1759. On the right is one of Gorham's Rangers. It is not clear how long they wore the black and blue uniform of the rangers at Québec, but by 1761 they had adopted a most practical reversible uniform of red coats turned with brown, with brown caps and linings, which could be worn either way out. They also wore leather jockey caps with an oak leaf or branch painted on the left side. Besides their weapons, the rangers also had powder horns with small straps and small pouches with straps. (David Rickman © Osprey Publishing Ltd)

from both Montréal and Québec. Naturally enough, with the exception of some of the Québec City militia, they had neither uniforms nor colors, although the militiamen of the three governments were distinguished at a very basic level by the issue of tucques or knitted woolen caps – white for Trois-Rivières, red for Québec, and blue for Montréal.

Uniquely in this campaign the French had the services of a *Corps de Cavallerie*, organized by Montcalm, a former cavalryman himself, in June 1759. Dressed in blue coats faced red, and bearskin caps "to give them a martial look," the troopers, some 200 strong, were Canadian volunteers and the officers regulars. Their commander was Captain de la Roche-Beaucourt, who had previously served in the Montcalm cavalry regiment.

Montcalm had one company of regulars belonging to the *Corps Royal de l'Artillerie* and two companies of colonial *Canonniers-Bombardiers*, supported by substantial numbers of naval gunners and militia. There was no shortage of guns, but most of them sat in emplacements and no more than four were actually dragged up on to the Plains of Abraham for the climactic battle.

The garrison of Québec City proper, as distinct from the field army covering it, comprised a disparate collection of units. In the first place there were piquets

Corps in Canada 1750s–60s

On horseback is a trooper of the *Corps de Cavallerie*, 1759–60. He wears the cavalry's uniform of a blue single-breasted coat with red collar and cuffs, possibly with red turnbacks, and apparently with bearskin caps. Officers wore white uniforms. The corps was reported well armed and equipped with saddlery. In the foreground is a fusilier of the *Compagnies Franches de la Marine*, dressed, as many soldiers on campaign in the wilderness were, in a mixture of Canadian and American Indian clothing. The *capots* were probably grey-white as they were frequently made from uniform coats. The headdress may have often been the military forage cap. Indian-style breechclouts, *mitasses*, and moccasins were worn below the belt. On the right is a sergeant of the *Compagnies Franches*, equipped to serve with the metropolitan army battalions. He carries a musket and bayonet like his men. In the background is a militiaman of the "Royal-Syntaxe" Company in 1759. The Royal-Syntaxe was so called because it was made up of 35 students from the Québec City Seminary. The student-militiamen probably wore their school uniform, a blue *capot* piped white with a white sash and a tricorn. On the right is a militiaman of the *Milice de Réserve*, 1752–60. These "reserve" companies, one in each city of Montréal and Québec, were ordered by Governor-General Duquesne. They consisted of wealthy

bourgeois merchants led by gentlemen. They wore a scarlet uniform with white cuffs and waistcoat. (Eugène Lelièpvre © Osprey Publishing Ltd)

drawn from the *troupes de terre*: one each from La Reine, Guyenne, Berry, Béarn, La Sarre, Royal-Roussillon and Languedoc numbering about 250 in total. The Québec City militia had a theoretical strength of 840 men and there were about another 1,000 seamen, marines, and naval gunners landed from the ships trapped in the river by Saunders' fleet, which with their officers made a total of some 2,200 combatants in September 1759.

SIEGES AND ENGINEERS

Sieges of forts and fortresses were common during the French and Indian War, as a siege was often the only decisive way to defeat the enemy and take control of an area. Many forts were subject to sieges, once if not several times during the conflict. Moreover, the last major engagements of the French and Indian War were sieges. The major French fortresses, Québec, Montréal, Louisbourg, and New Orleans were all capitals of the surrounding area, and seats of government. They were tremendously important to the protection of New France, and the fall of any one of them practically ensured the fall of the entire area. Except for New Orleans, all were besieged during the French and Indian War. Québec had resisted capture in 1690 but fell in 1759; its henceforth British garrison would resist in 1760, and again (against the Americans) in 1775–76. Louisbourg fell twice in the 18th century, in 1745 and 1758, after great sieges. Montréal held the last French army in Canada when it surrendered in September 1760.

MILITARY ENGINEERS AND FORTIFICATIONS IN THE 18TH CENTURY

Both the British and French armies at this time had access to specially trained engineers who designed and oversaw the building of fortifications. The British Army was supplied with engineers by the Board of Ordnance, which had a variety of functions in the 18th century, including supplying all required hardware to the army and navy, training and administering the Royal Artillery, and as engineers. From there it was a short step to supplying fortifications. As an organization it was quite independent, and its officers were, strictly speaking, not part of the army. In the early days, it was common for engineer officers to simultaneously hold military commissions in regiments of the line,

and commoner still for regimental officers to fill in as engineers when trained personnel were wanting. The British Army considered the standard work on fortifications to be John Muller's 1746 treatise *Elements of Fortification.* In practice the army's fortifications were often much less elaborate than those described by Muller and other experts. The British didn't build any large fortresses like the French instead they built smaller forts on the frontier.

In contrast, the theoretical education of French engineers in the age of Louis XIV (1643–1715) and Louis XV (1715–74) was remarkably good by the standards of the day and covered aspects of engineering, tactics, architecture, fine arts, and town planning. Since the Renaissance, the French had studied and developed the leading designs of fortifications in Europe, including the ideas of the Italians and Dutch, both leaders in military architecture over the centuries. The French approach was more systematic than elsewhere and as

Fortifications in North America

Following the discovery of America by Columbus in 1492, European colonists built their style of fortification in the New World in an attempt to ensure their safety and consolidate their conquests. The Spanish and Portuguese were the first to build sizable forts, some of which evolved into fortified towns – fortresses – as their settlements grew. The French and the British came later to North America and thus the establishment of their large permanent settlements only got under way during the 17th century. The British colonists rapidly outgrew their small stockaded settlements along the North American coastline, but did not build elaborate fortifications to protect their towns. The settlers of New France, however, did. Thanks to relentless explorers and traders, the land mass of New France was enormous, extending from the Gulf of St Lawrence to the Rocky Mountains in the west and from the Great Lakes to the Gulf of Mexico in the south. But as impressive as it may have looked on a map, New France remained a weak colony in terms of population, which was sparse and scattered, and colonial garrisons were integral to the protection of the fragile empire.

The fortresses of New France were extraordinary in their variety. Québec was a formidable natural fortress; the defenses of Louisbourg were almost transposed from Vauban's textbooks; Montréal had a substantial wall; and New Orleans was eventually also protected by moats and redoubts. Although quite different in fortification style and extent, Québec, Montréal, Louisbourg, and New Orleans all had one thing in common: their strategic importance was tremendous and the fall of any one of them would almost certainly cause the fall of the surrounding area. Any enemy who wanted to take New France had to take its fortresses first. To ensure that was unlikely, French engineers worked to adapt their knowledge of siege warfare in Europe to a completely new terrain, and produced new defense systems and outlying forts which could protect French possessions in North America.

early as 1604 a nationwide administrative regulation concerning fortifications was put in place. This brought an increasing professionalization of military engineering, which coincided with the advent of Sébastien Le Preste de Vauban (1633–1707), one of the greatest engineers in military history. Part of

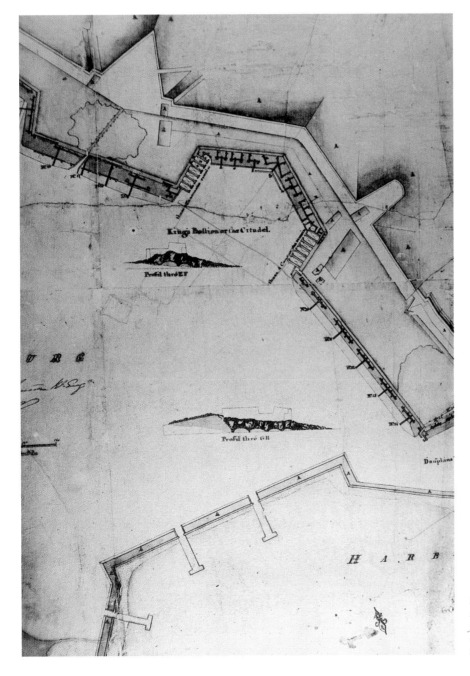

Detail from a British plan and section of Louisbourg showing the fortifications reduced to piles of rubble by 1761. (Photo René Chartrand)

213

Artillery was crucial during a siege. This iron 24-pdr French marine artillery cannon is mounted on the King's Bastion at Louisbourg. All the guns in Louisbourg at the time of its siege were naval models from the French navy. Most were probably the 1703 model, which remained in general use until 1766. (René Chartrand)

Vauban's remarkable success was due to his pragmatic approach; he was not merely a theoretician with skills in geometry, he was also a veteran military engineer in the field who conducted some 48 sieges during his career. Vauban's elaborate systems of fortifications thus combined and enhanced designs proven effective in actual siege warfare, hence their renown. Louis XIV, recognizing Vauban's great talent, made him national superintendent of fortifications and tasked him with building or repairing a multitude of forts and fortresses all over France. This vast public works project, which went on for decades, required numbers of qualified engineers. Previously, engineers in France had been more or less gifted amateurs who largely acquired their knowledge from engineering books published mostly in Italy and in Holland. Louis XIV felt that military engineering was a state secret and that Vauban's manuals on fortifications, on the ways to attack and defend fortresses, should not be published. Thus, those selected to be military engineers had no printed manuals from Vauban; instead part of their training was to make a manuscript copy of Vauban's treatises, which they would keep as their main reference work afterwards.

In France, the men responsible for designing and building fortifications were the *Ingénieurs du Roi* (the King's Engineers). These were highly skilled and educated individuals who held royal commissions to practice their art in government service. They combined the skills of architecture, military and civil engineering, and urban planning. The King's Engineers also had military officers' commissions to provide them with a rank within the military structure. They were employed as staff officers and would also be found in the entourage of a colonial governor or governor-general.

Under Marshal Vauban's leadership, the King's Engineers formed a sort of small independent ministry whose staff was spread all over France and its colonies. After the death of Vauban's successor, the Marquis d'Asfeld, in 1743, the engineers' independence came to an end. Most were absorbed into the army in France with others going to the navy. As the navy was responsible for the colonies in America, there were hardly any changes for the engineers posted to the various towns, who continued to be called the King's Engineers and wear their scarlet uniforms. During the French and Indian War, metropolitan army engineers were sent to Canada and other colonies and served mostly in the field with Montcalm's army. The colonial King's Engineers continued to be mostly preoccupied by fortifications, sometimes quite far into the interior of the continent.

Engineers were active in Canada from the early decades of the 17th century, and a regular establishment of engineers under a chief engineer was set up in the 17th century. A French military engineer landing in New France came with an education suitable for siege warfare in Europe. He was now faced with a "New World" offering very different strategic and geographic conditions into which he simply had to adapt. A good example was Chief Engineer Chaussegros de Léry. A veteran of European campaigns during the War of the Spanish Succession, he landed at Québec in 1716 with a complete knowledge of Vauban's system. In a site such as Louisbourg, local topography allowed the building of Vauban-style fortifications. But in Canada, as de Léry quickly perceived, many elements rendered Vauban's system questionable. Distance and a sparse population meant that military forces would move by water rather than by land and that manpower to build enormous bastions and glacis was not available. Thus, his first major work, the design to enclose Montréal with a reveted rampart, was a radical departure from the ideal star-shaped fortress in Flanders and resembled far more an early 17th-century fortress without the extensive outworks.

Engineers didn't only play an important role in building fortifications, they were often crucial to the success of a besieging army as well, offering advice on the best way to attack the city, weak points, the building of entrenchments, and positioning of artillery. However, when things went wrong, as with the ill-planned attack on the French field fortifications at Ticonderoga, the engineer could be blamed for a commander's mistakes.

SIEGES IN THE FRENCH AND INDIAN WAR

Although the outcome of sieges in this period were affected by similar factors, in an extreme environment like the wilderness of North America certain variables – such as the proximity of a relieving force, the availability of supplies to both the garrison and besieging force, and the season – were more important than in Europe. The French siege of Québec, in the spring of 1760, was a stalemate until it became apparent that ships of the Royal Navy would arrive before ships carrying French reinforcements.

The defenses of Québec. In 1745, a new line of fortifications further west was started and these are the present-day walls of Québec on the landward side. Except for the glacis and earthworks outside the wall that were never finished, this 1752 plan by Chief Engineer Chaussegros de Léry shows the city essentially as it was when General Wolfe's army besieged it in 1759. De Léry also drew in future streets and rectangular city blocks in the upper city's west side, and future square city blocks bordered by walls and bastions in the vacant lots of the lower city's northeast area. (National Archives of Canada, C-21779)

At the siege of Louisbourg, artillery was the main offensive weapon employed to take the city. Carefully sited batteries were employed to slowly erode the fortifications protecting the town, and destroy many of the buildings inside. At Québec, artillery action was less decisive, and it took a pitched European-style battle in front of the walls, following widespread devastation of the area around the city, to convince the French that holding out longer was not a viable option. When the besieged fort was smaller, artillery bombardment could often destroy the entire fortification in a few days, as at Fort Oswego. The failure to deploy artillery at Ticonderoga left the British assaulting the French lines unassisted. If a second attempt at placing a battery on Rattlesnake Mountain had been made successfully, the outcome of the battle might have been very different.

A view of Québec from the north, 1759–60. At left is the unfinished Redoute Royale, built from 1712 and nearly completed on the unfinished line of fortifications started by de Beaucours. The Ursuline sisters' convent and college are in the center. The ramparts built from 1745 are behind the viewer and cannot be seen. What can be seen is that the area between the old and the 1745 ramparts was left largely vacant and used to keep livestock. (Print after Richard Short; National Archives of Canada, C358)

WINNING NEW FRANCE
QUÉBEC, 1759

By spring 1759, an attack on Québec was expected daily, and so the city defenses were strengthened, a task employing thousands of men. Montcalm's aim was to stop the British long before they were close enough to attack the fortifications, and so perhaps the most impressive of the efforts was the fortification of the Beauport Shore, where both precedent and common sense indicated the British might land. The cliffs along its whole length between the St Charles and Montmorency rivers were fortified with a series of 18 batteries and "redans," or earthwork forts, for the most part linked by entrenchments. While the defensive position was reasonable, Montcalm suffered from insufficient resources. The shortage of men was partially alleviated by calling out the militia and even incorporating some of them in the ranks of his own regular regiments, but as soon as the British did manage to force their way into the upper river he found himself overstretched. The second problem was a shortage of supplies. The war thus far had consumed all the available food, and as the summer advanced this particular problem grew more acute as the flow of supplies from the settlements below Québec had been stopped by the British. Of those farmers above the city, many were serving in the militia and were therefore unable to raise crops. In the short term the army was able to cope; no-one was starving, but they were very much living hand-to-mouth. As a result there was no surplus to allow any significant stockpile to be created. This would limit Montcalm's strategic options when the final crisis broke.

Before Wolfe arrived at Québec, he was reliant on intelligence he had received about the fortress which indicated that the only practicable avenue of approach was from the western or landward side, which was covered by a quite inadequate line of fortifications. That this appreciation of the fortifications was inaccurate would not be discovered until Wolfe arrived in front of the walls on September 13. From the very outset, Wolfe considered the possibilities, and indeed the

Attack at Montmorency Falls. In the foreground the Royal Navy ships can clearly be seen giving fire support to the troops on the beaches. In the distance are British artillery firing at Québec from the south bank of the river. (National Archives of Canada)

advantages, of landing a substantial force somewhere above the city. His initial assumption was that he would be able to establish a beachhead on the Beauport Shore, just downstream from Québec, then fight his way across the St Charles River before swinging around to attack the city from the south, even though this was the very route that had been unsuccessful for a force of New Englanders trying to take the city in 1690. His second option was to get a detachment up the St Lawrence River, land them several miles above the town, and then entrench. This second option was obviously a much more attractive prospect, but it was by no means certain that it would be possible to get past Québec and into the upper river. He therefore proceeded on the assumption that he would have to effect his initial landing somewhere on the Beauport Shore. This was the only realistic plan Wolfe had to work with until he actually arrived on the spot and was able to make a proper reconnaissance of his objective. It is of interest that one of the Royal Navy navigators who aided with this reconnaissance was a young James Cook of later fame.

THE CAMPAIGN BEGINS

The first British troops landed on the Île d'Orléans on June 27. Wolfe soon discovered that the French had anticipated his arrival and were busily digging in above the Beauport Shore in precisely the area where he had hoped to effect his landing. Nevertheless, he began landing his army in earnest, unhindered by a poorly executed French attempt to destroy the fleet with fire-ships on the night of June 28. The Île d'Orléans served as a reasonably secure base-camp, but he needed

The mightiest site on the continent

The most formidable fortress in North America was the city of Québec. The site had been an Indian town when the French explorer Jacques Cartier arrived and named its imposing 300ft cliff Cap Diamant (Cape Diamond) in 1535. The area that would become Québec was the triangular site atop the cliff, on the north bank of the St Lawrence River, at the point where the river widens dramatically into a great estuary. On one side of the city was the broad cliff-girt river itself, and on another was a much smaller tributary called the St Charles River. Cartier built a small fort, the first fort constructed in Canada. A substantial settlement, the first permanent one in Canada, was begun in 1608. Initially a trading post, it expanded over the years. The town was taken by English corsairs in 1629, and returned to the French in 1632 after a peace treaty. The ensuing century saw improvements to the fortifications, particularly the enclosing of the city; and several failed sieges by the British and Thirteen Colonies. The fall of Louisbourg in 1745 came as a shock to the people of Québec, and improving the defenses became the order of the day. Although the war ended in 1748 without an attack on the city, alert stayed high, and the fortifications continued to be strengthened.

The city's fortifications during the siege of 1759 were reasonably extensive, but certainly not very elaborate. From 1745, the city's landward side was enclosed by a line of bastioned ramparts that were reveted with stone (1). A small redoubt with a powder magazine was positioned at the highest point on Cape Diamond (2). In 1759, the walls extending from the Cape Diamond Redoubt to the Potasse Demi-bastion were completed and equipped with guns, but they were mounted in the several bastions' flanks for enfilade fire and could not fire at the enemy at long range. Furthermore, the ditch and glacis were only finished in front of the Saint-Jean bastion and the Potasse Demi-bastion facing north. The rest of the perimeter was unprotected by a ditch and glacis and was thus considered the city's weak side by the French commanders.

In the upper town, the batteries west of the fort and the Château Saint-Louis were improved during the 1740s and had 16 guns and two mortars in 1759 (3). The most extensive batteries were sometimes called the Grand Battery (4). Because the river level was very shallow, fewer guns were needed on the eastern side of the cliff, but in all, some 66 cannons and seven mortars were mounted between the Côte de la Montagne and the Potasse Demi-bastion. Near the intendant's palace was a narrow jetty (5) that, in 1759, had a chain going across to the Beauport Shore so as to prevent enemy raids by longboats into the St Charles River. Slightly further north were the Saint-Roch and du Palais suburbs (6), which had 25 guns mounted in their newly built shore entrenchments.

The lower town featured five shore batteries facing south to sweep shipping on the narrows of the St Lawrence River. The most westerly battery was the small La Reine Battery; then, heading east, was the King's Shipyard

to bring his men much closer to their objective if they were to fight. Dalling's Light Infantry and the advance elements of Monckton's brigade were therefore put ashore at Beaumont, on the undefended south shore of the St Lawrence, on the evening of June 29. The rest of the brigade landed there next morning and despite some harassment from Canadian militia in the woods marched westwards to seize Point Levis, almost opposite Québec itself. Initially this landing was no more than a preemptive move to stop the French placing a battery on the promontory, which would be able to prevent British ships moving past the city. However, on July 2, Wolfe carried out a reconnaissance along the south shore and discovered that it would be possible to establish a battery at Pointe aux Peres. This was just to the west of Point Levis and would allow the guns to fire directly into Québec, the tactic used to such good effect at Louisbourg. The same day, reconnaissance by the

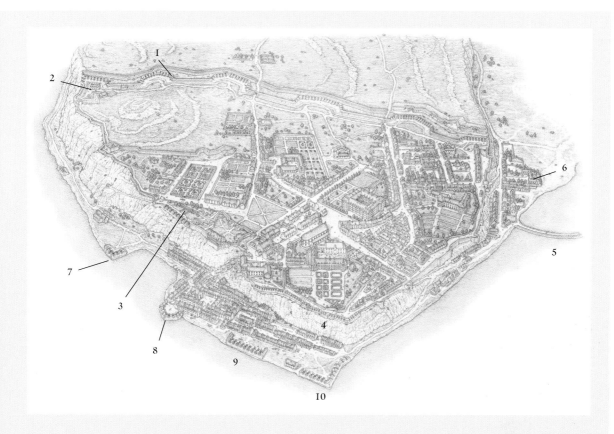

Battery (7). Past the "Cul de Sac" cove was the most advanced of the lower town's batteries, the bastion-shaped Batterie Royale with about ten guns (8). Then came the first Dauphin's Battery (9) built in 1709 and the second Dauphin's Battery (also sometimes called Saint-Charles) corner battery at the turn of the point (10) started in 1757 and never quite finished. (Donato Spedaliere © Osprey Publishing Ltd)

Royal Navy discovered the previously unsuspected Beauport Bank, a wide expanse of rocky shallows that would prevent ships coming in close enough to the Beauport Shore to provide the necessary naval gunnery support for a landing there. Without fire-support a landing there would probably have little chance of success. This information caused Wolfe to turn his attention, as he had anticipated might be necessary, to the area above the city.

Reconnaissance upstream found that a landing at Saint-Michel appeared practicable and so in the early hours of the morning of July 9 all of the army's grenadier companies were landed a short distance below the high falls at the mouth of the Montmorency River. As soon as the beachhead was secure, Townshend's brigade followed. With the diversionary force now in place the second phase of the operation had to be delayed until the navy managed to wrest control of the basin and get above the city. While they were waiting for the fleet, two of Murray's battalions and the rest of the guns were brought ashore at Montmorency. On July 15, the grenadiers were concentrated on the Île d'Orléans. Wolfe's plan for the landing involved a brigade-sized diversionary attack led by Monckton against the Beauport position in order to distract attention away from the main attack at Saint-Michel. While this diversionary plan had its advantages, the weakness of Wolfe's idea lay in the fact that he was clearly overstretching his forces.

In the event the attempt to run ships past Québec into the upper river was not actually made until the night of July 18. One ship went aground, but two ran safely past Québec and into the upper river accompanied by two sloops and two transports. Reconnaissance of the land above Québec followed, showing possible difficulties in the campaign ahead, but notwithstanding the risks Wolfe decided to proceed with the Saint-Michel landing. On the morning of July 20 the consolidated grenadier companies at the Île d'Orléans made ready, and orders were sent for Monckton to embark part of his brigade and all his light infantry immediately. Instead of mounting an elaborate, and probably futile, diversionary attack at Beauport, they were to proceed directly upriver to secure the beachhead at Saint-Michel.

Then, just as suddenly, the whole operation was cancelled. This abrupt change of heart reflected badly on Wolfe and furnished his numerous critics with yet more ammunition. However, it is clear from his dispatches to Pitt that he had good reason. The success of the operation obviously hinged on the speedy establishment of a beachhead and concentration of forces at Saint-Michel before Montcalm arrived. This was dependent on transporting Townshend's and Murray's brigades upstream on the tide faster than the French could march overland. The situation was completely changed when French guns, presumably accompanied by troops, appeared in the area. If the initial landing was seriously opposed or heavily counterattacked before the rest of the army could be brought up, then the whole operation would not only fail, but it would probably incur such heavy losses that the army would be forced to withdraw out of the area altogether. The French guns that prompted this decision were, in fact, largely unsupported and there were only a few militia in the area, but Wolfe could not possibly know this, indeed it is obvious that he was particularly uneasy about his lack of reliable knowledge on the French. In a bid to gain more information, he sent his quartermaster-general, Lieutenant-Colonel Carleton, even further up the river to reconnoiter. It is unlikely that Carleton learned very much of any use and, after a planning conference on July 23, Wolfe's attention turned in earnest to the Beauport Lines. However, he seems to have been far from convinced of the chances of achieving anything there. He led a reconnaissance in force up the Montmorency River, because a crossing higher up the Montmorency might allow the army to get into the rear of the Beauport Lines and thus avoid a costly frontal attack. In the meantime, he hoped that his party could seize and hold the ford until Townshend brought the rest of the troops up. Unfortunately, Wolfe's party did not find a suitable ford, and came under heavy attack twice by American Indians allied to Montcalm.

MONTMORENCY FALLS

Thwarted in his attempts to maneuver around the French army, both above and below Québec, Wolfe was at last faced with the distinctly unpalatable prospect of tackling the Beauport defenses head-on. For the most part the chain of redoubts and entrenchments was sited on top of the wooded cliffs overlooking the shore. Wolfe's attention was still drawn to the seemingly isolated redoubt on the beach that was to have been Brigadier Monckton's objective in the abandoned diversionary attack. His original plan seems to have been to transport four companies of grenadiers to the beach on landing vessels, while keeping an infantry reserve on boats. The grenadiers would seize the redoubt and see what sort of reaction this produced. At the same time the light infantry and rangers would mount a demonstration at the ford above Montmorency Falls, where the Canadians and American Indians were camped.

The attack had to be delayed due to a flat calm, but on July 31 the operation went ahead. Initially, it went to plan, until the boats were run ashore and it was realized that the redoubt was much higher up the beach than expected, and was in fact adequately covered by the entrenchments above. Wolfe himself came to judge the situation. He decided that the heavy fire incoming from the French indicated a certain disorder and confusion in the enemy ranks, prompting him to take the fateful decision to mount a frontal assault on the lines. Although there were certain advantages in the situation, the beach and hill were steep and uneven, and the numerous enemy were safely entrenched on the heights above. Unfortunately the tides imposed a delay on Wolfe's new plan as they had to wait for the tide to drop before the other brigades could ford the Montmorency below the falls. This delay compromised Howe's demonstration against the upper ford and gave the French time to shift two battalions of regulars across from there to support the men in the threatened trenches, thickening the French line from their center to their left. The renewed attack was a disaster, and when a violent thunderstorm stopped all firing Wolfe shut down the operation, evacuating as many men as possible by boat, while Wolfe and the greater part of the 78th Highlanders marched along the beach and crossed to safety by the Montmorency ford. It had been an expensive exercise that cost 210 killed and 230 wounded. Wolfe recorded his thoughts on the attack: "the grenadiers landed ... their disorderly march and strange behavior necessity of calling them off and desisting from the attack ... many experienced officers hurt in this foolish business." Next day Wolfe minced few words in an order that managed

QUÉBEC, JUNE–AUGUST 1759

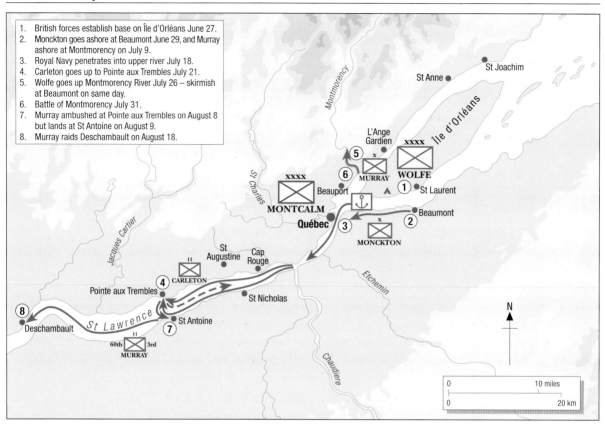

1. British forces establish base on Île d'Orléans June 27.
2. Monckton goes ashore at Beaumont June 29, and Murray ashore at Montmorency on July 9.
3. Royal Navy penetrates into upper river July 18.
4. Carleton goes up to Pointe aux Trembles July 21.
5. Wolfe goes up Montmorency River July 26 – skirmish at Beaumont on same day.
6. Battle of Montmorency July 31.
7. Murray ambushed at Pointe aux Trembles on August 8 but lands at St Antoine on August 9.
8. Murray raids Deschambault on August 18.

to rebuke the grenadiers for not following orders, and yet at the same time encourage both them and the rest of the army to do better next time. Wolfe displayed a much less certain touch in dealing with his higher-ranking colleagues in the recriminations that followed – there had already been several serious clashes with Townshend since landing, and the disaster at Montmorency would have exacerbated these difficulties for Wolfe.

INTO THE UPPER RIVER

On August 3, Murray led most of his brigade up the river to assist Rear-Admiral Holmes in destroying the remaining French warships, and above all to try to open a line of communication with General Amherst. Murray's first attempted landing was repelled by the French regulars, resulting in over 100 casualties. His attempt the next day resulted in a landing on the south shore at Saint-Antoine. He reported to Wolfe that the river was now too low for the navy to penetrate high enough to find the French ships. Nevertheless, on the

18th he rowed further upstream under cover of darkness to Deschambault, where he destroyed a depot containing the spare kit of Montcalm's regular battalions. Some of Bougainville's men eventually turned up, but only managed an ineffectual harassing fire. By now Wolfe had grown impatient and not a little anxious about the large number of boats which Murray had taken with him. Orders were sent recalling him and, leaving the 3/60th Foot and the ships above Québec, he eventually returned to Point Levis on August 25 with decidedly mixed news. Captured prisoners had given him the welcome news of the fall of Fort Niagara, and the abandonment of forts Carillon and Saint-Frédéric. However, there was no word from Amherst and certainly no sign of his breaking through.

Thwarted in all his attempts to outmaneuver or to bludgeon his way through the French defenses, Wolfe turned to a more cautious and circumspect policy in August, awaiting the arrival of Amherst's army. Unable to bring the French army to battle in the open, he took on the civilian population instead. To his prolonged bombardment of the near-defenseless city was now added a series of destructive raids by the rangers up and down the shores of the St Lawrence. At the time Wolfe publicly justified this policy as being in retaliation for attacks on sentries and foraging parties by local militia, but it was a policy long planned. He also justified it as a policy to provoke Montcalm into coming out to fight, but this must have been a slender hope. While destroying the Canadian settlements did have some military justification, it cannot disguise an abiding impression that these punitive raids were born of frustration as much as policy. This theory is supported by evidence of a temporary collapse in Wolfe's health at this time. Throughout his life Wolfe complained constantly of the state of his health and he is often portrayed as a man strong in spirit, but cursed with a weak and sickly constitution. Yet the evidence indicates that the real causes of his illnesses were psychological rather than pathological, particularly as the best known of his recorded periods of illness coincided with periods of acute personal stress. At Québec, he became ill as his first truly independent command was going seriously wrong, with heavy losses to the army, little progress, and disagreements with his brigadiers. In these circumstances it is perhaps not so very surprising that his physical health once more gave way under the strain.

Notwithstanding these problems, Wolfe was about to rouse himself for one more attack. He was well aware that if the city was not taken before the end of September, the fleet and most of the army would have to withdraw from the river before the advancing pack-ice sealed its mouth. He seems to have been considering another attack as early as August 11 and a week later was impatient for Murray to return in order to put it into operation.

Ordinarily Wolfe was not a believer in councils of war, preferring to make decisions himself. However, despite his unhappy experience of such councils at

After realizing that the redoubt below the Beauport Lines was not as opportune a target as he had hoped, Wolfe altered the plan, which involved the grenadiers waiting several more hours in the boats. At last, with the tide falling, the British ships renewed a brisk fire. Unfortunately when the grenadiers were finally ordered in, their boats promptly grounded, incurring a further delay. It was feared that the boats would be stranded if beached, so once close to the beach the men had to go over the side, and form up in waist-deep water. After landing, the grenadiers were supposed to wait for reinforcements; however, as soon as they landed they came under fire from the upper battery and attacked without waiting. The French gunners took to their heels, but heavy fire from the trenches above forced the grenadiers to take shelter in or behind the redoubt. Moreover, they now discovered that the lower slopes of the hill were covered with an abbatis. Unable to go forward and unwilling to fall back, the grenadiers started to take heavy casualties. At this point an extremely violent thunderstorm suddenly burst over the battlefield, reducing visibility to a few yards and stopping all firing. The men were evacuated, leaving many wounded on the beach where they were later killed by Montcalm's American Indians. (Gerry Embleton © Osprey Publishing Ltd)

Rochefort, the bedridden commander formally asked on August 28 for his brigadiers' written opinion on three different plans to take Beauport. The first of the three seems to have been Wolfe's own plan, which involved him leading a considerable detachment on a night march through the woods. The other two were merely variations upon the plan that had gone so badly wrong on July 31, each addressing the faults of that day to some extent. The brigadiers were quick to point out the failings of the first plan, and were not keen on another attempt on the Beauport Lines. Instead, they respectfully advocated evacuating the Montmorency camp and effecting a landing somewhere above the city. Wolfe accepted this plan, though he was clearly not very optimistic about the outcome.

In accordance with a plan drafted by the brigadiers, the guns were withdrawn from the Montmorency position on September 1, and most of the troops followed next day. Apart from a 600-strong detachment left to guard the stores and hospitals on the Île d'Orléans, the army was then concentrated at Point Levis, on the south shore. Once that had been done, the batteries there were left in the charge of Lieutenant-Colonel Burton, while everybody else marched upstream as far as the Etchemin river and embarked on the ships waiting there.

Although the ships were by that time anchored off Cap Rouge, some 13 miles

QUÉBEC, 1759

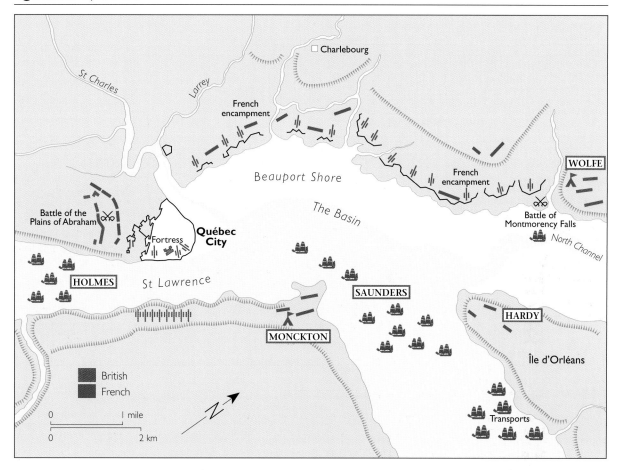

above Québec, orders for a landing still further upriver were issued on September 8. The first attempt at landing was postponed by heavy rain. Wolfe at this time seems to have been low, and passive. However, on September 9 his old spirit suddenly reasserted itself, and he found a suitable landing place at the Anse au Foulon, only a short distance away from his earlier objective, Saint-Michel. It was well-placed for a landing, depositing the army on the enemy's doorstep, and giving them the benefit of surprise. Wolfe could also bring the rest of the forces over from Point Levis and the Île d'Orléans for the assault. Moreover, at the Foulon there was a narrow road traversing the cliff. It was steep and apparently at least partially blocked by an *abbatis*. Once cleared however, Wolfe would have the means to move his troops and guns swiftly up from the river to the Plains of Abraham, the large plain to the west of Québec. On the assumption that the troops immediately available would be wholly inadequate, he could then either seize Québec by a *coup de main* or engage Montcalm in the open as he hurried to its rescue.

THE ANSE AU FOULON

At the time the man ultimately responsible for ensuring the security of the Anse au Foulon, Colonel Louis-Antoine de Bougainville, was at Cap Rouge with the bulk of his flying column, reinforced by grenadier companies belonging to Montcalm's five regular battalions. He was supposedly watching the British ships, but was absent when the heavily laden boats began dropping down the river with the tide at about 2.00am on the morning of September 13. The unfortunate officer actually on the spot, Captain Louis de Vergor, did not raise the alarm, as he was under the impression this was a scheduled French convoy of supply boats. The convoy had been cancelled, but Bougainville had failed to inform de Vergor.

Wolfe's intention was to land just to the west of the Foulon. Once ashore, a forlorn hope of volunteers under Captain William Delaune would seize control of the vital road. It would certainly be guarded, but as events proved Wolfe was quite justified in anticipating that 24 determined regulars with fixed bayonets would be able to seize it from a handful of militiamen.

Yet again Wolfe was betrayed by a lack of knowledge of the river. They were relying on the ebbing tide to carry them out of Bougainville's reach and ensure that they could all get safely ashore before he came marching down from Cap Rouge, but it had carried the boats much too far downstream. When Howe and his light infantry came ashore at about four in the morning, he very soon realized that he was in the wrong place. With every passing minute increasing the likelihood of the French discovering what was going on, he took a famous decision. Delaune and his forlorn hope were quickly sent off back along the beach to find the road, while Howe himself led three companies directly up the face of the cliff. This had formed no part of Wolfe's original plan, for it involved a hazardous climb as the men laboriously dragged themselves up the treacherous loose shale slope by tree roots and branches. On the other hand, it did have the merit of surprise, for they eventually scrambled to the top behind the French piquet posted at the head of the road. Equally fortunately, one of the first on the spot was a French-speaking officer, Captain MacDonald, who convinced a sentry that they were a large command coming to take the post, and told him to call the men of his party who were ranged along the hill.

The French did not remain deceived for long, of course. In the growing light the British boats became clearly visible and a battery at Samos briefly opened fire before being dealt with by Howe's light infantry. In the meantime, Wolfe was pushing his men up the road as fast as they landed. Montcalm had earlier sworn that 100 men well posted could stall an army, but de Vergor's men were scattered up and down the shore, and Montcalm had not reckoned with the British seizing control of the road. Its capture enabled Wolfe to establish his army on top of the cliff far more quickly and easily than anyone could have anticipated.

"Wolfe and his army scaling the heights to the Plains of Abraham." Although the cliffs appear more alpine than convincing, this modern print does at least correctly depict most of the troops ascending by means of the narrow road. (National Archives of Canada, C-1079)

Unfortunately, once Wolfe had his men atop the cliffs any thoughts he may have had of an immediate assault on the city had to be abandoned as he now saw for the first time that the new, stone-faced enciente stretched right across the peninsula. An assault might, nevertheless, be possible as there was neither ditch nor glacis in front of the walls. First, however, he was going to have to fight a battle.

THE PLAINS OF ABRAHAM

The situation at this point was very fluid indeed and in consequence no doubt rather tense. Wolfe was now finally in a position to assault the city, but he could not do so immediately. As a result he would undoubtedly have to first face a counterattack by Montcalm, and precedent suggested his response would be swift. Eventually, Bougainville's men would also arrive from Cap Rouge.

Initially, Wolfe formed his men with their backs to the river, in order to be able to deal with a French counterattack from any direction, but finding no

OPPOSITE *Montcalm leading his troops on the Plains of Abraham. (C. W. Jeffreys, National Archives of Canada, C-073720)*

opposition he marched out on to the Plains of Abraham. The weather was showery when he finally halted at about 6.00am and wheeled into a new position, facing Québec, with the river St Charles to the left. The battlefield was essentially an open field rising very gently toward the Buttes a Neveu, and in which neither side could subsequently claim any advantage from the terrain. On first taking up this position, Wolfe still only had the battalions that comprised the first flight, drawn up in a single line, but once the rest of the army came up he redeployed his forces in a shallow horseshoe formation. The brigade organization having been abandoned, Monckton as senior brigadier was given charge of the right, while Murray had the notional center. In fact, Murray actually commanded the left of the firing line, for Townshend's left wing was refused in order to face northwards on a line parallel to the Sainte-Foy road. This was done to counter the growing numbers of Canadian militia assembling on that flank, but it may also have effectively denied the road to the French army. Similarly, the 35th Foot, in a semicircular formation, were covering the right flank against more Canadian militia infesting the bushes lining the clifftop.

This image of the battle of the Plains of Abraham is accurate in depicting the road from the Foulon, and the way in which the city was dominated by the high ground of the Plains. (National Army Museum, Chelsea)

A surprising number of men had been left on the transports or on the beach, and as many as 600 of the light infantry were flung out in a screen to protect the rear of the army from the inevitable approach of Bougainville's column during the battle. Thus the six battalions forming the main battleline probably mustered no more than 1,768 bayonets. In addition there were at least two brass 6-pdrs,

which had been dragged up the Foulon road by Williamson and his gunners. The tactical formation adopted was interesting. Most accounts record that the battalions were drawn up only two ranks deep, rather than three, although the 78th Highlanders may have been drawn up in the usual manner. It is not clear whether this reduction in depth was done in conformity with Amherst's standing, or was simply an ad hoc expedient to cover the required frontage.

While they awaited Montcalm's arrival with his regulars, the substantial numbers of Canadian militiamen already arrived on the Plains engaged in fairly intensive skirmishing and eventually Wolfe ordered his men to lie down. He is often accused by later writers of recklessly exposing himself at this stage, but this was a necessary condition of the battle. Wolfe had to fight on foot, which imposed a fair number of important constraints. Not for him the luxury of remaining on horseback behind the lines, with aides-de-camp delivering orders and reports. Wolfe was restricted to a walking pace, with a severely curtailed visual range. In order to see anything he had to be on the spot, and basically in the front line. In the circumstances, he found it preferable to see things for himself rather than rely upon messengers. Shortly before the battle proper began, he visited Townshend to reassure himself as to the security of the left flank. That done he passed along the line to take up a position on a low rising ground which gave him a good viewpoint of the whole field.

In contrast to the determined efficiency being displayed that morning by Wolfe and his officers, the Marquis de Montcalm was panicking. Despite the earlier movement by most of the British troops to the ships some miles above Québec, the French commander had remained convinced that Wolfe still intended, ultimately, to fight his way ashore at Beauport. He was certainly encouraged in this happy belief by a noisy demonstration mounted in the basin by the boats of Admiral Knowles' ships on September 12. But having vainly stood to in expectation of a landing on the Beauport Shore until just after dawn, the Marquis was disagreeably surprised to receive reports of a landing at the Foulon.

Montcalm acted immediately. While it may seem odd that he did not delay to concentrate his forces before attacking Wolfe, he knew that even if the British threat to the Sainte-Foy road prevented a physical junction with the troops from Cap Rouge, he could rely on Bougainville to provide a diversion. More crucially, Montcalm did not know where Wolfe's army was. As far as he knew, they could have been about to storm Québec, in which case delay could risk the city, and there was perhaps an even stronger prospect of Bougainville and the other forces above the city being cut off and destroyed. Failure to support them or worse still lose the city was unthinkable, and he was heard to mutter "C'est une affaire sérieuse." He really had no option but to march at once and interpose his men between the redcoats and the city. This he accomplished successfully enough. It was after his troops had deployed in front of the city that things really started to go wrong. For some reason he convinced himself that the British were digging in, and was presumably encouraged in this belief by the late arrival of Williamson's gunners, who were themselves no doubt accompanied by seamen and perhaps other reinforcements as well. It must certainly have appeared clear that the longer he delayed the stronger the British were getting. Conversely, he had no knowledge of Bougainville's whereabouts. Indeed there was no certainty at all that he could effect a junction with him.

There were by this time seven infantry battalions making up Montcalm's hastily formed line. On the right was a skirmish line of colonial militia. The outermost of the formed battalions was a provisional unit of *Compagnies Franches*, then two regular battalions. All three, commanded by Colonel de Senezergues of La Sarre, were deployed in line formation, presumably three deep. The two regular battalions that formed the center were deployed in column under Montcalm's personal command. The left wing, under Colonel de Fontbrune, was again deployed in line, and also comprised just two battalions. On this wing also were militia operating in the scrub. It is difficult to establish with any certainty just how strong Montcalm's army actually was. In addition to the ordinary wastage to be expected in the course of the campaign, his regular battalions had earlier been stripped not only of their grenadier companies, but also of at least two piquets apiece, one serving with Bougainville's force, and another in the city garrison. Overall, it seems there were about 3,500 men present on the field. There were also guns with Montcalm, though estimates conflict over the number.

The slight advantage in numbers which Montcalm might have enjoyed was negated by a crucial difference in tactical doctrine. While British officers strove to control their men's fire, French officers took a more relaxed attitude to musketry, actively encouraged what was called a *feu de billebaude*, which amounted to the men firing at will. On the whole, moreover, the French favored rapid offensive movements relying upon the bayonet, and for that a column formation was preferred. This tactical philosophy may go some way to explaining why Montcalm now decided to fight. Sooner or later if he did not attack, it is reasonable to suppose that Wolfe would have attacked him, and having no great confidence in the ability of his men to win a static firefight in the open Montcalm intended to pierce the British center with a column attack.

At about 10.00am Montcalm waved his men forward. As the French advanced, the battalions on each wing opened an ineffectual fire on the waiting British and by all accounts quickly fell into disorder. The ranks of the five regular units had been padded out with conscripted militiamen and there are suggestions that, having fired, these men promptly went to ground or even ran away. The British battalions, on the other hand, waited until the French came within 40 yards range, when they opened up with a steady fire. In the center, the 43rd and 47th Foot momentarily held their fire in accordance with Wolfe's

In the center is Major-General Wolfe, studying his plans at Québec. There was no regulation dress for general officers at this time, and Wolfe's choice for in the field was a severely practical red coat and waistcoat and breeches. He wears a black armband, as he was in mourning for his father during the Québec campaign. To his right are a captain in the Royal Navy, and an officer of the Royal Artillery. On his left are men of the 78th Highlanders. (Gerry Embleton © Osprey Publishing Ltd)

patent method for demolishing French column attacks. The method worked as planned, and as the smoke thinned out all the way along the line it revealed the French army broken and in flight.

Wolfe unfortunately did not live to see his victory. He was shot in the first few moments of battle while standing on the low rising ground on the right of the line. As he lay dying his last orders were for Burton to lead Webb's Regiment to pursue the fleeing French, and stop their escape by taking the bridge over the St Charles river. While a particularly dramatic climax to his career, Wolfe's death at the very moment of victory came at an extremely inconvenient time, since Monckton was shot through the lungs at about the same time, and four other officers, including Carleton, were all wounded as well in the brief exchange. With Monckton down, command therefore devolved upon Townshend, but with so many other staff officers wounded it took some time for the brigadier to learn of the fact. In the meantime, it fell to Lieutenant-Colonel Hunt Walsh of Webb's 28th Foot to carry out his general's last order and initiate a fairly disorderly pursuit of the fleeing French.

Whether, in all the confusion, Burton ever received Wolfe's last message is not known, but Brigadier Murray tried, on his own initiative, to seize the bridge. Unfortunately, the attempt foundered when he and the Highlanders came under heavy fire, sustaining many casualties. Meanwhile, a minor crisis was developing behind them. Finding at last that he was now in command, Townshend returned to the center, where he realized that pursuit had left the troops in great disorder.

He re-formed the men, and as this was effected, Bougainville appeared with his troops in the rear of the British. Townshend marched the rest of the army back to confront Bougainville, who took the hint and drew off again without engaging. In the meantime, with the St Charles bridge still in their hands, the rest of the French were able to escape.

Nevertheless, the French casualties were quite heavy enough, at about 600 men and 44 officers in total. As in the British army, a significant number of senior officers went down. The most prominent amongst them was Montcalm himself, badly wounded by a canister round during the retreat and dead by the following morning. Both his brigadiers were also killed. On the British side Townshend reported a remarkably similar loss of 658 of all ranks, of whom around 60 were killed. While the close similarity in the number of casualties may appear surprising, it appears that most of the British losses were incurred when Murray was ambushed during the pursuit, while the French lost most heavily during the main firefight.

Following the battle, despite Bougainville's desperate efforts to throw supplies and reinforcements into the city, Québec surrendered to Townshend on September 18, and almost immediately afterwards the prospect of ice closing the mouth of

Edward Penny's painting is the most accurate depiction of James Wolfe's last moments on the Plains of Abraham. He is supported by Volunteer Henderson and attended by a surgeon's mate named Hewit. The identity of the standing grenadier is unknown, but the officer bringing news of victory is Lieutenant Henry Browne, also of the Louisbourg Grenadiers. (Ashmolean Museum, Oxford)

the St Lawrence forced the Royal Navy to withdraw from the river. With the ships went Wolfe's corpse, the wounded Monckton and, with rather less excuse, Townshend as well. Québec was entrusted to a perilously weak garrison under Murray, while further upstream the Chevalier de Lévis rallied the remnants of Montcalm's beaten army for one last gallant offensive to retake the city.

THE FRENCH SIEGE

The romantic, and wildly inaccurate, version of Montcalm's death. Not only does he lie on a mattress in the open field rather than in the Ursuline Convent, but the uniforms are of a much later date and the surrounding savage characters in this death scene seem to have originated from much further away than Acadia. (National Archives of Canada)

Only too aware that if Québec remained in British hands the war was lost, Lévis advanced in the spring before the snow had melted, gambling on retaking the city while Amherst's forces still lay in winter quarters. By scraping together every man he could lay his hands on, he marched north with no fewer than 6,910 effectives, nearly 4,000 of them regulars. His arrival was anticipated, but Murray's initial hopes of preventing him landing at Cap Rouge were frustrated by bad weather. All he could do was maintain a chain of outposts to give him some early warning and keep his sickly army under cover in Québec itself. Warned of Lévis' arrival on the night of April 26, 1760, Murray sallied out at daybreak next morning with half the garrison and succeeded in withdrawing his outposts in the very face of the French advance.

Perhaps taken aback by this vigorous response, Lévis proceeded so cautiously that Murray resolved to repeat the experiment next day. Like Montcalm before him Murray regarded the defenses of Québec as untenable against a regular siege, especially since his garrison was very sickly – some 700 men had died since the departure of the fleet and hundreds more were unfit for duty. He was particularly keen to secure the high ground of the Buttes a Neveu, which in some measure dominated the walls. He had contemplated forming an entrenched camp there, from which to defend the city, but the weather and season persuaded him otherwise.

By the last days of April conditions were scarcely any better, for while the snow was melting fast the ground was now waterlogged; but with the crisis upon him, Murray marched out on April 28 with some 3,866 effectives. They carried equipment for entrenching and no fewer than 20 light guns and two howitzers. To capture Québec, Lévis first needed to take the Buttes and Murray intended that he should pay a heavy price for them. His appearance surprised Lévis, who was still advancing very cautiously and had only just begun to deploy his forces. Understandably reluctant to entrench his already sickly army on the sodden Buttes, Murray took the very soldier-like decision to seize the moment and attack. By catching Lévis off-balance not only would he decisively deny him the high ground, but might in the process gain a victory even more decisive than Wolfe's.

The ruins of Québec following the siege of 1759. (National Archives of Canada)

Wolfe's method for demolishing French column attacks was hugely successful on the Plains of Abraham on September 13, 1759. Wolfe had ordered the regiments to load with an extra ball, and the French infantry fled in disorder after the center regiments delivered a close and heavy discharge which they could not withstand. (Gerry Embleton © Osprey Publishing Ltd)

The battle of Sainte-Foy started well for the British, but gradually the line became disorderly, as the various attacks and counterattacks unfolded. Lévis continued to persevere, launching heavy column attacks on both wings. Murray's artillery superiority had initially compensated for the fact that he was outnumbered by nearly two to one, but as the battle went on his gunners experienced more and more trouble bringing ammunition up through the mud and slush. In addition, some of the men were fighting almost knee-deep in the muck. Realizing the tide was turning, Murray gave orders to break off the action and retire into Québec. All but two of his guns had to be spiked and abandoned, and he recorded 292 killed, 837 wounded and 53 prisoners. Murray has been widely criticized for fighting, but if the ground had been firmer, however, he might indeed have gained the victory he sought despite the odds. In the event, he did at least get his army away in good order, which was probably no mean feat. Lévis for his part admitted to losing 193 killed and 640 wounded, which was certainly too high a price to pay for failing to destroy the British army. Having found them in the open his objective should, as he readily admitted, have been to drive the British away from the city as Montcalm's men had been six months earlier. Having carelessly exposed his army to defeat at the outset, his subsequent attacks were poorly coordinated.

Although he did finally order one of his brigades to try to get between the British and the city, the movement seems never to have even come into action.

Ironically, Murray's battle was probably unnecessary, for Lévis had only one 24-pdr and was desperately short of ammunition for all his big guns. However, his intimate knowledge of the weak spots in the city's defenses meant that when he unmasked his batteries on May 11, they concentrated on the Glacière Bastion, which began crumbling within a matter of hours. However, the new embrasures opened in the walls by the British enabled their gunners to direct a heavy counterbattery fire on the French, which proved depressingly effective. Next day Lévis was forced to restrict his guns to firing a mere 20 rounds a day. All now depended on whether the Royal Navy or French reinforcements would be the first through the ice and into the river. A single British ship, HMS *Lowestoft*, appeared on May 9, but Lévis doggedly clung on to hope until the evening of May 15 when two more British warships arrived. The following day they attacked and destroyed the French frigates supporting Lévis' army and he was left with no alternative but to retreat. Québec was now safely in the hands of the British.

Montcalm was shot during the battle in front of Québec on September 13, 1759. Held in his saddle by a soldier on either side, he rode his black horse through the St Louis Gate, bleeding heavily. He died some twelve hours later after settling his affairs, and receiving the last sacraments. (Print after Louis Bombled, photogreaph René Chartrand)

THE FINAL ACT
MONTRÉAL AND THE TREATY OF PARIS

THE CITY OF MONTRÉAL

Montréal was the capital of the district of Montréal, and in 1760, it was the only major French fortress left in the colony of Canada. Montréal was founded in 1642 by a group of fervently Catholic settlers. The settlement initially consisted of a fort, a chapel, and some houses. Like the majority of settlements in North America, its early years were dogged by constant raids by local American Indian tribes. In time the original religious nature of the town was overtaken by the activities of traders, and eventually of soldiers as Montréal became the main military garrison of Canada. This shift was due to the exceptional strategic position of the town. It was situated where the Ottawa River, flowing from the northwest, joined the St Lawrence River. Not far to the east, the Richelieu river, flowing from Lake Champlain to the south, joined the St Lawrence. This provided exceptional river highways to the heart of the continent. Most of the vital fur trade was carried out on the Ottawa River route. Great convoys of canoes bearing all sorts of manufactured goods for the Great Lakes American Indians, who were assembled at Michilimackinac, would come back laden with valuable furs. Convoys would land at La Chine, the traders' village west of Montréal. It was impossible to go on further to Montréal because of the great rapids that lay between La Chine and the city.

The town remained unprotected until the late 17th century, when a palisade wall was built around it. Over the ensuing years the defenses were extended and improved. In 1713, it was decreed that Montréal should have a stone rampart, and Gaspard Chaussegros de Léry arrived as chief engineer in 1716. Work to strengthen Montréal's fortifications started the following year and continued slowly over the following decades, and by 1744, Montréal was a fortress with a reveted stone wall. An unusual feature of Montréal's defenses was the string of about thirty outlying forts erected in the second half of the 17th century, when the Iroquois staged many successful raids. The forts were built all around the town to control its approaches as well as on the south shore of the St Lawrence River. The great majority of them were fairly modest with wooden stockade walls; however, four of them were substantial stone structures featuring masonry walls and medieval-looking round or square towers at the corners. None of these fortifications were meant to resist an attack by a European enemy equipped with siege artillery. Rather they were designed to provide shelter for settlers in the vicinity and to resist attacks by American Indians, and on occasion New England militiamen. Many of these forts had detachments of regular soldiers until the 18th century, as well as guards of militiamen. Near each fort, at the river's shore, was a spot to make an alarm bonfire if the enemy was sighted. This alarm would be relayed in succession to Montréal where a cannon would be fired to warn soldiers and militiamen to prepare for action. By the mid-18th century, only three of the forts had small detachments of troops from the *Compagnies Franches*. However, more troops were stationed around Montréal during the war.

ADVANCE ON MONTRÉAL

Following the failed French siege of Québec, General Amherst decided to attack Montréal with another of the multi-pronged attacks that had worked so well for the British previously.

A View of the Passage of the Army under the Command of his Excellency Major General Amherst down the Rapids of St Lawrence River for the Reduction of Canada in the Year 1760, *a contemporary watercolor by Captain Thomas Davies. (National Archives of Canada, C-00577)*

The defenses of Montréal in 1760

Chief Engineer de Léry chose to follow the previous outlines of the city, which formed a very long and narrow rectangle. Under such circumstances, a Vauban-style fortress design was impossible, but de Léry may have been influenced by some of the 16th- and 17th-century town fortifications erected in his native Provence. De Léry's design followed the former log palisade as far as possible. The walls on the landward side were wider than those on the waterside, as an attack from the river was considered most unlikely. A ditch and glacis were also built on the landward side. As conceived by de Léry, the relatively narrow rampart was not meant to withstand heavy artillery fire as the chances of an enemy appearing with heavy siege cannons were thought to be very unlikely. However, its parapets with embrasures could provide exceptionally heavy fire to repulse a mixed raiding force. On the north side of the eastern end was a small hill with the little "citadel" on top. The gates and sally ports on the edge of the St Lawrence River must have been the busiest, as this was the main trading place in Canada. Fortress Montréal in 1760 was well protected against a strong raiding party, but had not been designed to withstand a European-style siege. (Donato Spedaliere © Osprey Publishing Ltd)

After Murray and his troops had been resupplied and re-formed in Québec, he was ordered to advance along the St Lawrence, approaching Montréal from the northeast. Murray and 2,400 regulars embarked for the trip on July 2, followed by a reinforcement of just over a thousand men from Louisbourg. The second prong was a mixed force of 3,400 under the command of Brigadier William de Haviland, which marched from Lake Champlain in August, traveling up the St John River and then northwest toward Montréal. The third prong was a force of 10,000 led by Amherst. The army of regulars and provincials advanced from Fort Oswego on August 10, moving to Fort Frontenac, then up the St Lawrence River to attack from the west.

Murray's force managed to avoid a 2,000-strong French force at Trois-Rivières on the St Lawrence, and landed just north of Montréal at Sorel. The French forces in the area started to gather to try to destroy his force, but Murray sent out rangers and other units with proclamations for the militia to lay down their arms. Many did, after hearing reports that those who refused to surrender were being burned out of their houses. By the end of August, most of the French forces opposing Murray had dispersed.

De Haviland successfully cut off Bougainville's force of 1,000 from their lines of communication with Saint-Jean and Chambly, stranding them on the Île aux Noix. His troops roamed the countryside, forcing Bougainville to withdraw towards Saint-Jean. When he reached Saint-Jean, he met up with other French forces and staged a further withdrawal towards Montréal. The French troops facing de Haviland were also beginning to suffer desertion losses. De Haviland continued to move toward the St Lawrence. Forward units of Murray and de Haviland made contact in early September.

Amherst fought several small French units on his march up the St Lawrence, but the rapids outside Montréal were more of a hindrance, and his army arrived battered at La Chine, 9 miles from Montréal on September 6. The noose around the city was slowly drawing tight.

The foundations of Montréal's 18th-century ramparts toward the Saint Laurent Bastion with part of the city's center as backdrop. (René Chartrand)

An east view of Montréal, giving a good indication of what the city would have looked like in the mid-18th century. (National Archives of Canada, C-2433)

The Marquis de Lévis commanded 3,000 troops in Montréal, but he recognized that his force was slowly disappearing as the British advanced. Murray had crossed the river and was cutting off the city from the east, while Amherst set up camp to the west. De Haviland's force was approaching from the south. Amherst's column began to move heavy artillery from La Chine. With the French forces melting away, Vaudreuil held a council of war with the senior French military officers. Negotiations with Amherst began, and on September 8, the capitulation was signed.

In spite of the French fighting record over the last few years, Amherst refused to allow them the honors of war so they could not march out with drums beating, colors flying, and holding their muskets. The French officers were mortified, but the number of deserters from their ranks had left them without options. Angered by Amherst's pettiness, General Lévis and many of his officers and men gathered together that night, reputedly on Île Sainte-Hélene. There, the glorious and battle-worn silk colors were brought around a fire, held high for all the men to see, and then slowly lowered into the flames. It is said that many a French soldier angrily broke his musket that night. Amherst apparently inflicted such harsh conditions because he felt that the French had behaved very badly during the war, particularly their failure to prevent the

Montréal in September 1760. This print, first published in the Royal Magazine *in December 1760 gives a rather crude view of the city. The anonymous artist was obviously impressed by the fortifications as the walls are prominent in this image and every embrasure has a cannon! A garrison-size British flag flies over the small citadel at right. (National Library of Canada, NL 15805)*

American Indians allied to their cause from committing atrocities. Some French officers found this reasoning hypocritical following the devastation the British had inflicted on the population in and around Québec the previous year in actions which had not only involved their allied American Indians, but their regulars as well.

On September 8, 1760, the French troops lined up in Montréal's Place d'Armes and the last French army in Canada surrendered. Following the surrender, Amherst sent Rogers' Rangers and the 60th Regiment to occupy the French forts in the west, Detroit and along the Great Lakes. The troops were to accept the surrender of the French forces in the region, and meet with American Indian leaders to explain that the British were now in control of the area.

THE TREATY OF PARIS

The capture of Montréal more or less brought the French and Indian War to an end, but the larger conflict dragged on for another two years, until the Treaty of Paris was signed by France, Great Britain, and Spain on February 10, 1763. A second treaty, concluded between Austria and Prussia, was signed on February 15, 1763, and war around the world was eventually over.

In the late summer of 1762, the British mounted a campaign to recover Newfoundland and its valuable fishing waters from the French. The capture of Signal Hill, one of St John's most formidable defenses on September 15, 1762, was crucial to the campaign. (Steve Noon © Osprey Publishing Ltd)

The Treaty of Paris awarded to Britain all of France's lands east of the Mississippi including the Ohio Valley, Québec, and Cape Breton. France was only allowed to keep two small islands of its North American possessions. In return, France received Guadeloupe and Martinique, which had been lost during the fighting. Britain also received Florida from Spain, in return for the Philippines and Cuba. The result of this was to leave Great Britain as the only major European power on the Atlantic seaboard of North America, controlling the entire coastline from Newfoundland in the north to Florida in the south.

A VOLLEY THAT SET THE WORLD ON FIRE
THE CONSEQUENCES OF THE FRENCH AND INDIAN WAR

The principal outcome of the French and Indian War was that France was nullified as an adversary in North America. To the casual observer of 1763, Britain was in undisputed control of North America east of the Mississippi river. As is often the case though, the reality was not nearly as clear cut.

THE SEVEN YEARS' WAR

The conflict in North America was connected to the Seven Years' War. Anticipating the conflict by a year, it acted as one of the spurs to the eventual

The Prussians inflicted a heavy defeat on the Franco-German army at the battle of Rossbach, Germany, on November 4, 1757. (Anne S. K. Brown Military Collection, Brown University Library)

outbreak of hostilities in Europe and on the Indian subcontinent. Many of the participants had viewed the Treaty of Aix-la-Chapelle in 1748 as a temporary truce, and all sides involved had spent the intervening years working on a series of treaty agreements to disband the alliances of the War of Austrian Succession, and developing their specific aims. The skirmishes in North America in 1755 and 1756 strained relations between France and Britain to the limit, but it was actually the French invasion of Minorca in 1756 which sparked the formal declaration of war between the two countries. It soon became apparent that the struggle between the two countries was going to engulf the continent of Europe, and Prussia, Austria, and Russia began to mobilize their forces that same year. By 1757 treaty agreements had committed all forces to war, and the first global conflict began.

The Seven Years' War had elements of total war in terms of the commitment of resources on the part of all combatants, which in the long term meant that, because countries were putting all they had into simply continuing to fight, any gains became secondary. In the extreme, this meant that a country such as Prussia was fighting for its very survival. The Seven Years' War dragged on for another two years following the end of hostilities in North America. The final years of the Seven Years' War were marked by both military and financial exhaustion, and a growing will to end the conflict.

Further to their gains in North America, under the Treaty of Paris Britain became the dominant European power in the Carnatic and Bengal regions of India, for while Pondicherry was returned to the French, it could not be fortified. Belle Isle was given back to France in return for Minorca, and the British returned Goree in West Africa, in exchange for Senegal. France also evacuated all of the German territories of George III and his allies. Britain returned Cuba and the Philippines to Spain in return for Florida and withdrawal from Portugal. After

An anachronistic image of Major Donald Campbell, the commander of Fort Detroit during the American Indian uprising, negotiating with Pontiac during the siege in 1763. After this discussion, the assembled warriors wanted to kill Campbell and his men. Though some of the men escaped, Campbell was tortured to death. (Library of Congress)

the Treaty of Hubertusburg, all the borders of 1756 were reinstated. Following the war, Prussia eclipsed Austria as the major German state, Russia began to be considered a significant European power, but France ended the war as a shell of its former self. The expenses incurred during the war put France in a very difficult financial position, and attempts at financial reform were not as extensive, or successful as the military reform implemented. Military needs and the construction of a new fleet strained the budget to breaking point in the 1760s. Successful involvement in the American Revolution brought more financial burdens, and the French Crown's mounting debts and attempts to get it under control are often cited as some of the main causes of the French Revolution.

THE INDIAN UPRISING

Following the Treaty of Paris, Great Britain was in undisputed control of eastern North America. However, problems arose almost immediately in the newly acquired areas of the Ohio Valley, and the lands west of the Appalachians. These areas had previously been overseen by French forts, and there had been a smattering of French settlers in the region, but their presence had impacted little upon the local American Indian tribes. Yet with the area under British control, colonists were tempted to push westwards to open up the interior for settlement. Obviously the American Indians in the area objected to this, and the determination of the colonists to continue despite their objections led to an uprising known as Pontiac's War, in 1763–64.

When Amherst sent soldiers to inform the American Indians of the new British hegemony over their lands, he was very particular about the way they were to go about it. Soldiers were not allowed to give the tribes gifts or weapons, a policy which offended the American Indians who until recently had been fighting for the French, and expected to be offered gifts for promising loyalty to the new government. The soldiers were warned not to give offense to any one group, and maintain the peace at all costs. However, their actions disappointed those allied to the French during the war, and alienated the Senecas, who had fought for the British, by failing to keep their promises made during the war. The British had signed agreements ensuring that lands west of the Alleghenies would only be used by the American Indians for hunting. Trading of European goods in these areas would be cheaper, and furs and skins would sell at higher prices.

As early as 1761, representatives of tribes, including members of the Six Nations, demanded a meeting with the governor of Pennsylvania. The representatives were disappointed that the British were not keeping their promises, as settlers were moving into the area reserved for hunting, goods were still being sold at high prices, and furs were not appreciating in value. Furthermore, the American Indians were concerned that they were being surrounded by forts, and this would eventually exterminate their tribes. American Indians who had fought for the British were also not allowed to move into the areas previously belonging to the French. This irked many American Indians, who felt they had scores to settle with the French-allied tribes, and who wanted access to the rich hunting grounds in the Ohio Valley.

The white colonists felt that they had every right to settle wherever they wanted. Lieutenant-Colonel Bouquet soon became very unpopular for arresting whites operating illegally in the region. A later set of orders stated that gifts could be given to American Indians who brought in illegal white settlers. These settlers then had to demonstrate their purpose for being there and present proper paperwork. If unable to do so, they were arrested, and subject to military law. White settlers were furious that, as they saw it, American Indians were being favored over them. The continuation of this policy soured relations between regulars and colonists.

Because of the large areas the soldiers were trying to control, white settlers managed to settle and hunt in the areas reserved for the American Indians without detection, and the Indians in the region became increasingly restless. Soon clashes between American Indians and settlers became more regular.

The Black Watch at Bushy Run, 1763, a painting by C. W. Jeffreys. (National Archives of Canada, C-073726)

By 1761, the Senecas were holding meetings with members of the Delawares and Miamis to discuss attacks on the frontier region forts. They did agree that they were not ready for an all-out rebellion. French settlers in the area were also fanning the flames by meeting with chiefs and discussing a possible return of the French to the region. By the following year, the British were in a difficult position, set between the white settlers and American Indian tribes. Bouquet requested more troops, but most of the troops from North America were involved in amphibious campaigns in the Caribbean so sufficient reinforcement was not possible.

The tension escalated into a full-scale uprising by the American Indians in late 1762, when two Seneca warriors killed two white settlers. The Senecas sent war belts to the western nations as the signal to begin hostilities. The uprising, however, was not an unanimous effort. Members of the Senecas, Ottawas, Hurons, Delawares, and Miamis participated, but no tribe involved all of its warriors. None of the western tribes raised the war belt.

The purpose of the uprising is not completely clear. The aim seems to have been to seize all British forts and posts, but this was not consistently carried out. Particularly at the beginning, the effort was not coordinated, but instead seemingly consisted of unconnected attacks on forts by groups of warriors. The conduct of Pontiac, an Ottawa chief who commanded a village near Fort Detroit, is a good example of how the uprising was not as widespread or organized as it could have been. Pontiac agreed with the other chiefs about the state of affairs, but he organized a campaign against Fort Detroit on his own. Because the fort was so important, the British hailed him as the leading war chief, and named the war after him, even though this was the only action that he participated in.

Pontiac besieged Fort Detroit in May, and overwhelmed a relief force at the end of the month. Other forts along the Great Lakes and Ohio Valley were subsequently attacked by other American Indian tribes. Some were seized by surprise attack, others were able to repel the attacks long enough for the garrison to slip away. A Seneca war party was received into Fort Venango by the British, only to turn on the garrison and massacre them. This betrayal destroyed relations between the British and their former allies. By the end of June, all of the British forts along the frontier and in the newly claimed territories had been seized except for forts Pitt, Detroit, and Niagara. American Indian war parties also headed east toward Fort Bedford, but were unsuccessful in capturing it. Fort Pitt was surrounded in late June, but not attacked until late July. The British managed to repulse the attack, when it came, knowing that it was critical to hold Fort Pitt, as well as Niagara and Detroit, as jumping-off positions for the reconquest of the Ohio Valley and Great Lakes region. Bouquet and his headquarters received word of the attacks by late May.

On July 28, a relief column of 200 men arrived at Fort Detroit, but was carrying few supplies or provisions for the fort. On July 31, the column marched to destroy the American Indian camp and lift the siege, but they were ambushed and all but destroyed at a creek named Bloody Run. The siege of Detroit continued.

All available troops were sent to Philadelphia to stage an expedition to relieve Fort Pitt, but many of the troops had now been transported to the Caribbean or discharged, so Bouquet's force of men from the 42nd, 77th, and 60th regiments of Foot, and some rangers, only numbered some 500 men. Bouquet's units moved towards Fort Pitt, but the American Indians besieging the fort had heard of the movement, and deployed east to ambush them. They met at Bushy Run, some 25 miles from Fort Pitt. Skirmishes on the morning of August 5 alerted Bouquet to the possibility of an ambush. He deployed his troops in circular defensive positions and awaited the attack. It came at 1.00pm, and lasted throughout the afternoon and evening. Despite many casualties,

Lake Champlain from Fort Ticonderoga as seen by Henry James Warre, a British tourist who visited the site in 1842. A few overgrown stones can be seen in the foreground. (National Archives of Canada, C-31270)

Bouquet's force held out. The following morning, the warriors attacked again. They mistook Bouquet's shortening of the line for a retreat, and launched a disorganized attack. This enabled the British to pour heavy fire into the Indian force, and attack them with bayonets. The remainder of the Indians withdrew from the field of battle. It is not certain whether Bouquet engineered the entire maneuver, but he had used the situation to his tactical advantage. Both sides lost about 50 men killed and 50 wounded.

Fort Pitt was relieved on August 10, but the fighting continued, with the siege on Fort Detroit not lifted until October, and then mainly because the American Indians had lost interest in continuing the siege. Detroit was still in dire need of supplies. The tension in the region that provoked the uprising eventually forced the British government to proclaim a policy concerning the newly conquered territories. The Royal Proclamation of 1763 was an attempt to resolve several outstanding issues in the region conclusively, but it was still somewhat ambiguous. The proclamation declared that the French settlements north of New York and New England were to become known as the new colony of Québec, that Florida was to be divided into two new colonies, that all three new colonies were to operate under English law, and that all other land not encompassed by the three new colonies was to belong to the American Indians. Colonial governments that claimed land in the region, such as Pennsylvania and Virginia, were no longer allowed to grant lands in the area. Only Crown representatives could negotiate with Indians over the sale of land.

BUSHY RUN, 1763

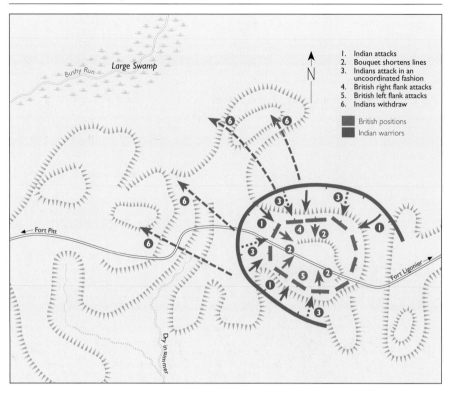

Large Swamp

Bushy Run

N

1. Indian attacks
2. Bouquet shortens lines
3. Indians attack in an uncoordinated fashion
4. British right flank attacks
5. British left flank attacks
6. Indians withdraw

British positions

Indian warriors

Fort Pitt

Fort Ligonier

Dry in summer

No whites were to settle the region, and any whites already present in the region were ordered to withdraw to east of the Appalachian Mountains. White traders were allowed to cross into Indian territory, but only if carrying a license from the commander-in-chief. The proclamation was vague about what French inhabitants of the Indian territory should do. The proclamation did end the uprising, but at the same time established a whole new set of problems with colonists from the Thirteen Colonies who wished to settle in the region, which contributed to the tensions already developing.

Amherst was replaced in late 1763, but his strategy for 1764 was carried out. The siege of Fort Niagara was lifted in early July, after William Johnson managed to reach agreement with all but three of the chiefs besieging the fort. The American Indians were granted several concessions, including the right to lodge complaints at Fort Detroit, and a schedule for setting values on goods and skins. Following this peace conference, Bradstreet left with his force to subdue the three tribes still in rebellion, and spread the word that hostilities with the other tribes were at an end. Bouquet moved into the Ohio Valley to subdue any remaining American Indian hostility and receive any white captives. By the end of the year the campaigns were complete and peace was restored to the frontier.

THE AMERICAN REVOLUTION

The French and Indian War had highlighted existing tensions between the British government and the Thirteen Colonies, and added new ones. The American Indian uprising had raised several issues relevant to the security of new British territories. Great Britain's methods for dealing with these considerations further alienated the subjects of the original Thirteen Colonies. Already aggrieved by the tensions that had arisen during the war, the colonists were outraged by the government's use of armed troops to prevent the westward expansion and settlement they felt was their right.

In winning the French and Indian War, the British government had amassed considerable debt, and the continued military presence in North America was stretching funds further. However, the Thirteen Colonies did not feel it was their responsibility to pay for the war, and they had no intention of contributing funds

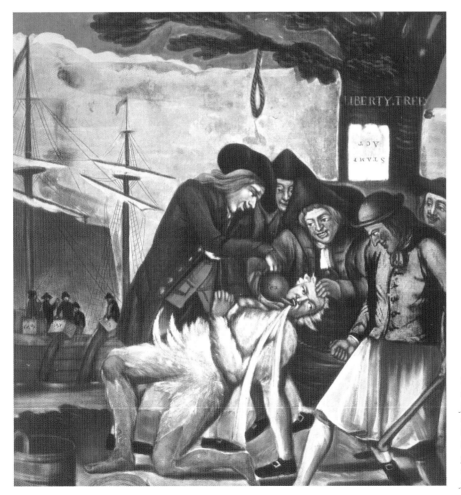

The Bostonians paying the excise man at the Boston Tea Party. Tarred and feathered, the British official is drowned in tea. The acts introduced by the British government, including the Tea Act of 1773 put considerable pressure on the American colonists and fired a passion for independence from the British Crown. (Topfoto)

The "Boston Massacre" came about on March 5, 1770, when a group of local men began to taunt a British sentry. Some regulars arrived to support the sentry, and the following few minutes left five Boston men dead, shot by British regulars. The event was utilized by Americans campaigning for independence. (Topfoto)

for the upkeep of security along the frontier, which they felt was solely there to stop the westward movement of settlers. Before the war, the British government had maintained a policy of minimal interference with the colonies, but now they tried several ways of compelling the colonial governments to pay to support the British Army's presence in North America, and debate on this and related issues raged between London and North America from 1764 until 1775. The colonists found the Québec Act of 1774 particularly galling, as it gave the colony of Québec administrative rights over the new territories in the Ohio Valley, and east of the Mississippi, areas which settlers in Pennsylvania and Virginia felt were theirs.

The numerous grievances harbored by the Thirteen Colonies had developed by 1775 into open rebellion against the British Crown. The redcoats had gained significant tactical expertise during their task of protecting the colonies against the French. However, while some of the regulars found themselves in action against Pontiac, others were "axed" as an economy measure, and by the time the American Revolution came around, more of the reforms that had been instituted during the French and Indian War had been forgotten, and most of the senior officers had never fought in North America. Those who had done so generally had a low opinion of the fighting capabilities of the Americans following negative experiences with provincials during the 1750s. In general, the British almost completely disregarded the large numbers of veterans in the colonies who had served in the provincial and regular units during the French and Indian War. They disparaged the Americans' ability to fight a war as a unified entity and to their detriment they failed to realize the potential of the professional army raised by the fledgling United States in 1775; an army shaped and led by the very men who had fought alongside the redcoats for so many years.

APPENDIX
FRENCH AND INDIAN WAR SITES TODAY

Commemorations of the 250th anniversary of the French and Indian War began in 2004 and will be ongoing throughout the decade. There will be reenactments of battles and encampments, exhibitions, and other events at many of the battle sites and elsewhere in the United States and Canada. Full details of all planned events, along with information about visiting the sites associated with the war can be found on their website: www.frenchandindianwar250.org

An exhibition, "Clash of Empires," will tour the Senator John Heinz Pittsburgh Regional History Center, Pennsylvania, The Canadian War Museum, and the Smithsonian Institution. For more details see their website: www.pghhistory.org

Following are details of some of the principal sites covered in the text.

Lake George

Amherst rebuilt Fort Carillon in 1759, renaming it Fort Ticonderoga. This fort was captured by the American revolutionaries in 1775 and reoccupied by the

The remains of Fort Crown Point. General Amherst ordered this substantial fort built in 1759 to guard against a possible French counterattack. The stone walls of the quarters (left) and the main men's barracks (right) are preserved. (René Chartrand)

British in 1777. Thereafter, the fort was abandoned and the battle site, once a clear field, gradually became overgrown. Today the low mounds that form the remains of the entrenchments on the heights are in the middle of a forest. Here and there are a few monuments including a tall cross, a reproduction of one erected by Montcalm to commemorate the victory, and a fine stone memorial to the Black Watch. The whole area is now a fine park with the restored Fort Ticonderoga at its center, and the view from the fort is majestic.

The site of the French Fort Saint-Frédéric, and the ruins of Fort Crown Point which Amherst built in 1759, are nearby. At the other end of the lake is Fort William Henry on a small rise, open May 1 to October 31 each year. There are guided tours, and the museum holds artifacts found during excavations in the area. http://www.fort-ticonderoga.org/ http://www.fwhmuseum.com/

Louisbourg

At Louisbourg, what was once a sizable fortress was reduced to little more than a pile of rubble on an abandoned peninsula. In time, it became a national historic site with a small museum. However, in the two decades following 1961, the fortress was reconstructed and incredibly the fortress town of Louisbourg

The first building to be reconstructed at Louisbourg in the 1960s was also the largest in the town, and indeed in 18th-century North America. This massive building which combined official residences, church, and barracks, comes to about 365 feet long. (René Chartrand)

stands again today as it was in the mid-18th century. It is a major tourist attraction and with the Cape Breton Highlands National Park, it draws visitors to the eastern end of Nova Scotia.

For anyone visiting Fortress Louisbourg today, there is a lot to see. It is probably the best and most accurate reconstruction ever attempted on such a scale. Outside the fortress walls, there are also many vestiges showing foundations of destroyed buildings, such as the Royal Battery. If one goes round the harbor and up to Lighthouse Point, the reward is a splendid view of the harbor entrance, and the fortress town of Louisbourg exactly as it was in the mid-18th century.
http://fortress.uccb.ns.ca/

Montréal

After 1760, Montréal's walls seemed less relevant to a successful defense, and more of an obstacle to businessmen as the city expanded rapidly, and the walls were demolished in the early 19th century. Montréal is now Canada's second largest city and over the last two decades small parts of its ramparts' foundation have been rediscovered and preserved. The network of outlying forts also fell into ruin and disappeared except for a few stone vestiges.
http://www.montreal.com/tourism/index2.html

The site of Fort Duquesne is now a park in the middle of Pittsburgh. The outline of the fort can be seen traced on the ground behind the fountain. (René Chartrand)

Monument to Montcalm and Wolfe in Québec. (René Chartrand)

The Ohio Valley

Although in 1754–55 the battlefields of the Ohio Valley were an unsettled wilderness accessible only by narrow American Indian trails, it is now easy to drive to all the battlefields of the area.

Jumonville Glen and Fort Necessity are near the village of Farmington in Pennsylvania, and are both National Historic Battlefields administered by the US National Park Service. Jumonville Glen is probably the site that has remained least changed since the war, and interpretation panels are useful to understand the situation in 1754.

The Fort Necessity National Battlefield is nearby. The fort has been rebuilt following archaeological excavations in 1952–53. There is an interpretation center nearby, and all the features of the battlefield are well marked. The Bushy Run battlefield site outside Pittsburgh has a visitor center and provides tours of the site to explain the 1763 battle.

The site of the battle of Monongahela was cleared in 1855, totally built over with heavy industries in the town of Braddock in the later 19th and early 20th centuries. For a time, it was a booming town, and the Monongahela river itself was rerouted as a canal. Finding features of the battlefield now is a challenge, particularly as some of the topography was leveled when the industries were built. The area bears almost no resemblance to the natural sites described in battle reports. The meeting place of the Monongahela and Allegheny rivers is now a park in the center of Pittsburgh, where a plaque marks the center of Fort Duquesne and the fort walls are outlined on the ground. Further back is the outline of the larger British Fort Pitt, built after Fort Duquesne was blown up, which has a museum in a rebuilt bastion.

http://www.fortpittmuseum.com/
http://www.nps.gov/fone/

Québec

Following the cession of Canada to Britain and the American siege of 1775–76, Québec's fortifications were steadily improved and a large citadel was finally built in the 1820s. Three large forts were also built on the south shore in the 1860s. Following the withdrawal of the British garrison in 1871, there was pressure to demolish the walls and batteries. Thanks to the efforts of the heritage-conscious governor-general of Canada in the 1870s the ramparts were preserved, and today Québec is the only walled city in North America. The rampart that was erected is essentially the same that can be seen in present-day Québec. Great efforts have been made to preserve the heritage of this exceptional city, and it was declared a World Heritage Site by UNESCO in 1985.

The Beauport Shore is mainly built up, although the Montmorency Falls remain impressive. The battlefield on the Plains has largely been built over, except a small part of it is now an ornamental public park, with a monument to Wolfe.

The only place where any sense of the 1759 battle can still be felt is the cliff above the Foulon. Wolfe's landing place has long since disappeared under a modern ocean terminal, and the crucial Foulon road has been graded and widened. However, the actual cliff face scaled by Howe and his men remains largely as it was in 1759.

http://www.quebecheritage.com/en/

SELECT BIBLIOGRAPHY

PRIMARY SOURCES

Anderson, F. (ed.), *George Washington Remembers: Reflections on the French and Indian War* (Lanham, Maryland, 2004)

Amherst, J., *The Journal of Jeffrey Amherst 1756–1763*, edited by J. C. Webster (Toronto, 1931)

Bougainville, L. A. de, *Adventure in the Wilderness: The American Journals of Louis Antoine de Bougainville*, edited by E. P. Hamilton (Norman, Oklahoma, 1964)

Bouquet, H., *The Papers of Henry Bouquet*, edited by S. K. Stevens et al, 6 vols (Harrisburg, 1951–54)

Knox, H., *Historical Journal of Campaigns in North America, 1757–1760* (New York, 1914)

Loudoun, J., *General Orders 1757* (New York, 1899)

Rogers, R., *A Concise Account of North America* (London, 1765)

Rogers, R., *The Annotated and Illustrated Journals of Major Robert Rogers*, annotations by T. J. Todish, illustrations by G. Zaboly (New York, 2002)

Wolfe, J., *Instructions to Young Officers* (London, 1768)

SECONDARY SOURCES

Anderson, F., *Crucible of War: The Seven Years' War and the Fate of Empire in British North America 1754–1766* (New York, 2000)

Brumwell, S., *Redcoats: The British Soldier and War in the Americas, 1755–1763* (Cambridge, 2002)

Brumwell, S., *White Devil: A True Story of War, Savagery, and Vengeance in North America* (New York, 2005)

Chartrand, R., *The French soldier in Colonial America* (Ottawa, 1984)

Chartrand, R., *Canadian Military Heritage* (Montréal, 1993, 1995)

Duffy, C., *The Military Experience in the Age of Reason* (London, 1987)

Fowler, W., *Empires at War: The French and Indian War and the Struggle for North America 1754–1763* (New York, 2005)

Fry, B. W., *An Appearance of Strength: The Fortifications of Louisbourg* (Ottawa, 1984)

Fuller, J. F. C., *British Light Infantry in the Eighteenth Century* (London, 1925)

Gallay, A., *Colonial Wars of North America 1512–1763: An Encyclopedia* (New York & London, 1996)

Halpenny, F., *Dictionary of Canadian Biography: 1741–1770* (Toronto, 1975)

Hamilton, E. P., *Fort Ticonderoga: Key to a Continent* (Boston, 1964)

Hibbert, C., *Wolfe at Quebec: The man who won the French and Indian War* (London, 1999)

Houlding, J. A., *Fit for Service: The Training of the British Army 1715–1795* (Oxford, 1981)

Jacobs, W. R., *Wilderness Politics and Indian Gifts: The Northern Colonial Frontier 1748–1763* (Lincoln, 1950)

Johnson, M. and Hook, R., *Macmillan Encyclopaedia of Native American Tribes* (London, 2000)

Katcher, P., *Armies of the American Wars 1715–1815* (London, 1975)

Kennett, L., *French Armies in the Seven Years' War* (Durham, North Carolina, 1967)

Leach, D. E., *Arms for Empire: A military history of the British colonies in North America* (New York, 1973)

Leach, D. E., *Roots of conflict: British armed forces and colonial Americans 1677–1763* (Chapel Hill, North Carolina, 1986)

McLennan, J. S., *Louisbourg: From its Foundation to its Fall 1713–1758* (London, 1918)

Middleton, R., *The Bells of Victory: The Pitt-Newcastle Ministry and Conduct of the Seven Years' War* (Cambridge, 1985)

Pargellis, S. (ed.), *Lord Loudoun in North America* (New York, 1968)

Pakman, F., *History of the Conspiracy of Pontiac, and the war of the North American Tribes against the English colonies after the conquest of Canada* (Boston, 1851)

Parkman, F., *Montcalm and Wolfe* (New York, 1884)

Reid, S., *Wolfe: The Career of General James Wolfe* (Staplehurst, 2000)

Richards, F., *The Black Watch at Ticonderoga and Major Duncan Campbell* (Glen Falls, New York, 1930)

Selesky, H. F., *War & Society in Colonial Connecticut* (New Haven, 1990)

Stacey, C. P., *Quebec, 1759: The siege and battle* (Toronto, 1959)

Steele, I. K., *Guerrillas and Grenadiers: The Struggle for Canada, 1689–1760* (Toronto, 1969)

Stotz, C. M., *Outposts of the War for Empire* (Pittsburgh, 1977)

Ultee, M. (ed.), *Adapting to conditions: War and society in the eighteenth century* (Alabama, 1986)

INDEX

References to illustrations are shown in **bold**.